Clark Howard's

CONSUMER SURVIVAL KiT

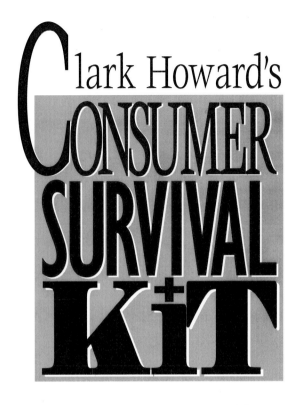

Clark Howard's CONSUMER SURVIVAL KiT

REVISED AND EXPANDED EDITION

Clark Howard and Mark Meltzer

LONGSTREET PRESS
Atlanta, Georgia

For Rebecca, Nancy and Connie,
who inspire us to do our best

Published by
LONGSTREET PRESS, INC.
A subsidiary of Cox Newspapers,
A subsidiary of Cox Enterprises, Inc.
2140 Newmarket Parkway
Suite 118
Marietta, GA 30067

Printed in the United States of America
2nd printing 1996
Library of Congress Catalog Card Number: 94-74241
ISBN 1-56352-200-4

Book design by Laura McDonald

Contents

When I wrote the first edition of the *Consumer Survival Kit* two years ago, I had no idea whether anyone would buy it. Thankfully, people have loved it and bought it in great numbers. That's why we've created this second, revised edition.

Readers of the *Consumer Survival Kit* have had a big role in determining what new material would go into this second edition. I discovered that you wanted more information about investments—and you'll find that presented here in a very easy-to-understand format.

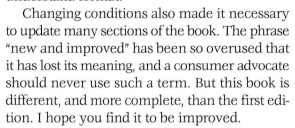

Changing conditions also made it necessary to update many sections of the book. The phrase "new and improved" has been so overused that it has lost its meaning, and a consumer advocate should never use such a term. But this book is different, and more complete, than the first edition. I hope you find it to be improved.

This is also the first edition of the *Consumer Survival Kit* to be distributed nationally, so many readers may not know how I entered the consumer arena. I started out as a travel agent, opening a chain of travel agencies that I sold in 1987. Thanks to my travel experience, the *Consumer Survival Kit* is one of the few consumer books that also includes advice on travel.

After I sold my travel agency, I moved into radio, first as host of a travel show, then as host of a wide-ranging consumer show in Atlanta. I'm proud to say that my career has grown in three directions. I have a three-hour daily consumer radio show, and I'm a TV reporter for the ABC-TV affiliate in Atlanta. I also write one travel column and one consumer column each week for the *Atlanta Journal & Constitution*.

Every day on my radio show, I speak with consumers looking for solutions to the day-to-day consumer problems we all face, and advice on how to stay out of financial trouble. Every day I hear what you're concerned about, who is trying to rip you off, and how. Many of my best suggestions,

to help you be smarter with your money and avoid ripoffs, are in this book.

I've written the *Consumer Survival Kit* to help anyone who's ever thought about joining a health club or buying a timeshare and for anyone who's ever opened a savings account or had a credit card. This book is for people who have bought a car or had one repaired, who have bought a house or rented an apartment, or have taken a vacation. In short, it's for everyone, because we all want to get the most out of the money we earn, whether to spend it, save it, or invest it.

Consumer protection laws differ from state to state, and I've included a number of examples in this book to show you how the rules can vary. I was surprised myself at how little of this book needed to be adapted for a national audience. My advice on buying a car or remodeling your home is the same whether you live in Boston or Boise.

The basic law of consumerism also remains the same—you are your own best police officer. It doesn't matter what the law says when scam artists try to get into your wallet, because it's very hard to recover money after it's been stolen. Instead of looking to law enforcement to help you after you've been taken, learn how to protect yourself and your money.

You can read the *Consumer Survival Kit* from cover to cover, or you can turn to a chapter that's of immediate interest to you. If you're thinking about buying an extended warranty for a new appliance, turn to the section on extended warranties in the Ripoffs chapter. If you're thinking of a trip to Europe, turn to the Travel chapter. There's plenty of valuable information here, and I've also included key phone numbers you can use to get more help.

In the Workbook chapter, you'll find a sample credit report and a drop-dead letter you can use to stop collection agencies from harassing you. There's also a worksheet you can use to document your consumer problems, the phone calls you make, and the letters you write in your efforts to solve these headaches.

As you read this book, you'll see how much I loathe wasting money, whether it's a few cents at an overpriced vending machine or a few hundred dollars on a health club membership. I hate to hear that other people have wasted money or been taken by a system that is often so unfriendly to you, the consumer.

My successes and failures in investments have taught me many lessons. I've learned that you should invest only in things you understand and over which you have reasonable control. Take the time to make wise decisions and then monitor your investments so you know when, if necessary, to get out.

I wasn't always as concerned with saving money as I am today. I enjoyed a comfortable life growing up. But my comfortable cocoon was shattered during my freshman year at college, when my father lost his job. Looking back, I consider it to be one of the best things that ever happened to me, because it forced me to take control of my future. Now I try to help others do the same. I hope this book helps you win more of life's everyday battles.

Clark Howard

Acknowledgments

Putting together a book like this requires a lot of help, and I'm grateful to the many people who were so willing to provide it. A couple of people deserve special thanks: Kim Curley, executive producer of my radio show and Nancy Deubell, the wife of my co-author, Mark Meltzer.

Kim's knowledge and skills were a valuable resource as we researched the many details presented here, and they were vital in making this work as thorough and accurate as possible.

Many of Nancy's ideas became elements of this book and her input helped make it more complete and readable. She also did a lot of less glamorous but important work.

I'd also like to thank Suzanne Comer Bell, our editor at Longstreet Press, whose many comments and ideas have made the book better and easier to read.

More than a dozen people and organizations provided expertise in specific subject areas, particularly those listed below. My thanks to them all.

Joni Alpert

Dan Blake

Milton L. Brown, Jr.

Deb Elvin

Steven L. Hale

Neal Howard

Jerry Hunt

Gary E. Jackson

Mike Kavanaugh

Daniel H. Kolber

Mac the Mechanic

Elizabeth Manley

Robert G. Martin

Michael Perling

Phoenix Travel

Piedmont Hospital

Jack Sawyer

Joe Turner

There are plenty of books, newsletters, magazines, and online services for the sophisticated investor, and plenty of commission salespeople are waiting and willing to sell investment products to the rest of us.

But it shouldn't be difficult for you to make wise investment decisions for yourself, without a commission salesperson and without having to snooze through volumes of investment research data and recommendations.

There's one golden rule to keep in mind whether you're buying something, investing your money, or using credit—treat time as your ally. The best way to avoid making a bad decision is to not make a quick decision.

In this chapter, I'll give you easy-to-understand information to help you invest for your future. I'll also give you tips about dealing with debt, protecting your money in a divorce, why you need a will, and how to choose a lawyer and an accountant.

Long-term Investing —

If there's any key principle to successfully building long-term wealth, it's that you put money aside regularly. One of the best places to invest that money is in no-load (no-commission) mutual funds, which allow you to own a piece of corporate America, with less risk than owning individual stocks. In a capitalist society such as ours, the wealth goes to those who own companies—the stockholders—not those who work for them.

Your No. 1 investment priority should be funding your own retirement, because you can't rely on the traditional vehicles that may have helped fund your parents'—or grandparents'—retirement. Their generations had a strong Social Security system and pension plans that were fully funded by their employers.

Today's working Americans will get only a small portion of the funds necessary for retirement from Social Security, and the employer-paid pension largely is a thing of the past.

The guarantee of a company pension has vanished partly because of changes in the way we work. Our parents often worked for one company for 20 to 40 years. Today, people often work for a number of companies during their careers, switching jobs when better opportunities come along. The tradition of an unofficial lifetime contract between employer and employee has disappeared, and with it the traditional security blanket many companies had provided. Without the government or a paternalistic corporation to fall back on, you have to be much smarter and more aggressive in planning for your retirement.

To properly fund your retirement, you'll need to save about 10 percent of your pay, throughout your working life. If you start saving in your 20s, you'll be leaps and bounds ahead of everyone else. But if you're 45 and haven't saved anything for retirement, don't be fatalistic and do nothing. Just start now and try to set aside 10 percent of your pay.

There are several investment vehicles that you should consider when putting aside money for retirement, including the 401(k) plan, the Individual Retirement Account (IRA), the Simplified Employee Pension (SEP), and the variable annuity. All charge a 10 percent penalty if you withdraw the money before age 59 1/2.

No matter which of those investment vehicles you select, you have to choose a specific investment. That list of choices includes fixed-income investments like a bank certificate of deposit, purchases of individual stocks or bonds, or mutual funds, which buy hundreds of stocks or bonds for you.

I'll describe the investment vehicles first, then the specific investments and how to buy them.

The 401(k) Plan

The principal retirement vehicle of the 1990s is the 401(k) plan. It's basically a tax-sheltered investment account, set up by your employer, to help you accumulate money for retirement. The 401(k) is the best way to build a retirement nest egg, because you can painlessly set aside money for your future, and you can take the money with you if you switch jobs.

The 401(k) provides several significant advantages. Most important, many employers match or partially match the money you contribute to your 401(k) plan. So if you contribute $100 per month to the plan, they'll contribute either $25, $50, or $100. With most investors trying hard to get a 6 to 10 percent return on their money, a vehicle that gives them an automatic return of 25, 50, or 100 percent, thanks to the employer contribution, is sensational.

The money you put into your 401(k) plan is deducted from your before-tax (or gross) income, so participating in the plan lowers your tax bill for the year. In addition, you don't have to pay taxes on the interest or dividends your money earns until you withdraw the money at retirement. Sheltered from the corrosive effect of taxes, your investment can grow faster than money in a traditional savings or investment account.

Since 401(k) contributions are deducted from each paycheck, making the contributions is easy to do. Participating in a 401(k) plan is an incredible deal for those who are lucky enough to have the opportunity.

To take full advantage of the benefits of a 401(k) plan, you should put as much money into the plan as your employer allows. The more you put in, the bigger the annual tax deduction, the faster your retirement nest egg grows, and up to a point, the more your employer contributes.

Each company's plan is different, but many will match your contribution up to 6 percent of your pay. In most cases, you may add additional funds, usually up to 10 percent of your pay. The extra money won't be matched, but it still will grow tax-deferred. If you can't afford to contribute the maximum amount your company permits, at least put in the maximum amount the company matches.

People often make the mistake of borrowing against their 401(k) plans, an option that is permitted in many plans. It's true that you borrow the money from your own fund, and pay it back with interest to the same fund. But borrowing from the plan, particularly when the purpose is something like a vacation, is a bad idea. You pay the money back to your own account, with interest. But the loan causes the fund to grow more slowly than it would have if all the money had been fully invested in a stock mutual fund. So borrowing reduces the amount that will be available when you retire.

The greater risk is that you will quit your job or be fired. When that happens, the borrowed money is due immediately. If you can't pay it back, the IRS treats the loan as an early distribution of your retirement money. You'll have to pay a 10 percent federal penalty on the total, plus ordinary state and federal income tax, for that tax year. On average, you'll have to pay 46 percent of the money you borrowed in taxes and penalties. If you've already spent the money, you may not even have the money to pay the taxes.

The Individual Retirement Account (IRA)

If you don't have an employer-sponsored retirement plan, then you should take advantage of IRA accounts, which allow you to shelter up to $2,000 a year from income tax. Just as with a 401(k), the money is deducted from your gross income and grows tax-free. However, there is no employer match.

Within an IRA, you can choose to invest wherever you wish. You can go into stock mutual funds, bond mutual funds, certificates of deposit from a bank, insurance company products, or any other investment. Think of the IRA as a house, and the specific investment as a room within the house.

The Simplified Employee Pension (SEP)

If you're self-employed, or have some self-employment income, you have the right to take advantage of a fantastic retirement plan called a SEP, or Simplified Employee Pension. A SEP is a kind of super IRA, a tax-sheltered plan which allows you to invest a much greater amount of money than an IRA does.

With a SEP, you can contribute up to 13.08 percent of your net earnings from self-employment for the calendar year, up to $30,000 a year in most circumstances. You figure your net income at tax time, after deducting expenses, and calculate your maximum SEP contribution from the net. You figure the amount you may contribute, deposit the money in your SEP account, and note the SEP contribution on your tax form.

Let's say you earn $50,000 annually in net income as a full-time, self-employed individual. You can contribute up to $6,540 to the SEP. If you work part-time for yourself as a landscaper and earn $10,000 after expenses, you can contribute $1,308 to a SEP—even if you have a 401(k) plan at your regular job. You're not eligible to open an IRA if you have a 401(k) plan.

The simple, one-page application form to start a SEP can be obtained from any discount broker, broker, or mutual fund company.

Employees of some businesses also may participate in a SEP. The law requires that if a business owner sets up a SEP, he must allow employees to participate in it. This type of SEP may be funded by the employer, the employee, or both. Contributions are tax-deductible.

Annuities

Once you've put all you're allowed to into a 401(k) plan, a SEP, and/or an IRA, you're out of tax-deductible investment vehicles. So your next priority is a tax-sheltered form of retirement savings. The best of those is a tax-sheltered retirement annuity, an investment vehicle that has become hugely popular in the last several years. There's no limit on what you can contribute per year, and while there's no tax deduction for the contributions you make, the earnings grow tax-free until retirement, just as with an IRA.

You can put money into a variable annuity in a lump sum or through periodic contributions. There's usually a minimum investment to open the account.

You can withdraw the money in a lump sum at retirement, or receive regular payout checks, beginning at retirement.

So far, life insurance companies have had a monopoly on annuities. There are some court cases under way that may strip the insurance companies of that monopoly. That would be great for consumers because the insurance industry has used its monopoly to charge enormously high fees on annuities, so high that they defeat the very tax advantages that make a variable annuity attractive.

I expect that banks eventually will enter the variable annuity business, and that competition will help force down these outrageously high fees. Usually I make fun of banks, but compared to the insurance industry, banks are the height of efficiency.

Despite the problem with insurers, there are some good choices for variable annuities today. A number of companies have set up low-fee variable annuities, in cooperation with insurers, and the list is growing rapidly. Companies offering the low-fee variable annuity include USAA Life Insurance Co., Janus Capital, Charles Schwab Corp., Scudder, Stevens & Clark Inc., Vanguard Group, Fidelity Investments, and

T. Rowe Price Associates. The minimum initial investment with most of these plans has been $2,500 or $5,000. But these may come down with increasing competition.

Remember, an annuity is a long-term investment, one that you'll keep for at least 15 years. That's when compounding—continually getting "interest on your interest"—combines with the benefits of tax-sheltered growth to build your nest egg dramatically.

To open a variable annuity, you contact the company of your choice at its 800 number, and they'll send you a kit that includes the application form and a full description of the plan. You'll find the numbers at the end of this section, and in the Phone Book chapter of this book.

Rainy Day Account

Your first investment priority should be to put as much money aside as possible into a tax-deferred plan. If you've reached the limit of saving in these plans, and you still have money you wish to put aside, the next priority is to develop a safety net for you or your family, in the event that you suddenly find yourself with unexpected expenses or a loss of income.

Any form of periodic savings plan will help you build a rainy day account. You can use a payroll deduction plan or an automatic transfer from your checking account. It doesn't matter if the money goes into a savings account, the purchase of Series EE savings bonds, or into shares of a mutual fund. The most important thing is to put aside a certain amount of money each month.

Saving for College

Besides saving for retirement, the most common long-term savings goal is for a child's college education. I had a call once from a couple who were leaving the hospital with a two-day-old baby, and wanted to put money aside for their child's college education. I was gratified to hear that they were thinking ahead.

Unfortunately, they hadn't yet started saving for their own retirement.

There are so many different ways to pay for college, but you can depend only on yourself to pay for your retirement or for sudden financial crises. Thus, I see a child's college education as the third priority. The strategy is the same as the periodic savings for your own personal safety net. That is, put aside a certain amount of money per month for your child's college costs.

Where the Money Goes

Once you've selected your investment vehicle for retirement—401(k), SEP, IRA, or variable annuity—you need to choose a specific investment within the retirement fund. The best choice is stock and bond mutual funds, which give you the safety of diversity and the growth potential you must have to build a sizable retirement nest egg.

Stock mutual funds are the most efficient way for you to own companies, far better than investing in individual stocks. Mutual funds limit your risk by giving you a small part of a big basket of companies. So if one company fails or encounters trouble and suffers a sharp decline in its stock price, as happened to IBM a few years ago, it barely affects your diversified holdings. In that way, you benefit over time from the natural growth of corporate America and the profits it generates.

The problem for so many people is that they fear the short-term loss that can be generated from investing in stocks. Any mutual fund can have a bad year or two. But over periods of 10 years and longer, most good funds will easily beat "safe" fixed-rate savings vehicles. In fact, when you look at any 10-year period from the 1920s to today, stock market investors have received an average annual return of 10.6 percent. That includes the huge market losses in the Great Depression and the 1987 market crash.

You can enhance your chances of investing safely with a simple technique called dollar-cost averaging, which eliminates the dilemma of trying to time the market's peaks and valleys. You make regular contributions to a mutual fund, perhaps $50 a month, or divide a lump sum into 12 or 18 monthly deposits.

Without dollar-cost averaging, market dips are a real danger. If you invest $12,000 in stocks and the market plunges the next day, you're in trouble. But if you invest the same $12,000 over a 12-month or 18-month period, it doesn't matter what the market does. If prices go down, your $1,000 a month buys you more shares of stock. If prices rise, your portfolio increases in value. Over the long haul, given the historical tendency of the stock market to climb, you should do quite well. Dollar-cost averaging dramatically reduces risk.

Here's a great example of why you should use dollar-cost averaging. My brother invested $100,000 in a stock partnership in September 1987. The October 1987 stock market crash occurred a few weeks later, and when it did, he lost 40 percent of his money in three days. It took years for prices to climb to the point that he made back the $40,000 he had lost. If he had used dollar-cost averaging to invest over a 12-month period, he would have put $8,333 into the market in September 1987 and lost $3,333—instead of $40,000—when the market crashed. The second $8,333 he put in would have bought him a great many more shares, as would subsequent deposits, because the crash made each share of stock cheaper. When the market eventually took off again, he would have made a fortune. It's too hard to guess where the market is headed, and with dollar-cost averaging you don't have to try. A 401 (k) plan offers automatic dollar-cost averaging.

Your 401(k) plan may offer anywhere from three to ten investment options, including a money market investment, some form of fixed-income investment, a bond mutual fund, and one or more stock mutual funds. The worst thing you can do when you're saving for retirement is put any of your money in the fixed-income investment. Fixed-income investments, like a bank certificate of deposit or a 401(k) plan's Guaranteed Income Contract, grow too slowly to meet your retirement goals. They're good places to keep money that you're going to need within a few years. But they will not be able to far outpace inflation and are a poor choice for a long-term investment. The best strategy is to choose several of the stock funds or funds that own both stocks and bonds. It's okay to include a fund that owns bonds alone, but a bond fund should represent no more than 20 percent of your retirement portfolio.

Your options in an IRA or SEP are nearly unlimited. So you'll need some background to help you sort through the myriad of mutual fund choices. My best advice is to go to a bookstore and buy one of several excellent, comprehensive guides to mutual fund investing. Two of my favorites are *The Handbook for No-Load Mutual Fund Investors*, by Sheldon Jacobs, and the *Guide to Mutual Funds*, by the American Association of Individual Investors.

But if you feel intimidated or overwhelmed by the prospect of reading an entire book on mutual funds, let me offer some basic strategies. These aren't the only right answers, but they are the kind of things that have worked well for people and keep them from being frozen by investment fear or apathy.

Index Funds

Most mutual funds have a professional manager, whose goal is to outperform the broad market by carefully buying top-performing stocks. For that professional management, mutual fund investors pay an annual management fee, which usually ranges from 0.5 percent to 2.0 percent of their investment in the fund.

One interesting kind of mutual fund, an index

fund, operates with a different strategy. Instead of using a professional manager to pick stocks, the index fund aims for safety and growth by buying a very broad range of stocks or bonds, usually 500, 1,000, or 2,000 individual stocks or bonds. Instead of guessing where to put the fund's money, they own virtually everything.

Some index funds aim to match the performance of the Dow Jones Industrial Average, the Standard and Poors 500, or other widely followed market indexes. Bond index funds often mix long-term and short-term government and corporate bonds.

The management costs for index funds are near zero, and their performance often is very good to excellent. Buying a mixture of index funds is an easy, low-cost investment strategy.

Here's one idea that will give you a widely diversified portfolio as to the number of stocks and the type of investments you own. Put 30 percent of your money into a 500-stock index fund, 30 percent into a broad-market index fund (it will usually own 2,000 to 4,000 stocks), 20 percent into an international index fund, and 20 percent into a bond index fund. With that portfolio, you've bought the world: you've bought the biggest companies in the country; you've bought virtually all the publicly traded companies in the United States; and you've balanced some of your equities with ownership of corporate debt, or bonds.

With this strategy, you can buy all your funds from one mutual fund company. You'll probably want to pick the company with the lowest costs. Buying is as simple as calling one of the mutual fund companies and asking for a catalog of their funds. Or you could ask for a prospectus on their 500-stock fund, their international index fund, their broad-market index fund, and one of their bond index funds. If there are several bond index funds, ask for a prospectus on the intermediate-term fund. That would be a fund that buys bonds with maturities from three to 10 years. I think an intermediate-term fund works best for people who are buying bonds just to balance their portfolio. Short-term bonds (less than three years) don't make sense in a long-term retirement portfolio.

You can put as much effort into assembling an investment portfolio as you want. Using an assortment of index funds is a low-tech answer for people who want to invest but are fearful of or uninterested in making a lot of decisions.

To set up a portfolio, just call the mutual fund house you choose and they'll send you an application form. Fill it out and you're in business. If your money already is in an IRA account, you may be able to shift it into the investments you select by telephone.

If you have to transfer money from a bank IRA or roll it over from a 401(k) account, put the money into the mutual fund company's Money Market fund while you're deciding on your portfolio mix. Then call them and move the money to the funds you choose.

You can move a lump sum directly into the investments you choose, but that carries some risk. Instead, use dollar-cost averaging. Put the lump sum into the company's Money Market fund, then transfer a portion every month into the specific investments you've selected.

You're not necessarily giving up anything in performance by choosing an index fund, because the fees associated with an index fund are so low. Investment experts believe that an actively managed fund must outperform the market by 2 percentage points in order to compensate for the transaction costs and higher management fees. So a brilliant fund manager would have to achieve a 9 percent return just to keep up with an index fund that gains 7 percent, after fees are considered. However, some experts believe that a managed fund might be a better choice if your investment window is less than five years.

If you want to invest in mutual funds but are afraid to make any decisions, you can choose one of the catch-all "multifunds" available from several mutual fund houses. Fidelity Investments, the largest of the mutual fund companies, has the Fidelity Asset Manager. It's an all-purpose fund, managed by a professional money manager, that divides its investments among stocks, bonds, and cash. The normal mix is 40 percent stocks, 40 percent bonds, and 20 percent Money Market instruments, a middle-of-the-road basket of investments.

For investors thinking about retirement or other long-term goals, there's Fidelity Asset Manager Growth, which is tilted more toward stocks. Its typical investment mix is more aggressive: 65 percent stocks, 30 percent bonds and 5 percent Money Market. Vanguard's version, Vanguard Star, has 62.5 percent stocks, 25 percent bonds, and 12.5 percent Money Market funds. T. Rowe Price's fund is called Spectrum fund. Several other no-load fund companies have similar products.

There are a number of plans specifically tailored to help with college savings. T. Rowe Price and Vanguard lower their minimum investments for custodial accounts, in which an adult holds the account on behalf of a child. T. Rowe Price drops its minimum from about $2,500 to $1,000. Vanguard allows an initial deposit of $500, rather than its usual minimum of $5,000 to $10,000, depending on the fund.

Another to consider is the Series EE College Savings Plan, which allows parents 24 years old or older to buy Series EE savings bonds in their name. If those bonds are used strictly to pay for a child's college education, then under certain income circumstances, they are free from taxes at the time of withdrawal. So it becomes a tax-free college investment. But there is one flaw: the issue of whether or not the bonds will be taxed is based not on your income in the year that you buy the bonds, but

on your income in the year your child goes to college. It's tough to look in a crystal ball and see what your income will be in 12 to 18 years, and that's why the Series EE savings plan has not been successful.

There are a lot of choices in mutual funds—Fidelity itself has hundreds of funds—and if you like to read about all of them, have fun. But I want to caution you about becoming so overwhelmed by the choices that you do nothing.

If you want to spend a few hours getting some background, *The Handbook for No-Load Mutual Fund Investors* is very readable and will help you make decisions. But here are some basic things you should know.

The primary fees associated with mutual funds are sales loads, a hidden sales fee called a 12b-1 charge, and a management fee.

I don't think it ever makes sense to pay a significant load charge to buy a mutual fund. There's a vast selection of no-load funds, and your chances of doing well with them are as good as with a fund that carries a load.

You should never buy any mutual fund from a commission sales person, such as a stockbroker. If you buy a professionally managed fund, you'll pay a management fee to the fund. Don't pay a second fee to a stockbroker for his advice. That goes double for an index fund. You get no professional advice with an index fund, so you certainly shouldn't pay a commission.

The loads you would pay if you bought from a stockbroker or financial planner could be as high as 8.5 percent. So if you invest $1,000, $85 comes off the top as a sales commission and the remaining $915 goes into your account. That's a lot of money to pay. Fidelity has low sales loads on some of its funds—3 percent or below—and no loads on most.

Some brokers and financial planners will misrepresent a fund as a no-load fund when it has hidden loads through the 12b-1 fee, a sales charge that's collected each year on your

- Tips on - Long-term Investing

● Your No. 1 investment priority should be funding your own retirement.

● Consider several investment vehicles when putting aside money for retirement: the 401(k) plan, the Individual Retirement Account (IRA), the Simplified Employee Pension (SEP), and the variable annuity.

● When you're investing for retirement, the growth potential of stocks is a better bet than conservative investments such as certificates of deposit, which barely keep up with inflation.

● To minimize the risks of investing in stocks, consider stock mutual funds. Mutual funds limit your risk by giving you a small part of a big basket of companies.

● Saving for a child's college education is a lesser priority than saving for your retirement.

● One low-tech investment strategy is to invest in an assortment of index funds. Some index funds aim to match the performance of the Dow Jones Industrial Average, the Standard and Poors 500, or other market indexes.

● Another alternative is to invest in one of the catch-all "multifunds" available from several mutual fund houses, such as the Fidelity Asset Manager.

Contact:
Fidelity Investments
82 Devonshire Street
Boston, MA 02109
617-523-1919
1-800-544-6666

INVESCO
7800 E. Union Avenue
Suite 800
Denver, CO 80237
303-930-6300
1-800-525-8085

Janus Capital
100 Fillmore Street
Suite 300
Denver, CO 80206
303-333-3863
1-800-525-3713

Morningstar, Inc.
225 West Wacker Drive
Chicago, IL 60606
1-800-876-5005

Charles Schwab Corp.
101 Montgomery Street
San Francisco, CA 94104
415-627-7000
1-800-648-5300

Scudder
P.O. Box 2291
Boston, MA 02107
617-439-4640
1-800-225-2470

T. Rowe Price Associates, Inc.
100 E. Pratt Street
Baltimore, MD 21202
410-547-2308
1-800-638-566

Twentieth Century
4500 Main Street
P.O. Box 419200
Kansas City, MO 64141
816-531-5575
1-800-345-2021

USAA Life Insurance Co.
USAA Building
San Antonio, TX 78288
1-210-498-6505
1-800-531-8000

The Vanguard Group
P.O. Box 2600
Valley Forge, PA 19482
610-669-1000
1-800-662-2739

Reference:
The Handbook for No-Load Mutual Fund Investors
by Sheldon Jacobs ($49)
1-800-252-2042

Guide to Mutual Funds ($24.95)
The American Association of Individual Investors
625 North Michigan Avenue
Suite 1900
Chicago, IL 60611
312-280-0170

funds. This fee, which might be 1 percent of your investment, could turn out to be more costly than an upfront load, because you pay it every year. Plus, you pay not only on your initial investment, but on your investment gains.

Over a 10-year period, a $10,000 investment in a mutual fund growing at 10 percent would be worth $25,937. The same investment in the same fund, but with a 12b-1 charge of 1 percent, would grow to $23,674. That's a difference of $2,263, about the same as investing in a fund with an 8.5 percent upfront sales load.

The management fee is the money you pay to have a professional money manager buy and sell stocks for your mutual fund. You'll pay this fee annually, on the total amount invested, with every mutual fund. But it will be lowest with an index fund, for which management duties are insignificant. The management fee for index funds generally is less than 0.5 percent.

Paying more could be worth it if the fund delivers. If over both a 5-year period and a 10-year period, a fund with a high expense ratio has outperformed greatly a fund with a lower expense ratio, it may be worth paying the higher expenses.

Fidelity's heralded Magellan fund, managed for years by Peter Lynch, has a 3 percent upfront sales load and a 1 percent annual management fee. But the fund was such a great performer—it grew at an annual average of 27.4 percent from 1975 to 1993—that investors happily paid the charges.

However, Magellan points up a risk of choosing a fund for a name-brand manager like Lynch, who retired in the late 1980s. If the manager of your fund leaves, there's no guarantee that the fund's performance will be similar to its past results.

If you choose your own mutual funds, it's a good idea to choose an assortment of funds that have different investment goals. So while you might want some money in an international fund, don't put all of your money into one. Putting some money into several different types of funds will give you better long-term growth.

If your goal is to build a personal savings fund, for personal use or for a child's college, a good strategy is to put a set amount of money each month into a mutual fund. For this kind of investment plan, a good choice is one of the all-purpose "multifunds." Some mutual funds have a minimum monthly payment that's too high for many budgets. But four mutual fund families allow you to put in as little as $50 a month—Janus, INVESCO, T. Rowe Price, and Twentieth Century.

If you understand the basics I've discussed here, you won't be intimidated by anything you see in a prospectus or a book on mutual funds. If you want to study mutual funds in intricate detail, subscribe to "Morningstar," an information service that will provide you with all you ever wanted to know about mutual fund investing. Or ask to see Morningstar's reports at your local library.

Short-term Investing —

Investing for retirement is a low-risk proposition, because an investment window of 10 or more years smooths out the ups and downs of many growth-oriented investments.

Short-term investing is trickier. You need investments that fluctuate very little in value, so the money will be there when you need it. Let's say you put $5,000 into a mutual fund and, in the third year, the value of your investment drops 10 percent. That's no problem in a retirement portfolio, because the fund's value in 1998 is far less important than its value in say, 2028, when you retire. But you could get burned if you have to cash in the investment in 1998 and take a substantial loss.

If you have an investment window of three years or less, stay conservative and consider yourself a saver, rather than an investor. A couple of good options are bank certificates of deposit and short-term Treasury securities, both of which are fully guaranteed.

Each of us has the ability to buy Treasury bills direct from the U.S. government, through the regional offices of the Federal Reserve Bank. Treasurys are sold in a variety of terms: three months, six months, one year, two years, three years, five years, seven years, ten years, and thirty years. The longer the term, the higher the interest rate you'll get, but the greater the risk that a sharp run-up in inflation could erode the value of your investment. Most people buy Treasury securities with a term of five years or less. That makes a lot of sense if the purpose of the investment is to park your money for a few years.

Treasurys compete with banks for your money. There are times when Treasury investments will pay more than banks, and there are times when Treasurys will pay less than banks. In April 1994, I bought three-year Treasurys at an interest rate of 6.54 percent, which was 1.5 to 2 percentage points higher than bank interest rates. But a year earlier, Treasurys weren't a great deal at all. Treasurys pay more when the government has a greater need for money, to fund the annual federal budget deficit, than banks have to acquire money for loans to consumers. When loan demand is high, banks will pay more.

To buy Treasurys, you open a Treasury Direct account at a regional office of the Federal Reserve Bank. If you live in a city with a Federal Reserve Branch, you walk in, fill out a short form, and hand it to a teller with a check. A minute later the teller will hand you a receipt and you're done. If you don't live near one of the 36 regional Federal Reserve branches, you can do the transaction by mail. Call or write to the nearest Fed office, or the Bureau of the Public Debt in Washington, and they'll send you a kit.

The beauty of buying Treasurys direct from

the government is you pay no commission. People who don't know about this program might needlessly pay a commission to a stockbroker or a bank to invest in Treasurys. That could eat up most of the advantage of buying them.

There are some conditions to the Treasury Direct program. You need a cashier's check if you're buying T-bills with maturities of one year or less. Otherwise, a personal check is fine. Treasurys of one year or less have a $10,000 minimum. Two-year and three-year Treasurys have a $5,000 minimum, and Treasurys with maturities of five years or longer have a $1,000 minimum. In addition, the hours you can buy Treasurys direct are somewhat narrow, usually from 9:00 A.M. to 2:00 P.M.

If you think Treasurys are for you, buy the *Wall Street Journal* and check the approximate interest rates for three-month and six-month T-bills. The rates are listed in a daily chart called the "Treasury Yield Curve." The rate you will receive is based on the amount investors bid at auctions. Three-month and six-month Treasurys are usually sold each Monday. The longer-term Treasurys are sold monthly or quarterly. Two-year and five-year Treasury notes are issued during the last week of each month. Three-year and ten-year notes usually are issued on the 15th of February, May, August, and November. Thirty-year Treasury bonds usually are issued on the 15th of February and August.

Most people who buy Treasury Direct in person buy the morning the securities are auctioned or the day before. If you're buying by mail, you might have to buy a week before the auction.

The difference in Treasury bills, notes, and bonds primarily is in their maturities. Three-month, six-month, and one-year Treasurys are called bills. Two-year, three-year, five-year, and ten-year Treasurys are called notes, and thirty-year Treasurys are called bonds. There's one other significant difference. T-bills are sold at a discount from par. So, just as with a savings bond, you pay less than the face value for the T-bill. A $10,000, six-month T-bill might cost $9,700. The difference in what you pay and the face value is the "interest."

If you can't meet the minimum deposits for the Treasury Direct program, or you simply prefer bank certificates of deposit, you can get the best return by "laddering" your savings. If you're investing $5,000, use $1,000 to buy a one-year certificate of deposit, $1,000 for a two-year CD, $1,000 for a three-year CD, $1,000 for a four-year CD, and $1,000 for a five-year CD. When the one-year CD matures, use the $1,000 to buy a five-year CD, and do the same the next year when the two-year CD matures. If you continue this process, each of the CDs will be for five years, giving you the best interest rate on your money. But instead of having all $5,000 locked up for five years, you'll have access to one-fifth of your money each year.

Investment decisions are more difficult if you want to put money aside for a moderate period of time—three years to ten years. Experts traditionally have advised "safe" stock and bond investments for this investment window. But you can get burned even with these. Many people who invested in short-term bond funds, for example, suffered dramatic losses not long ago when the value of the bond funds took an unexpected drop in value. They tried short-term bond funds for a 4 1/2 percent yield, instead of 2 percent in an interest checking account, and were stunned when they lost 6 percent of their money. That was unusual, but it can happen.

More often, people with an investment window of three to ten years will do well with short-term bond funds or "balanced" funds, which own both stocks and bonds. But you still have more risk than with a long-term investment horizon.

I see a lot of advertisements for tax-free municipal bonds, but I'm not at all sold on them for most taxpayers. A lot of people buy municipal bonds because they hate to pay the government taxes. It's fine to feel that way, but disliking taxes shouldn't be the basis for an investment decision. If you're in the 15 or 28 percent tax bracket, you may be better off with a taxable investment than with a tax-free investment. You get a lower yield on a tax-free municipal bond than with a taxable corporate bond, and the tax advantage often isn't sufficient to make up the difference. Tax-free municipal bonds are a good choice if you're in the top tax bracket and want an investment that produces a steady, current income. But the top tax bracket includes less than 2 percent of all taxpayers.

If you're 60 to 70 years old, you have several factors to consider when making investments. You have a short investment window, because you might need access to your money in less than ten years. You also want your investments to generate income. But you need growth, too, because there's a good chance you could live another twenty years.

The solution is to invest a portion of your money to generate income, through high-dividend stock or bond funds, and a portion with an eye toward the future. In *The Handbook for No-Load Mutual Funds*, mutual funds expert Sheldon Jacobs suggests that even retirees should have 60 percent of their investment portfolio in stocks (and 40 percent in bonds). You might find that too aggressive for your taste.

Jacobs suggests a retirement portfolio with 35 percent in a variety of stock funds, 25 percent in internationally oriented stock funds, and the remaining 40 percent in bond funds.

In a portfolio for investors within ten years of retirement, Jacobs suggests a more aggressive approach, with 50 percent in stock funds, 25 percent in international stocks, and 25 percent in bonds. And in a younger person's "wealth-builder" portfolio, he suggests 65 percent in stock funds, 30 percent in international, and 5 percent in aggressive growth stock funds.

- Tips on - Short-term Investing

● If you may need your money in a few years, it's important to choose less volatile investments.

● Good options for people with an investment window of three years or less are bank certificates of deposit and short-term Treasury securities.

● Under the government's Treasury Direct program, you can buy Treasury bills, notes, and bonds directly, either by mail or at any regional branch of the Federal Reserve Bank.

● A good strategy with certificates of deposit is "laddering," buying certificates of different maturity and constantly rolling over the funds.

● If you have an investment window of three to ten years, you could try short-term bond funds or "balanced" funds, which own both stocks and bonds.

● Tax-free municipal bonds are generally a good idea only for investors in the top tax bracket.

Contact:
Bureau of the Public Debt
Division of Customer Services
Washington, DC 20239
202-874-4000

Stockbrokers and Other Investments —

Buying shares of stock in a single company is a risky way to invest your money, and it's riskier still because of the dangers of dealing with stockbrokers.

Stockbrokers may seem like unbiased investment advisors. But in truth they are commission salespeople, whose job is to get you to buy and sell stocks because these trades generate commissions for the broker and the brokerage firm. There is an inherent conflict of interest between the investment products that would be most suitable for you and the ones that can generate big commissions for the stockbroker.

If you choose to do business with a full-service broker, make certain to state your investment objectives very clearly on the brokerage agreement you will be asked to sign. If you're a conservative investor who does not like risk, state it. If you like a moderate amount of risk, state that. And if you have no fear of risk, indicate that you're willing to try risky investments. If you fail to state very clearly in that brokerage agreement what level of risk you're willing to take, you can get burned later.

If you ever notice an unusually high level of trading activity in your account, you must act immediately. This ripoff, called churning, is done to generate commissions from unnecessary trades. If trades are made that you have not authorized, or if the broker is doing anything else you don't like, rush a letter to the stockbroker stating that the activity in your account is unauthorized by you and all trading activity should stop immediately. Have someone at the brokerage sign to acknowledge receipt of the letter. Then send a letter to the brokerage house demanding an immediate meeting with the branch manager. Document every phone call that takes place with the broker if you feel the broker has violated your trust. Finally, if you feel you have been cheated by your account being churned, immediately send a certified letter to the brokerage house stating that your account has been churned and that you want all money returned to you, including all commissions unfairly earned and any losses suffered on unsuitable investments.

When you sign your agreement with the stockbroker, it probably will contain a clause saying you will not sue the stock brokerage and you will agree instead to arbitration to resolve any disputes. Make sure you cross that phrase out, put your initials by it, and insert the following sentence: "I reserve the right to sue X brokerage in the event that I have a dispute with the firm." If the broker won't agree to this, don't do business with that broker.

Complaints against brokerages are staggering. As of mid-1995, Prudential Securities had paid more than $1.4 billion in fines and settlements stemming from its sale of limited partnerships to investors. The investors alleged they were cheated.

The problem is that stock brokerages are really just sales organizations, not investment houses. The branch manager is judged by how much volume he pushes through his office. Each broker is judged by how much commission he drives through. At sales meetings, they'll have some new investment products and the manager tells the brokers to sell them hard because extra commission is being paid on them. The brokers then get on the phone and work their accounts, telling clients why this product is such a great deal and why it will make a fortune for the client. The brokers write a ton of orders and the clients get duped. Prudential, it was alleged, sold people $1.46 billion worth of limited partnerships that were anything but good investments. Huge commissions were earned by all. Then the customers started screaming.

I received a huge number of calls about People's Financial Resources, an investment scam set up to bilk church members. The head of this operation, Donald P. Clark, got to know local pastors and won permission to make financial presentations to members of the church. In the presentations, Clark would promise to draw up a will for somebody, give some financial planning advice, and get some investments started, for a total of $1,800 to $2,000 per person. The red flag was his promise that the investments would earn inordinately high rates, 12 percent or more. His favorite targets were young widows and others who had come into some money recently and didn't know what to do with it.

Because the presentations were made in the church, most people never questioned the organization's legitimacy. But investors started getting suspicious when they tried and were unable to withdraw part of their money. The Securities and Exchange Commission and local authorities in two states all acted to shut down the company's operations, but the money was lost. Donald Clark's brother, Ken, pleaded guilty to five counts of securities fraud and was sentenced to fifteen years in jail for his role in the scam. Donald Clark agreed to plead no contest to federal civil charges of fraud and to pay back $6.2 million of the $20 million taken from investors. But it wasn't clear whether he had the money or not.

The moral is, be careful when you're investing money. Don't buy securities from someone who isn't registered with both the National Association of Securities Dealers and the regulating authority in your state.

I've had a number of experiences with investments in my own life, both good and bad. I invested in a video rental concession in a major supermarket and lost all my money when the general manager embezzled from us and skipped town. I also was involved in an experimental car company in which I lost my investment.

I've had other ventures that have been very successful. I invested in a commuter airline that went from being privately held to publicly traded. I've done quite well as one of the original investors in a community bank. And I've done extremely well buying troubled real estate, including foreclosures, relocations, and even estate sales of real estate.

Here are a few of the things I've learned:
* Don't invest in businesses you don't know anything about.
* Don't buy individual stocks unless you just think it's fun to do. It's too risky to place your money in just a few companies.
* If you're going to take a major stake in a business, don't do so without having some voice in how that business is operated.

But my most important advice on investments is the simplest—if you do not understand an investment, do not buy it. Just because a friend, a relative, or an investment counselor tells you to invest in something, don't do it unless you fully understand the investment. People violate this investment rule often, even though it makes the most basic sense. Then they're shocked when their money disappears. People get seduced by risky, trendy, and confusing investments such as oil and gas limited partnerships, wireless communication limited partnerships, futures, and commodities trading. Don't rely on the promotional literature for such investments. Investigate further before you buy.

The most important time to be conservative with your money is when you win the lottery or receive an inheritance or a large settlement of a lawsuit or claim. People who are lucky enough to come into a large sum of money have a tendency to want to gamble with it. That's the opposite of what you should do. The best approach is to be as conservative as you possibly can. If you receive a large amount of cash, you shouldn't increase your spending or change your lifestyle dramatically, or that money will soon disappear. If others know, everybody's going to be at your door trying to sell you the greatest new business venture, the greatest new investment, or a resort property you don't need. So batten down the hatches. That's the one time when it's okay to lock the money in the bank and let it earn the market rate of interest.

One fellow I met seemed determined to give away a large amount of cash. He had just won the lottery and came to talk to me at a trade show about the three-wheel car company I was involved with. He told me this was a business he wanted to invest in because he believed it was the fuel-efficient car of the future. Here I was, one of the owners of the company, and we needed money. But while I would have loved to have had his money in the company, I told him it was a risky venture and that he should rethink his plans. He didn't appreciate the advice, but it was the best advice I could have given him. I've long wondered what ever happened to that man and whether he blew all his money.

Now the reverse sometimes happens. I've heard of people who have invested their winnings in a business and wound up with ten times the original sum. But that doesn't happen often. For every one entrepreneur who successfully invests his or her new money in a start-up business, there are probably a hundred who fail and wind up with nothing.

Credit Cards —

When the preapproved credit card applications arrived by the handful around America in the 1980s, few realized how easily debt could destroy a family's finances. That sobering lesson has been learned by many in the 1990s, as millions of jobs have been lost and family budgets built on debt have collapsed.

Too many were forced to turn to bankruptcy, while others have been fortunate enough to emerge from overwhelming debt and are determined not to make the same mistake again. A few years ago, I met a fellow at a gas station convenience store who told me a remarkable story. Two years earlier, when he started listening to my show, he had $26,000 in credit card debt and he hated answering his telephone. In those two years, he completely changed his lifestyle,

---

- Tips on - Stockbrokers and Other Investments

- Stockbrokers are commission salespeople whose job is to get you to buy and sell stocks because these trades generate commissions for the broker and the brokerage firm.

- If you choose to do business with a stockbroker, make certain to state your investment objectives clearly on the brokerage agreement.

- Monitor your account and watch for "churning," or unnecessary trading.

- Include in your contract a clause allowing you to sue the brokerage if you have a dispute with the firm.

- Don't buy securities from anyone who isn't registered with both the National Association of Securities Dealers and the regulating authority in your state.

- If you do not understand an investment, do not buy it.

Contact:
National Association of Securities Dealers
(Investments)
Disciplinary History: 1-800-289-9999
Licensing Information: 301-590-6500

---

wiped out all his credit card debt, and bought his own home. That made me feel great. In two years, someone who was drowning in debt and whose life was out of control wiped out the debt and reclaimed his life.

I look at debt as a disease and credit cards as one of the easiest ways to get sick. Nobody ever got wealthy borrowing money for gifts, clothes, restaurants, entertainment, or travel. When you purchase lifestyle with credit, you end up with huge obligations and no tangible assets. The meal is eaten, the trip is taken, and most of the clothes you bought at the mall end up sitting in your closet.

Credit cards are seductive. When you first get one in your hand, it seems to be a new source of wealth. But that wealth is really an illusion, because misusing a credit card actually lowers your standard of living over time.

Credit cards are okay if you use them for safety or convenience. In high-crime cities, it's good to carry a credit card rather than cash because, if your card is lost or stolen, the maximum cost to you is $50. Having been a victim of crime, I almost always use credit cards and carry only a minimum of cash. But I use credit cards only as a convenient, alternate method of payment and I pay the bill in full every month.

Two-thirds of all credit card holders use them the wrong way. They use their cards to purchase merchandise and then carry the balance, financing this new debt at extremely high rates of interest. Paying that interest is what siphons your money away. If you have $1,000 in the bank in a savings account earning 3 percent and you are paying 17.5 percent interest on a $1,000 credit card balance, somebody's doing real well and it's not you.

Some experts say you should pay for everything with cash. But if you track what you buy it doesn't matter how you pay. If you feel your spending is out of control, take a little notebook along with you and record every expen-diture you make for two weeks. Then put a code by each item. Put an "A" next to things you absolutely had to spend the money on. Put a "C" down when you're not really sure if you had to have it or not, and put an "F" by anything that you truly didn't have to have. The reason I use those codes is because people can relate them to school grades. You get an "A" for spending money correctly and an "F" for spending money incorrectly.

If you can discipline yourself to use credit cards only for convenience—knowing you'll pay the balance in full each month—choosing a card is easy. All you need to do is get a card with no annual fee and a 25-day grace period between the day of the purchase and the day the inter-est meter starts running. That way, you can have the convenience of credit cards with no cost at all.

However, if you frequently carry a balance, the annual fee matters very little. Far more important is the interest rate, which will cost you a lot more money on a high balance than will any annual fee. Certain banks now specialize in credit cards with variable interest rates. Those cards tend to have high annual fees, but the rates, though not fixed at a certain level, tend to be lower than those of most cards. If you can't avoid carrying a credit card balance, at least make it less expensive by paying a lower rate to finance that balance.

If you pick a variable rate card, avoid those that attract you with an ultra-low teaser rate. Pick one that calculates its interest rate using a widely followed rate, such as the prime lend-ing rate. You'll know in advance how the rate will be figured. I received a mailer recently from a credit card company offering a very low interest rate—6.9 percent. But that rate was applicable for only 90 days. After that it jumped to 17.5 percent. So that card had no advantage.

One other thing I want to point out is that if you pay in full some months and carry a bal-ance during other months, avoid any card, such as the Discover Card, that has a "two-cycle" billing method. Using this technique, the lender adds the balance together for two months before computing interest and therefore severely punishes people who pay their bill in full some months but carry a balance other months. You're better off taking a card with a higher rate of interest than going with a card that uses the two-cycle method.

Credit cards have changed a lot in the last few years because nonbanks have entered the credit card business. Now that banks no longer have a cartel, you have such alternatives as the Universal Card from AT&T and other cards from General Electric and General Motors. Credit unions have become big issuers of cards because they often charge no annual fee and have low interest rates. If you have access to a credit union, go there first for a card.

These new issuers have changed the face of the credit card business, forcing other issuers to lower their rates. Market share has dropped for both American Express, which has a very, very high annual fee, and Citibank, which is the nation's largest issuer of VISA and MasterCard.

The AT&T and GM cards both have been hugely successful, the GM card because of the lure of being able to accrue $500 a year toward rebates on GM cars. If you always buy GM cars, this card is a smart choice as long as you don't run a balance on the card, because it does have significant interest charges. The AT&T card is a great choice for people who don't run a balance because there's no annual fee. The interest rate is a little lower than many other cards. The Discover Card suffered a drop in volume because, even though it has no annual fee, its interest rate remains extremely high. Discover has gone to a split rate system, under which people who charge frequently get a lower rate. But the rates are too high and Discover's heavily promoted "cash back" system provides little true benefit. As a result, the marketplace is punishing Discover. People

- Tips on - Credit Cards

● Debt is a disease and credit cards are one of the easiest ways to get sick. Nobody ever got wealthy borrowing money for gifts, clothes, restaurants, entertainment, or travel.

● Credit cards are okay if you use them for safety or convenience.

● Two-thirds of all credit card holders use them the wrong way. They buy things with money they don't have and finance this new debt at extremely high rates of interest.

● If you don't carry a balance, get a card with no annual fee and a 25-day grace period between the day of the purchase and the day the interest meter starts running.

● If you frequently carry a balance, get a card with a low interest rate. The annual fee matters very little.

● Don't carry more than two or three credit cards. They're unnecessary and can cost you up to $50 per card if they're lost or stolen.

Contact:
Ram Research
Card Trak
460 West Patrick Street
P.O. Box 1700
Frederick, MD 21702
1-800-344-7714

(For a comprehensive guide to low-interest credit cards, no-fee credit cards, and secured credit cards)

are slowly but steadily going to cards with lower rates.

A lot of people still carry too many credit cards in their wallet. It makes sense to carry a VISA and a MasterCard, but skip department store cards and gasoline credit cards. Department store cards have very high interest rates and are primarily a tool to get people into the stores to spend money. These cards are really an invitation to build debt for yourself.

Gasoline cards are similarly useless. Generally a business that takes a gasoline credit card will also take a VISA or MasterCard. Using a gasoline card or a department store card means there's an additional bill you have to pay, and if that card gets stolen, you're liable for the same $50 on it as any other card. If your wallet is stolen and you have two credit cards in it, your maximum risk is $100. If you have seven cards, your maximum risk is $350.

You don't want to carry just one card because if, for some reason, that company decides to lift your card, you are without credit. No two banks use the same credit standards, so you're better protected if you carry a VISA and a MasterCard, each from different institutions. I carry a VISA from my insurance company, a MasterCard from my credit union, and a Discover Card so I can use it at Sam's Club, which doesn't take any other cards.

Credit Problems —

If you misuse your credit cards, you'll eventually get to the point at which you are heavily in debt and you're just making the minimum payment on your credit card bills. By paying the minimum, you never work off the balance. All you're doing is paying interest on the early debt you took on.

Some advisers say you can tell you're in credit trouble if your debt payments exceed a certain percentage of your take-home pay, but I don't think anybody ever figures out those ratios, except when they're applying for a mortgage. You know how you feel. You need help if you're afraid to answer the phone or open the mail, you have trouble sleeping at night, or you're eating too much or too little.

Since I've been doing my radio show, there has been a steady increase in the number of callers who have money troubles. Most of these people were living a credit existence and had a change in their personal circumstances that caused their finances to collapse. They lost their job, got divorced, became ill, or had a problem with drugs or alcohol that made their debt unmanageable.

I have seen more credit trouble over the last few years not because people have taken on more debt; it's because more people have lost jobs and the family income has fallen. Couples today often rely on the income of both the husband and the wife, and if they lose either job a money crisis may soon follow.

When you get into financial trouble, you need to create a pyramid of priorities. The most important thing to pay is your mortgage or rent. The next priority is your car loan, and the third is your utilities, which keep your house functioning. After that you pay your unsecured creditors—credit card and loan companies.

Ironically, the most ferocious and frequent phone calls you'll receive when you fall behind on your bills will be from the credit card and small loan companies. The mortgage companies tend to react more slowly because their loans are secured by your home. The car loan people are only a little quicker; again, their loan is secured by your automobile. Because of these calls, people in credit trouble often throw money at the wrong source. The credit cards should always come last.

You have strong rights under federal law to prevent collection agencies from harassing you, although the law does not apply to the creditors themselves. The Fair Debt Collection Practices Act bars collectors from threatening to harm you, your reputation, or your property, and from using profane language or falsely claiming to be an attorney or a government representative. The law also prohibits claims that you will be arrested or imprisoned if you don't pay, and it prohibits late-night phone calls and repeated phone calls intended to harass you.

You can stop collection agencies from contacting you at home, at work, or at all by sending them a "drop-dead" letter. You'll find a prewritten drop-dead letter in the Workbook chapter of this book. It's a good idea to send it by certified mail, and don't forget to keep a copy. Once a collection agency receives it, the company can contact you only to acknowledge that it won't contact you again, or to notify you that it is filing a lawsuit. Under the law, if a company continues to harass you, you can sue it for actual damages and punitive damages of up to $1,000. The law is enforced by the Federal Trade Commission.

Beware of companies who say they'll help you get out of debt. A caller told me she was considering such a service. She was supposed to send a check each month to this company. The company would then subtract its fee—$15 a month plus $5 per credit card or loan—and distribute the rest to her creditors. The red flag was a line in the contract saying she wouldn't hold the company responsible if the company didn't send the money to her creditors.

A legitimate consumer service is available to help you when you can't keep the wolves from your door. It's called Consumer Credit Counseling and it is available in most areas. Consumer Credit Counseling is provided by a network of nonprofit organizations. They're funded, ironically enough, by the credit grantors, to offer people a method to honor their debts. Call the National Foundation for Consumer Credit Counseling to find a location near your home.

People who go to credit counseling generally fall into one of three categories. A third of the people who walk in the door are so far in debt or have such little income that credit counselors cannot be of help to them. These are the people for whom bankruptcy becomes a real option. The second third are not in nearly as bad a shape as they think they are and really just need help in setting up a budget and new spending priorities. These folks are helped through counseling at little or no cost to them.

Consumer Credit Counseling Service is best known for the way it helps the third group of people, those whose debts have grown beyond a manageable size but who have the ability to repay them within three years, with some help. A repayment plan negotiated by Consumer Credit Counseling requires some give on both sides. It requires the consumer to cut spending or increase income through a part-time job or more work hours. It requires the department stores and other lenders to reduce the amount of money owed or create more favorable terms for repayment.

When you feel it is hopeless, Consumer Credit Counseling can give you an honorable way to meet your obligations. That's what most people want. The sudden power people feel regaining control over their lives is wonderful. I remember one man who had just finished his repayment plan with Consumer Credit Counseling Service. He was near tears as he talked about the burden that had been lifted off him. That's the beauty of the process. This is not like the seductive TV ads that promote bankruptcy as an easy way out. This is a fresh start with dignity and hard work.

For a while, I heard some stories about credit grantors who refused to comply with the terms negotiated by Consumer Credit Counseling. Very few do that anymore, and those who do show themselves to be extremely foolish. If someone is right on the edge of being able to work out a successful repayment plan through Consumer Credit Counseling, and a shortsighted, mean-spirited credit grantor

- Tips on -
Credit Problems

● By paying the minimum payment on your credit cards, you never work off the balance. All you're doing is paying interest on the early debt you took on.

● When you get into financial trouble, create a pyramid of priorities. The most important thing to pay is your mortgage or rent. The next priority is your car loan, and the third is your utilities, which keep your house functioning. After that you pay your unsecured creditors—credit card and loan companies.

● If you need help, don't immediately file for bankruptcy. The best option is Consumer Credit Counseling, which can help you work out a debt repayment plan.

● If you've had credit trouble and want to reestablish credit, try a secured credit card, which lets you charge up to an amount you place on deposit with the lender.

Contact:
Federal Trade Commission
Publications Division
Washington, DC 20580
202-326-2222
(Ask for a copy of the brochure "Fair Debt Collection Practices Act.")

National Foundation for Consumer Credit Counseling
8611 2nd Avenue, Suite 100
Silver Spring, MD 20910
(301) 589-5600

Ram Research
Card Trak
460 West Patrick Street
P.O. Box 1700
Frederick, MD 21702
1-800-344-7714

(For a comprehensive guide to low-interest credit cards, no-fee credit cards, and secured credit cards)

doesn't go along, it's going to push the debtor into bankruptcy court and then the credit grantor probably is going to get nothing.

Citibank at one time was completely uncooperative with Consumer Credit Counseling and now they're on the team. Through their former mean-spiritedness, the number of their customers who filed for bankruptcy soared. So they changed their approach.

Some people worry that going to credit counseling will hurt their credit rating. Most of these people already have a flawed credit report and credit counseling really has a neutral impact. Plus, once you've completed a repayment plan, Consumer Credit Counseling will work to help you obtain one mortgage loan, one car loan, and one credit card. So, rather than being a negative, credit counseling has a reward at the end—the establishment of a responsible level of credit with the service's assistance.

If you have had credit problems and are trying to reestablish credit, I suggest you get a secured credit card. That's a credit card you get by posting a deposit with the lender, say $500. Then you're able to charge up to the $500 you have on deposit. The money you have on deposit earns interest and you have a credit card you can use like any other VISA or MasterCard holder. There are a lot of organizations that offer secured cards with very unfavorable terms and a precious few that offer secured cards at reasonable terms. The best ones tend to have a moderate annual fee, $35 a year or less, no application fee, and a grace period from the purchase date until interest charges begin. To get a list of lenders who offer reasonable terms on secured cards, contact Ram Research.

Perhaps you haven't reached the point of going to Consumer Credit Counseling and things have begun to improve. Maybe you got a job or a raise. Start digging out of debt this way. Take your unsecured debts and rank them by interest rate. Pay the monthly minimum on all credit cards and credit lines, except for the one with the highest interest rate. Throw every penny you can at that one each month until you've paid it off, then go to the second highest and extinguish that one. If you have six lines of credit, motivate yourself to cut it to five. That's much easier and more satisfying than trying to get rid of all of them at once. Try to set a realistic time period, within three years, to get rid of your debt.

Credit Reports —

A few years ago, finding a mistake on your credit report was no big deal, because a credit report was just one factor in determining whether you got a bank loan or credit card. Underwriting standards for loans were looser than they are now, and lenders considered other factors, such as your character, in deciding whether to grant you a loan.

Today, an error on your credit report can keep you from being able to get the loan you want, buy the house, or rent the apartment you want to live in. Those are big problems.

Loan approval standards are tougher now because of the financial upheaval in the lending industry. Bad loans caused many institutions to fail and forced others to tighten their loan qualifications. No longer are lenders doing home mortgages with little documentation required. The mortgage approval process, once loose and sloppy, has become tight and unforgiving. With personal loans and car loans, a few slow-payment marks on your credit report used to be sloughed off. Now they can lead to an almost automatic denial of credit.

This transformation was quite a shock to the credit bureaus, the companies that collect information on your credit history and issue a report to the lender when you apply for a credit line. For years, the credit bureaus operated in happy anonymity and knew that being somewhat accurate was good enough. Now, lenders want them to be totally accurate and they can't do it.

Complete accuracy is needed because the credit report has skyrocketed in importance. People going for a job interview, to rent an apartment, or to open a checking account at a bank now routinely must sign an authorization to release their credit report. If you've ever had problems with a bank, other banks won't do business with you.

Getting a credit report corrected is one of the most difficult and frustrating things consumers ever face. There are three major credit bureaus—Equifax, TRW, and Trans Union—and they don't share information. So even if you correct an error with one, you will have to do the same with the other two. After a month-long battle to get an item removed from your Equifax credit report, TRW and Trans Union may still show you to be a deadbeat.

Another stubborn problem is the way information is supplied to the credit bureaus. Let's say a credit card company incorrectly says you're a deadbeat and you convince Equifax to remove the error. A month later, the credit card company may send a new computer tape to the credit bureau and the error reappears on your credit record. If that happens, you have to ask the credit bureau to use suppression technology, which will prevent an item from ever reappearing on your report once it's been cleared up.

The biggest problem with the credit-reporting industry has been that your arguments get little weight when you challenge an item on your credit report. But the word of the credit card companies and other credit grantors is given tremendous importance. You have a right under federal law to challenge items on your credit report. The credit bureau then has a reasonable period of time, usually interpreted as thirty days, to decide whether that item should be removed. They simply forward your protest to the credit grantor. If the credit grantor reaffirms the information, the credit bureau takes the credit grantor's side, no matter what you say.

I've had many callers tell me their credit report listed a loan they knew nothing about. Someone else borrowed the money and didn't pay it back and somehow it wound up on their credit report. The consumer protests to the credit bureau and the bureau comes back and says the credit grantor has verified the loan was theirs. End of story.

Slowly, the credit bureaus are beginning to reform the method of dispute. If you have clear proof that a debt is not yours—perhaps a loan document with your signature forged—the credit bureau will remove it from your report. But they will do so only if you ask them. The real problem with the credit-reporting system is that there's no pressure point on the credit grantors, no way to penalize them for knowingly putting false information on your credit report. Let's say a bank puts something on your credit report and you have proof that it's wrong, but the bank still doesn't change it. Right now it's almost impossible for you to sue them to force the change. If there was a pressure point that a consumer could press to make an irresponsible or malicious credit

grantor suffer for its actions, then we'd really be somewhere.

The improvements made by the three major credit bureaus have been most obvious at Equifax. TRW is a defense contractor, a diversified company, and officials there don't pay that much attention to this part of their business. They've made a couple of changes. Trans Union is the smallest. They're leaving it to Equifax to set the trends for the industry. Equifax has made improvements because it fears public outrage could cause Congress to order severe changes in how it does business. Among those changes is a consumer service center Equifax opened to make access easier to the public. It's open from 8:00 A.M. to 11:00 P.M. Equifax and TRW now have toll-free numbers you can use to order a credit report.

Equifax is much more accessible to the public, and many people are relieved that the company no longer is as impossible to reach. But it's still difficult to resolve disputes and even harder to get errors removed from all three reports. One entrepreneur has even come up with a service that provides you with copies of all three of your credit reports for one fee. You'll find a sample credit report in the Workbook section of this book.

I strongly recommend that you spend the money to get all three of your credit reports six months before you apply for a home loan. That's very, very important. I receive so many distressing phone calls from people who are trying to get approval for a home loan and are stymied by a credit report problem.

I had a call from one fellow whose credit report was so messed up that he had to take two weeks off from work to straighten it out. He discovered, while refinancing his house, that someone he didn't know had used his Social Security number to obtain ten credit cards. The crook had fraudulently rolled up several thousand dollars in charges.

One way to avoid this potential disaster is

- Tips on -
Credit Reports

● There are three major credit bureaus that issue credit reports to lenders—Equifax, TRW, and Trans Union—and they don't share information. So even if you correct an error on one credit report, you will have to do the same on the other two.

● You have the right under federal law to challenge items on your credit report. The credit bureau then has a reasonable period of time, usually interpreted as 30 days, to decide whether that item should be removed. Unfortunately, the credit bureau almost always sides with the credit grantor.

● Get copies of all three credit reports six months before you apply for a home loan. An error on your credit report can take months to clear up. If your time is ticking away on a home closing and you can't get approved for a loan, you're going to lose the house.

Contact:
Equifax Information Service
P.O. Box 740123
Atlanta, GA 30374
404-612-2500
1-800-685-1111

(Send a signed written request with your name, address, and Social Security number. The cost varies. It's free if you have been turned down for credit based on an Equifax report.)

TRW Complimentary Report Request
P.O. Box 2350
Chatsworth, CA 91313
1-800-682-7654

(For one free credit report each calendar year, you must indicate you are asking for your "annual complimentary copy" and include your full name, address, and previous addresses for the past five years, Social Security number, year of birth, your spouse's first name, and a copy of your driver's license or a household bill.)

Trans Union
P.O. Box 7000
North Olmstead, OH 44070

(Call for information. Or send $15 and a signed written request with your name, address, previous addresses within the past five years, Social Security number, daytime telephone number, date of birth, and employer.)

to guard your Social Security number. Consider leaving your Social Security card at home, rather than carrying it in your wallet, in case your wallet is ever lost or stolen.

An error on your credit report can take months to clear up. If your time is ticking away on a home closing and you can't get approved for a loan, you're going to lose that house. With a car loan, time is not as important. You should go into your bank or credit union and get preapproved for a car loan just before you're ready to buy. You'll know immediately if there is a problem. It's not as much of an earth-shattering crisis if there's a reason you can't buy a new car. When you get knocked out of the housing market, it's traumatic.

401(k) Payouts —

When you quit a job or are fired, you may have to decide what to do about the money in your 401(k) retirement plan. Once upon a time, you would get a check from your company and had 60 days to put the money into an Individual Retirement Account, or another company's 401(k) plan, or face severe tax penalties. But so many people spent the money that the government changed the rules. Now if you take a check from your employer, 20 percent of your 401(k) money will be withheld to cover your potential tax liability. With 20 percent withheld, it's very difficult to put the full amount into an IRA.

Let's say you've had $10,000 in a 401(k) plan. You have 60 days to roll over the full $10,000 into another retirement plan. Because $2,000 of your $10,000 was withheld by the government, you have to redeposit not just the $8,000 you received, but write a check for $2,000 to make up the full balance. If you don't, the $2,000 you haven't rolled over will be considered a withdrawal and will be subject to a 10 percent early withdrawal penalty ($200 of the $2,000) plus normal federal and state income tax. The withdrawal penalty doesn't apply if you are 59 1/2 or older.

If you don't roll over any of the 401(k) payout into a retirement plan, then all $10,000 is subject to tax and the early withdrawal penalty. For most of us, that means $4,000 to $5,000 of the $10,000 would be eaten up.

One way to avoid any of these complications is a trustee-to-trustee transfer of your money. If you leave your job, instruct your former employer to send the retirement money directly to an IRA account at a particular mutual fund house or to any other financial institution that manages IRAs. Or have it deposited directly into the 401(k) plan at your new employer. If you follow this procedure, no money is withheld, no taxes are due, and your money continues to grow until retirement.

More and more in recent years, people have been tempted to spend their 401(k) payouts after being fired from a job. They worry about how they're going to pay the rent, buy food, and take care of their family. They spend the retirement money and then end up with a huge tax bill equal to 40 to 50 percent of the total payout. Sometimes, people find a job in three or four months and decide they don't need to spend the retirement money. But they're still stuck with the tax bill if they've taken their money out of the tax-sheltered environment and allowed 60 or more days to pass before rolling it over.

Here's what you should do if you're afraid you're going to need money. Transfer the money directly from your employer's 401(k) plan into an IRA. Make sure the IRA account is totally liquid, that is, money can be withdrawn from it at any time. If you use a mutual fund account, choose a money market mutual fund. Then, if you find you must have some of that money to live on, pull out what you need and leave the rest in the plan. If you do it that way, only the portion you've withdrawn will be subject to tax.

Here's another trick. If you lose your job late

in the year and you expect to have a lengthy period of unemployment in the following year, try to leave your money in an IRA until at least January 2. There are two advantages to that. First, your tax rate will be much lower if you don't earn much that year, so getting your retirement money won't cost as much in taxes. Also, the tax won't be due until the following April 15, almost 16 months later. So you'll have some time to get back on your feet. But make every effort not to spend more than half of your retirement money if at all possible. That way, you'll always have the other half to cover you in case you end up with a huge tax bill. Someone I know was unemployed and spent all her retirement money during her unemployment. She ended up having to borrow the money to pay the IRS.

When you roll the retirement money into an IRA, I recommend you do it using a procedure I outlined earlier called dollar-cost averaging. First, deposit the money into a money-market account inside the IRA. Then, with all the money safely under the IRA umbrella, divide it into roughly equal amounts and transfer portions of it from the money-market account into the stock mutual funds you've picked, over a 12- or 18-month period. If you have $12,000 to invest, you transfer $1,000 on the same day each month from the money-market account into the stock mutual funds, or $667 a month for 18 months. That way, you're protected from the sudden ups and downs of the market.

I got a pension fund distribution not long ago and deposited all the money with the Charles Schwab discount brokerage house, which allows purchase of certain no-sales-commission mutual funds. Schwab's plan is called the Mutual Fund OneSource. They've reach an agreement with several of the no-load mutual fund houses under which the broker's commission is paid to Schwab by the mutual fund. Customers buy without any sales cost, just as if they were buying directly from the mutual fund house. But they have the convenience of dealing with a brokerage house.

I transferred my money to Schwab's money market fund and I'm periodically buying into nine different mutual funds. My plan was set up so that I made an initial investment in each of the nine funds and put the rest in the money market fund. Each month for 18 months, a portion of my money is transferred into the nine funds. The minimum amounts to invest in this way are very low, but there are some perks for putting a larger sum in. Under Schwab's plan—and these things are subject to change—if you transfer $10,000 from a 401(k) plan or IRA, you pay no IRA custodial fees for life. And with the Mutual Fund OneSource, I can keep my account with one institution but buy mutual funds from a number of different mutual fund families.

Another strategy is to do a direct transfer of your retirement money and instantaneously buy the same holdings you had in the company-sponsored plan. You don't even have to worry about dollar-cost averaging because you've already done that by making payments out of every paycheck into the company's mutual fund.

One word of caution: If you transfer a 401(k) payout into an IRA, you might want to keep it separate from any previous or future IRA you may have. If you keep the 401(k) money separate, you are permitted to move it later into another company's 401(k) plan. If you mix funds, you lose that option.

I've heard horror stories from people who've been waiting years to get their 401(k) money after they are no longer working for the company. There are no rules requiring the employer to distribute the money within a certain number of months. Each plan has its own rules, listed under the distributions section of the summary plan and description. You can request a copy of the plan from your former employer or go to the employer's office and read it.

- Tips on -
401(k) Payouts

● If you leave a company and take a check for your retirement money, 20 percent of the money will be withheld to cover potential federal taxes. But you have to redeposit 100 percent of the money into an IRA account or another 401(k) plan within 60 days or lose nearly half of it to federal and state taxes.

● You can avoid withholding with a trustee-to-trustee transfer of your money. If you leave your job, instruct your former employer to send the retirement money directly to an IRA account or the 401(k) plan at your new employer.

● Don't spend the retirement money, or you'll end up with a huge tax bill. If you think you may need the money, put it in an IRA, then withdraw only what you need.

● Use dollar-cost averaging if you're going to put your money into a stock or bond mutual fund. Put the money into a money market IRA account, then transfer the money gradually into other funds over 12 or 18 months. This protects you from the ups and downs of the market.

● If you transfer a 401(k) payout into an IRA, keep it separate from any previous or future IRA you may have. This way you will be permitted to move it later into another company's 401(k) plan.

When I sold my travel agency in May 1987, the buyers wanted to continue contributing to the retirement plan. Then they decided they wanted to liquidate it. Incredibly, the process of handling the paperwork and coordinating between the new owners, myself, and the insurance company took 4 1/2 years. People were inconvenienced, but at least no one lost money because of the delay. The money remained in the plan, and the holdings of the employees continued to grow.

Finally, many employers will continue to manage your retirement money for you even after you leave. If you don't want the hassle of investments, it may be a smart thing to leave your 401(k) money in the care of your former employer.

Taxes and Investing —

People make a huge mistake when the primary emphasis of their investment is its tax value. You never know when such a decision will come back to bite you.

In 1984, I invested in a real estate tax shelter in Miami, Florida, the type of shelter that got extremely favorable treatment under the tax code. On paper, the limited partnership had huge losses, so investors ended up with more net benefit on their taxes than the amount of money they were putting in.

Well, in 1986, Congress changed the laws and eliminated the favorable tax treatment, forcing real estate ventures such as this limited partnership to stand on their own two feet as businesses. As a result, the shelter failed and the property was foreclosed upon. Not only did I lose all that I had paid in, but because of the foreclosure, all of my losses over the years had to be recaptured on my tax return in one year. In 1991, I had a tax bill of more than $50,000. It proved to me what I had always heard and ignored, that the underlying investment should first be sound. Then, if it has tax advantages, that's a bonus. Making an investment decision solely for tax reasons leaves you exposed to loss.

Here's another example. Many banks encourage people to borrow against their house, through a home equity loan, for a vacation, a boat, or a car. They consider this a smart loan, because you can deduct the interest paid on the loan from your income tax. On consumer loans, there is no interest deduction anymore.

This is another tax decision in which what appears to be smart in most cases is dumb. Your house should be treated as security. If you use it as a piece of collateral for a loan and you're unable to pay back the loan, you don't lose the boat or the memories of the vacation you took. You lose your house. To put your house at risk because of a tax advantage is an unwise decision. It's even worse if you're borrowing against your house for something that retains no value, like a vacation. The only reason to borrow against your house is to increase the worth of the house, say for a bathroom or kitchen addition or renovation.

The purchase of a home is another instance in which the tax advantages of the investment are frequently overstated. Home ownership is part of the American dream and part of the measurement of our success. But from a financial standpoint, buying a house is not always the smartest decision. The standard deduction is so large now that the benefit of itemizing deductions on your tax return—the main financial benefit of home ownership—has been significantly reduced.

Let's take the example of a family that earns $60,000 a year and owns a $90,000 house. Say they put $9,000 down and borrowed $81,000 on a 30-year, 8 1/4 percent fixed-rate mortgage. By itemizing their deductions, the family would owe about $5,545 in federal income tax. If the family took the standard deduction, they would pay $6,861 in federal tax. So the tax benefit to buying a house, for this family, is just $1,316 annually. That's not a huge amount of money compared to the cost of the purchase.

Sometimes, people have a sufficient sum of money to pay cash for a car or even a home. I've had calls from people who've received an inheritance and wonder whether they should use it to buy a home without a mortgage. My best advice is, go over the numbers with your accountant to see if you'd be helping yourself by paying cash for the house instead of putting the money into some other investment.

The interest on a car loan is no longer tax deductible, so unless you love paying interest, buying a car with cash is a great idea if you can afford it. My attitude is, we'd be a lot better off if people still bought cars for transportation, the way we did 30 years ago. Too many people today buy a car as a personal statement. If you can pay cash for a decent used car and therefore don't have to make a monthly car payment, you can do really well. Take the amount you would have used for the monthly payment, stash it in a car war chest and use it to pay cash for the next car you want to buy.

One of the most troubling tax decisions people make when April 15 rolls around is not filing their tax return because they don't have the money. If you can't pay, you should file your return anyway and attach an explanation. You're treated much differently if you fail to file than if you filed but can't afford to pay. Those who don't file can face potential criminal charges.

If you do file and can't pay, you should enter into negotiations with the IRS and the state for a payment plan. Generally, they will be reluctant partners in this process, so you need to give a complete explanation as to why a payment plan is justified. You will have to give a lot of information about your finances, but this is far preferable to burying yourself in a hole and hiding.

Once people don't file one year, they become afraid and they don't file in subsequent years. If you find yourself in that situation, you can go to the IRS and turn yourself in. They will help you recreate your tax return for those years. Surprisingly, people fail to file in many cases when they are due a refund. So you may not

- Tips on -
Taxes and
Investing

● In choosing an investment, the investment itself should be sound. If it has tax advantages, that's a bonus.

● Don't use home equity loans. If you use your house as collateral for a loan and you're unable to pay back the loan, you lose your house.

● From a financial standpoint, buying a house is not always the smartest decision. The standard deduction is so large now that the benefit of itemizing deductions on your tax return—the main financial benefit of home ownership—has been largely negated.

● If you can't pay your income taxes on April 15, file your tax return anyway and attach an explanation.

● If you have problems with the IRS, try the IRS problem resolution office. If that doesn't work, call or write your congressman or U.S. senator's constituent service office for help.

Contact:
IRS Problem Resolution
National Office
Taxpayer Ombudsman's Office
Washington, DC 20224
1-202-622-6100

be facing the financial albatross you suspect, and there is a tremendous feeling of relief when you do settle up.

Of course you may get some other feelings from dealing with the IRS. The agency has had a reputation for being uncaring and uncooperative, and many people believe that reputation is well deserved. Because of this, Congress forced the IRS to set up a program called problem resolution. Congressional constituent service offices had become defacto problem resolution centers. If someone had a problem with the IRS, they'd call their congressman, and his or her staff would work to resolve it. Congress got tired of dealing with so many IRS problems and forced the IRS to set up this program to provide better service to the public. The problem resolution office is supposed to create communication and find solutions.

I have to say I'm getting some distressing calls with complaints about problem resolution. One caller said problem resolution helped him set up a payment plan, but that the agency ignored it and placed a lien on his house. Still, you should start with problem resolution. If that doesn't work, call or write your congressman or U.S. senator's constituent service office for help. If you don't know the name of your representative in Congress, call another one and a staffer will be able to tell you how to reach him or her. Or call one of your U.S. senators.

Electronic Tax Filing —

Electronic tax filing has been touted as an easy way to do your taxes and quickly get back your refund. The IRS says consumers who use electronic filing will get their refund check in two or three weeks instead of six or eight.

Just the same, I don't like electronic filing. Because the system eliminates a lot of paperwork and data entry, it makes the IRS's job easier and lowers its cost of doing business. There's nothing wrong with that. What's very wrong is you have to pay an exorbitant fee to file in this way. When you use electronic filing, you have to fill out your tax forms, then bring them to a third party to be transmitted to the IRS. The fee for transmitting the information normally is about $35. With the preponderance of personal computers and modems in homes and offices, there should be a way for you to file electronically at no cost, without having to use an IRS-approved intermediary. The current system is inefficient and expensive and it's a hardship on the consumer.

Paying $35 to get a $500 refund five weeks early is throwing money away. If you asked a bank to let you borrow $500 for five weeks and the bank charged you $35, the effective interest rate for that loan would be more than 70 percent.

The double whammy is the cost of a rapid refund loan, which many consumers have received when they have filed electronically. Typically, the intermediary has charged $35 for the electronic filing and another $25 for a loan equal to the size of your refund. In that way, tax filers essentially have received a refund check in three or four days.

But the days of the refund anticipation loan may be over. Because of fraud in electronic filing, the IRS has stopped the practice of sending a notice to preparers that the return had been accepted. Because of that, refund anticipation loans will be more difficult to get and the wait will be longer. A longer wait eliminates the reason to get a refund anticipation loan, and I hope that will convince taxpayers to stop getting them.

You can tell electronic filing is profitable by the preponderance of businesses that offer this service. In addition to tax preparers, pawnshops and check-cashing stores perform electronic filing. Even office supply stores have it. It wouldn't surprise me if gas stations someday offer electronic filing. Businesses should beware, though. Increasing competition is sure to cut these huge profit margins, and eventually the IRS will develop the ability to take electronic filing directly from a home computer.

Until then, stay away from electronic filing. If you find yourself so cash pinched at tax-return time that you are willing to borrow money at

- Tips on - Electronic Tax Filing

● Electronic tax filing is an expensive way to get your tax refund a few weeks early. It's not worth the fee you have to pay.

● If you find yourself so cash strapped at tax-return time that you are willing to borrow money at such high effective interest rates, try some method to save money.

● If you keep getting large tax returns, ask your employer to withhold less money from your paycheck and put the extra few dollars in a shoe box or bank account.

such enormously high rates, please try some method of saving money. If you can put $10 a week in a shoe box, at the end of a year you'll have $500 and you won't have to borrow against your tax return. Of course, a shoe box that pays interest is always preferable.

If you keep getting large tax returns, your employer may be withholding too much money from your paycheck. The cheapest way to avoid paying an electronic filing fee would be to reduce your withholding and put the extra few dollars you get in the shoe box.

I know that many people use tax withholding as a method of forced savings. The government takes out an additional few dollars a paycheck and at the end of a year, it pays back a few hundred dollars as a refund. If that's the only way you can save money, I suppose it's okay. But you're essentially giving the government an interest-free loan. Don't make it worse by paying a fee for electronic tax filing and a refund-anticipation loan. If you do, you've hurt yourself too many ways.

Divorce —

People often get so caught up in the emotions of a divorce, they forget the financial aspects. I think that's human nature. I can tell you from personal experience that divorce is one of the most painful experiences you can go through.

Still, during this period when you are vulnerable emotionally, you are also vulnerable financially. You have to protect your financial interests by terminating not just the marriage but all joint financial obligations.

If you have credit cards that are jointly owned, the accounts must be paid off and closed, and each party should obtain credit in his or her own name. This is essential so that neither spouse is responsible for the other's bills. Even though the divorce decree says your ex-husband is supposed to pay the credit cards, sometimes he doesn't and the credit card companies come after you. I take this kind of call all the time.

If the credit card accounts are not closed, you can be hurt in two big ways. One, though you may have paid all your bills and maintained a great credit rating, your credit can be ruined and you can get knocked out of the credit market. That's trouble if you want to buy a home or a car.

Second, though you may not realize it, you are financially responsible for the credit card debt, even if your former spouse gets the merchandise. That's because a credit card agreement, like any joint credit agreement, is legally superior to the divorce decree. The contractual obligation continues regardless of what the divorce decree says. If you pay off and close those accounts, you have nothing to worry about. Otherwise, you have a time bomb waiting to explode, sometimes months or years later.

Your only recourse if your former spouse runs up debts and then reneges on the obligations is to call your divorce lawyer and file an action based on the divorce decree. But that doesn't change the fact that you owe the money to the credit grantor.

Another important asset to think about is your house. It doesn't matter if you sign over your rights to the house to the other partner. The obligation on the mortgage is where you're at risk. Before reaching a final agreement on the divorce, you need to know whether the person keeping the house can qualify for a new mortgage alone. If he or she cannot, the house should be sold so that neither party is responsible. If both of you remain on the loan, the one who leaves the house has no advantages and lots of disadvantages. You really have a problem if you can't sell the home.

If you're both listed on a car loan, the same problems can occur as with a house or credit cards. But there is a complication. If it's a five-year loan, and you're early or midway through the loan, the vehicle usually is worth less than the amount owed. If that's the case, you will need some additional money to refinance the loan or sell the car and pay off the existing loan.

Lawyers hate when I say this, but I believe strongly that couples should try divorce mediation, rather than immediately getting separate lawyers, going into enemy camps, and duking it out. Divorce takes such a tremendous emotional toll on the individuals involved, and the legal process, being adversarial, only increases the hurt, distrust, and anger. Some counties now require that mediation be used in all civil cases, including divorce, before the parties may appear in court. You can obtain a free list of mediators in your city by writing to the Academy of Family Mediators.

If children are involved and the parents fight about the divorce, they both have something to lose as the process marches on. I know of one couple that wound up in a shov-

- Tips on - Divorce

● You have to protect your financial interests in a divorce by terminating not just the marriage but all joint financial obligations. That includes credit card accounts, mortgages, and jointly held loans. Refinance the loans or sell the house or car.

● If joint accounts are not closed, you are legally responsible if your ex-spouse doesn't pay, no matter what the divorce decree says. Your credit can be ruined and you can get knocked out of the credit market.

● Consider divorce mediation, a less adversarial process than using lawyers, in which a mediator tries to get the two parties together to reach a fair agreement.

● If your ex-spouse is months or more behind in child-support payments, consider using a collection agency. But don't pay more than one-third the amount due in collection agency fees.

Contact:
Academy of Family Mediators
355 Tyrol West
1500 S. Highway 100
Golden Valley, MN 55416
612-525-8670

Child Support Enforcement
370 L'enfant Promenade, S.W.,
4th floor
Washington, DC 20447
(202) 401-9373

Children Support Services
P.O. Box 691067
San Antonio, TX 78269
1-800-729-2445

Reference:
Mom's House, Dad's House: Making Shared Custody Work, by Isolina Ricci (Macmillan)
The Parents Book about Divorce, by Richard Gardner (Bantam)

---

ing match at a shopping center after the father made off with the couple's two-year-old son in front of their young daughter. That's a tragedy for the whole family.

Another couple I know of tried mediation and now share joint custody of their five-year-old daughter. She spends four days each week at Mom's house and three days at Dad's house and everyone gets along very well. The parents live close to each other and in the same school district. Forget money for a minute and consider your relationship with your children and your children's future well-being. Mediation becomes a great tool to try for a divorce without much hostility.

However, divorce mediation is not the entire answer. A mediator merely tries to get the two parties together and to reach an agreement they believe is fair. But before a mediation agreement is final, each party should have it reviewed by an attorney who specializes in family practice law. In the end, you need a lawyer's expertise to point out elements of a proposed mediation agreement that may be unwise or unfair to you.

Child support is a major financial issue of divorce. It's almost a cliché now that the non-custodial parent doesn't pay child support. The fact is, lots of parents do pay it. But collecting child support, either because of underpayment or nonpayment, has become a major national problem. Generally it's the mother trying to collect child support from the father.

Many states have child-support recovery offices, but as a group they are abysmal failures, mostly because the case loads are so enormous. They can be good sources of information, however. They can tell you, for example, that the law allows you to collect back child support even after a child turns 18, and that you can go back to court during the child's lifetime and request an increase in support payments. But actually collecting the money can be next to impossible if the parent truly doesn't want to pay.

The difficulty in collecting child support has spawned a booming industry—child-support collection agencies. Some are traditional collection agencies that have gone into this as a sideline. Others do nothing but collect overdue child support. For a mother who's dealing with a father who has never paid or has not paid for months or years, this is an excellent idea to consider. You will give up a portion of the child-support money in collection agency fees—a third is typical—but if you haven't been getting checks, every dollar you get is found money. If a collection agency wants more than one-third of the total due, you should probably look elsewhere. You can find a collection agency that specializes in child support by contacting Children Support Services.

Finally, there's the problem of what to do about income taxes. One spouse generally accepts responsibility in the divorce decree for income taxes that may result from audits of prior year's tax returns. If your spouse is involved in a business, you may want to indemnify yourself in the decree from tax responsibilities of the business. But the IRS doesn't recognize such division of responsibility and may go after either spouse if more taxes are owed.

If the tax return hasn't been filed for the year prior to the divorce, you have the option of filing jointly or separately. You pay a higher rate if you file separately, but you should consider it because it can protect you from your spouse's tax liabilities for that year. After the divorce, of course, you are single and file separately.

Wills —

It's very important to have a will, but it's amazing how many people of all income levels don't have one. I think it's because people prefer to avoid the reality that they're going to die someday. They'd rather not think about their own mortality. The greatest favor you can do for your survivors is to stipulate, in your will, what you want to happen to your assets.

When you die without a will, most states write a will for you. In a legislated will, a state distributes your assets to your family based on its own formula. The thought of your money going to a relative you can't stand should be motivation enough for you to do a will. If not, think of the person to whom you would like to give most or all of your assets. They might not get the money because you haven't designated it in a will.

I remember one case involving a utility executive who had divorced and remarried, then died without writing a will. He left an estate worth $700,000. Because he had no will, the state divided the money equally among his two children and his second wife, about $225,000 each after expenses. He might have wanted it split some other way, but without a will, it was impossible to follow his wishes.

There's another case that illustrates the importance of having a will. A husband and wife with two small children were killed in a car accident, leaving insurance payments and other property worth $2 to $3 million. Because the couple had a will, a trust was set up to manage the inheritance, and custody of the children was decided according to the parents' wishes. Had there been no will, the state would have appointed a guardian for each child's property. Court permission would have been needed for many financial decisions, a cumbersome process that would have produced legal expenses of several thousand dollars per year for perhaps 15 years.

It's simpler than you think to create a will. For a will to be legal in most states, you have to be at least 18 years old and of sound mind. The will must be written, signed by you, and witnessed by two people who won't receive anything from your estate. That is the end of the mystery of a will. That's all you have to do.

If you want to have a will done by a lawyer, that's fine. Lawyers' fees for doing a will vary widely, depending on the complications of your estate and how much the particular lawyer charges per hour. To write my most recent will, I used a computer program called WillMaker. There are four or five other programs for personal computers that make this very easy. Mine took about 10 minutes to do. Then, I had the will reviewed by my lawyer. It costs significantly less to have a will reviewed by a lawyer than to have one drawn up by a lawyer. Here's the kicker. My lawyer did not suggest one change in the will I drew up using the computer program.

A will kit generally costs less than $20 from any good bookstore, and a computer program generally costs $50 or less. A lawyer may charge as little as $150 or as much as several thousand dollars.

You should do whatever is comfortable for you, either drawing up your own will, using a kit or program, or having a lawyer do it. But if you start doing your own will with a kit or a computer program and you reach a point where there's a question you don't understand or a procedure that does not make sense to you, or language that isn't clear, stop right there and go to a lawyer. If you have substantial assets or if there are children involved, it can be disastrous to agree to things in language you don't understand, or make decisions in your will that you haven't fully thought out. Those are the two big variables that you really have to be sure about.

If you have a great deal of assets, especially more than $600,000, don't do a will yourself. It is critical, in order to avoid very high estate taxes, to plan your estate with a lawyer who specializes in wills, estates, and trusts. Now most people laugh at the thought of having more than $600,000 in assets. But many times people forget the value of their life insurance, their home, and money in their retirement plans. It can add up quickly.

The state processes your will after you die and your assets are distributed through a procedure called probate. Probate usually is quick and routine, especially if the assets are below $500,000 or $600,000. But in some states, probate can be inefficient, expensive, or corrupt; it can take months or years, and court costs can seriously erode the value of the estate.

Some assets pass directly to a spouse or child if they are jointly owned. With a house, the deed must list one individual as owner and the other as "joint tenant with right of survivorship." If you merely list two people as co-owners, the deceased's 50 percent share of the house will pass to his or her heirs as specified by the will. It works the same way with a car.

For a bank account, generally joint ownership is all you need for the co-owner to have immediate access and ownership after the other dies. For stocks or mutual fund accounts, include "joint ownership with right of survivorship" on the papers. With life insurance, it doesn't even matter what's specified in your will, because the insurance contract is a superior document. The payment automatically goes to the designated beneficiary.

There are lots of unscrupulous folks out there trying to convince you that a will is terrible and a living trust is a godsend. A living trust is a method of avoiding probate and hav-

- Tips on - Wills

● It's simpler than you think to create a will. For a will to be legal in most states, you have to be at least 18 years old and of sound mind. The will must be written, signed by you, and witnessed by two people who won't receive anything from your estate.

● You can draw up your own will, using a kit or a computer program, or have a lawyer do it. Do what's comfortable for you. But if you start doing your own will and become confused, stop and go to a lawyer.

● If you have a great deal of assets, especially more than $600,000, don't do a will yourself.

● A living trust is an alternative to a will in which your assets pass immediately to your designee when you die. But it's complicated and expensive and few people need it.

ing your assets pass immediately to your designee outside of the probate process. A living trust is appropriate only in very rare circumstances, such as when someone owns property in several states and wants to avoid multistate probate. For example, you might own a home in Michigan and a retirement home in Florida.

Or, a living trust can be used if a person is in failing health and wants to turn over effective control while he or she is still able to do so. There generally is no tax advantage to a living trust, because the same inheritance taxes apply. If you do have a specialized situation that calls for a living trust, have a lawyer prepare it because it's a very complicated document. The cost will be many times more than a will. Less than 1 percent of the public needs a living trust.

There's another document you may have heard referred to as a living will. It's a form you fill out that lets hospitals know, when you are critically ill, whether they should use extraordinary means to keep you alive. The Supreme Court has ruled that hospitals must accept these written medical care instructions.

You should complete a living will so your family won't have to agonize over what should happen to you. In the Workbook chapter of this book, you'll find a real living will that you can use.

Funerals —

Another thing people avoid thinking about is the arrangements for a funeral. Most of us die keeping those thoughts to ourselves and leave our grieving loved ones to decide if there will be a funeral or a memorial service, a burial or cremation. At their weakest moments, when they are often overcome by sadness or guilt, they have to make some very difficult and personal decisions.

I've been on the funeral home sales tour and it's an awful experience. The funeral director, usually someone who is very pleasant and low-key, often starts by taking you through the casket area. The caskets are arranged from the most expensive, in the front and very well displayed, to the less expensive, which are in the far end of the room gathering dust. In many funeral homes, the least expensive caskets aren't even on display.

You're in an environment in which you're encouraged, gently but persuasively, to spend more money than you would have anticipated, at a time when you're most vulnerable. You have absolutely no ability to comparison shop at this point, because you've already designated the funeral home and had the body transported there. So you are their captive in negotiations over costs and services.

Do yourself and your family a favor by making those decisions yourself ahead of time. The most effective way to hold down the costs of these arrangements, and to improve the chances that your wishes will be carried out, is to join the Memorial Society in your area. You pay a one-time fee ($25 to $50) to join and can list your wishes and get negotiated prices for caskets and burial or other services. You set the budget and pick what you want. When you die, your family goes to the funeral home you designated and they pull the file specifying your arrangements and preset costs. The funeral homes are willing to give great prices to the Memorial Society in exchange for the high volume of business generated by their relationship.

I don't recommend that people prepay for a funeral or a cemetery plot. We've become such a transient population that it's foolish to prepay for funeral arrangements in a particular city. Circumstances could change and you might move to a different city. Not only that, but what happens if the funeral home goes out of business? Your money could go down the tubes. By joining the Memorial Society, you make all the necessary decisions, and prices are set, but funeral expenses are not paid until you die.

Choosing a Lawyer or Accountant —

Lawyers

I get very upset when people choose a lawyer based on a television ad. If you do that, there's no way to be sure you're getting a quality person. I don't recommend taking a referral from the bar association, either.

If you've ever used a lawyer for any reason and it was someone you liked and respected, ask him or her to suggest someone with the expertise you need. Don't take a referral as blind faith, but it's a good first step. A second way to find a lawyer is to ask friends, relatives, and colleagues to suggest someone they have used and liked.

But in all cases, interview the attorney as if you were interviewing someone to fill a job. Make it clear you are interviewing the lawyer to see if you are going to hire him or her. Most attorneys will give you 30 minutes of their time at no charge for this purpose. It's well worth the effort, because it's far easier to hire a lawyer than it is to fire one.

Be particularly cautious when you're hiring someone to represent you on a contingency basis. Typically in these cases, the lawyer will receive one-third of any settlement you receive but won't charge you an hourly rate along the way. It seems like a no-lose situation. But if you fire a contingency lawyer, he or she can come back and bill you for the hours spent work-

---

- Tips on - Funerals

● Most people die without making funeral arrangements, forcing their grieving family to make tough decisions and overpay on funeral costs. Join your local Memorial Society and make those decisions yourself, ahead of time.

● Don't prepay for a funeral. You could move to another city or the funeral home could go out of business.

Contact:
Funeral and Memorial
Societies of America
6900 Lost Lake Road
Egg Harbor, WI 54209
414-868-2729
(For a directory of memorial
societies in your area)

ing on your case. Let's say a lawyer puts in 20 hours on your case and charges a rate of $200 per hour. The lawyer could send you a bill for $4,000 and you would have to pay it.

If you fire one contingency lawyer and hire another, make sure you obtain a signed release from the first lawyer relinquishing any claims to the final settlement. As hard to believe as this may be, the first lawyer could pop back up and claim he or she is owed one-third of the settlement. You might have to pay a third to the first lawyer and a third to the second lawyer because you didn't get a release from the first lawyer.

Even if you're paying a lawyer on an hourly basis, you need to be careful whom you hire. The law has become extremely specialized, and no single lawyer can handle every job for you. You don't want to pay for a lawyer's on-the-job training. If you need specialized legal help, you want a lawyer who knows that particular field. If you are getting a divorce, you need a divorce lawyer. You don't want a general practice attorney who once handled a divorce for a cousin. If you need a will, you should choose a lawyer who specializes in wills, estates, and trusts. If you're going to sue somebody, you want a litigator. And if you're doing a real estate transaction, you need to get a real estate lawyer.

Chances are that nothing awful will happen if you pick the wrong lawyer to handle your case. It might cost you more in legal time because the lawyer's lack of knowledge means he or she will need more hours to get the job done. But the lawyer also could botch the case.

I dealt with one case in which the lawyer messed up badly enough that my caller could have lost $5,000. But to his credit, he took the steps to correct the error. When my caller originally sold her house, the buyer didn't have all the money needed to buy it. So the buyer entered into a second mortgage agreement with the seller for $5,000. That means if the buyer didn't pay, the seller would have the right to get her house back. But the lawyer forgot to record the second mortgage at the courthouse, so when the buyer resold the house, he never repaid the $5,000 to the original seller. When the seller called me, I pointed out the error to the lawyer, and he paid the $5,000 debt out of his own pocket.

Another lawyer spent 11 months in prison after embezzling money from clients. The clients had come to him to sue Audi over the Audi 5000, the car that was alleged to accelerate unexpectedly in some circumstances. The lawyer took up-front fees from victims and settlement money from Audi and pocketed all of it. One couple I talked with was referred to him by a lawyer they found in the telephone book. He took a $2,000 retainer from them and pocketed $7,000 in settlement money without their knowledge. He apparently bilked hundreds of people of millions of dollars.

A more common dispute with a lawyer is over the bill. If you have this concern, ask the lawyer for more information. Law firms today are being asked to justify every penny that's billed, and you have a right as a customer to demand a full accounting. If that doesn't resolve it, call the American Bar Association and ask about fee arbitration.

If your relationship with your lawyer turns adversarial, which is a most unfortunate circumstance, you need to document everything in writing to that attorney, just as he or she would do to you.

Accountants

I get so many complaints about lawyers and only a few about accountants. Still, it's a good idea to make the effort to find a good certified public accountant. One of the best ways to find a CPA is to ask people who own their own business.

I have a built-in bias against individuals

- Tips on -
Choosing a Lawyer
or Accountant

- Don't pick a lawyer based on a television ad or a referral from the bar association. If you do, there's no way to be sure you're getting a quality person.

- If you've ever used a lawyer whom you liked and respected, call him or her and ask for a referral to someone with the expertise you need.

- Always interview a prospective attorney as if you were interviewing someone to fill a job. Most attorneys will give you 30 minutes at no charge for this purpose.

- Be particularly cautious when you're hiring someone to represent you on a contingency basis.

- In choosing a CPA, an individual or small business often will do best with a small- to medium-sized local practice.

- If you interview CPAs who tell you how clever they are and how they are going to beat the IRS, hire someone else.

Contact:
American Bar Association
Attorney Complaints & Fee Arbitration
750 North Lake Shore
Chicago, IL 60611
1-800-621-6159

American Society of CPAs
1211 6th Avenue
New York, NY 10036
1-800-862-4272

or small businesses using one of the Big 6 accounting firms. You're a low priority to them, so you'll be placed with someone who is very inexperienced. There's so much turnover at the lower levels that you'll never get the attention you need. The ultimate insult is paying high fees for uncaring and inattentive service.

An individual or small business often can do best with a small- to medium-sized local practice. Like a lawyer, a CPA will generally give you 30 minutes of free time for an interview, if you ask for it. The most important questions you can ask are, "How many CPAs are there in the firm?" and "How long has each been with the firm?" If you hear that the people have been there a good long time, that speaks well for the firm. If there's a great deal of turnover in the personnel, that's an important warning sign to stay away.

It's important what questions a CPA asks you. You want to make sure the CPA is interested in your situation and is asking questions that address the concerns you have.

If you interview CPAs who attempt to be heroes, telling you how clever they are and how they are going to beat the IRS, that's a red flag. If instead they talk about prudent ways to reduce your tax exposure and liability, that's good.

The essence of my radio show is helping people solve problems. Many callers I talk with have been mistreated by a company or government agency and don't know what to do about it. I don't have a magic wand that forces companies to admit they're wrong and make amends, but I know what works.

In this chapter, I'll show you some simple techniques to make your voice heard. You'll be surprised at how effective they are and how easy they are to use. When cajoling and prodding don't work, you may have to go to court. I'll tell you how to file a case in small claims court—and how to collect on your judgment if you win.

This chapter also includes some important tips to guide you in returning merchandise to retailers, choosing a dry cleaner, and signing a contract. I'll tell you when it's critical to use a credit card and what you need to know when you purchase major items such as furniture, carpet, and jewelry.

Solving Problems —

Part of the trick to solving consumer problems is having a strategy you can use to get results. Too often, consumers get frustrated and just go away mad, and going away mad is not a solution.

Whether it's a business that's confounding you or the government, the first strategy to try is talking to somebody at a higher level. If a higher-level official is unresponsive, go still higher in the organization. Go as high as you can, either by phone calls or visits to the organization. If a salesperson won't help you, go to the manager. If it's a chain, go up the ladder to the regional vice president or the home office.

One of the big problems in corporate America is that those who have the most direct contact with the public are given the least amount of power to solve customer problems. I always shake my head when someone in the customer service department says there's nothing he or she can do. More and more, the companies that succeed are those that connect with the public and solve problems.

When front-line employees don't have the latitude to find solutions, customers get angry and sales plunge. One of the hot topics in corporate America these days is the empowerment of employees. Unfortunately, it seems to be more a topic for discussion than a reality in the workplace. So for you to get results, you have to get out of the normal loop and go straight to the decision makers who can actually solve problems.

If you reach nothing but dead ends on the phone, or you can't even find out whom to speak with, your next strategy should be documenting your attempts to solve the problem. Keep a log of the phone calls you make, whom you spoke with, and what was said. In the Workbook chapter of this book, you'll find worksheets to help you document the calls you make and the letters you write.

Letter writing is a lost art, but letters are a very powerful tool. I take dozens of calls from people who have complained repeatedly by telephone, then given up. I had one call from an apartment renter who wanted to move out after a problem with her landlord. She had tried to resolve the dispute by phone and got nowhere. But at that point she had no solid evidence that she had made any effort to find a solution. Writing letters not only gets attention, but it's a great method of documenting your efforts.

In your first letter, list whom you've spoken with about the problem, what attempts you've made to solve it, and what specific action you would like from the recipient of your letter. Give the person a specific period of time to deal with the problem. If you don't get a response by the allotted time, immediately send a second letter with a copy of the first attached. It takes very little time, but it's effective at working toward a solution.

Always keep a copy of your letters, and always, no matter what the situation, make the tone positive and friendly. Never write a nasty, angry letter. Words can hurt or help. Angry words send a powerfully negative message and may prevent you from getting any cooperation.

If you try to contact people by phone, in person, and by letter and you get nowhere, you have to look for another pressure point. If a U.S. government agency is ignoring you or not serving your needs, call the constituent service office of your congressman or U.S. senator. If it's a state agency, call one of your state legislators. And if it's a city, county, or town issue, call the elected official who represents you in those governments. Your elected officials know they can gain a loyal voter by taking care of your needs. That's why you turn to them.

I know a fellow who found out about a supposed mortgage loan default when he applied for a credit card. The Department of Veterans Affairs said this fellow had defaulted on a loan in another state. But it was a matter of mistaken identity. He had never defaulted on the loan—he had never even been to that part of the country. He wrote to the V.A. explaining that it was a mix-up, but the agency insisted he had defaulted. So he wrote to one of his U.S. senators, whose vote on federal appropriations helps decide the department's funding. The senator's office then contacted the agency on his behalf, and, not surprisingly, the matter was cleared up rather quickly.

If your problem is with a private organization and all attempts to resolve it have failed,

- Tips on - Solving Problems

- If you're having trouble resolving a problem with a business or the government, talk to a higher-level official. Go as high in the organization as you can.

- If you reach nothing but dead ends, your next strategy should be documenting your attempts to solve the problem.

- Write a letter detailing the problem and requesting some action to resolve it. If you don't get a response, send a second letter with a copy of the first attached. Always keep a copy of your letters and always make the tone positive and friendly.

- If a government agency is not serving your needs, call the constituent service office of your congressman, U.S. senator, or local elected official.

- If your problem is with a private organization and all attempts to resolve it have failed, try sending one last letter by certified mail. If that doesn't work, you may have to sue the business in small claims court.

try sending one last letter by certified mail. It's not necessary, in fact it's undesirable, to send your first couple of letters this way, because certified mail is a hostile gesture. Assume that the company has been negligent toward you, but not malevolent, and that your letter will get proper attention. Most times, if you are persistent, you will get results.

Even if a company doesn't satisfy you, remember that you have the power to vote with your wallet. If a business treats you poorly, spend your money somewhere else. In a consumer-driven society such as ours, that's the ultimate power.

Small Claims Court —

It's one of the true ironies in this country that more people recognize the name Joseph Wapner, the judge on the old "People's Court" TV show, than the name William Rehnquist, chief justice of the Supreme Court. Perhaps it's because people identify more closely with participants in Judge Wapner's version of small claims court than with the participants in a Supreme Court case.

Small claims court is a great place to turn when phone calls, meetings, and letters have failed to resolve a dispute. It works best when two parties have an honest disagreement. The process does not work as well if your adversary deliberately set out to cheat you.

Taking a case to small claims court is fairly easy. Before you file a case, send a letter by certified mail to the other party. The letter has to cover a few basic elements, including:

● How you've been harmed.
● Why that particular person or company is responsible.
● How much money you seek and why it is justified.

Write this letter in a friendly tone, because it may be read later by a judge. You want the judge to view you as a reasonable person who tried but failed to solve a problem and has turned to the courts for help.

You sue in the county in which your adversary lives, the county in which you were injured, the county in which the business is located, or the county in which the product was manufactured. You need an exact address so the party can be served notice of the suit. If the defendant is served and doesn't show up to argue his or her side, you win by default.

Call the clerk of the court in the county in which you'll be filing your case to find out that court's procedures. Some areas have a kit or brochure to help you. You'll pay a filing fee—generally less than $100—which you may recover if the judge rules in your favor. In most cases, you don't need a lawyer. In fact, some states prohibit lawyers in small claims court. The rules vary on other aspects of the process. New York State allows either party to appeal a small claims court verdict, but Hawaii and Arizona are among those that bar such appeals. Louisiana allows the losing party to pay in installments.

On average, you can sue for up to $5,000 in small claims court. But in Kansas, the limit is just $1,000. In Tennessee, you can sue for up to $10,000 in small claims court, up to $15,000 in counties with more than 700,000 residents.

There's a wonderful book available to help, *Everybody's Guide to Small Claims Court* (Nolo Press), which runs through the process in great detail.

Once you get your trial date, it's time to prepare your case. The most important things to remember are to be well organized and bring strong documentation. The judge wants to hear a short version of your story, so carefully think through the three points you stated in your certified letter. Try to provide documentation for each area: 1) how you've been harmed; 2) why that particular person or company is responsible; and 3) how much money you seek and why it is justified.

Bring letters you've written in the past, records of phone calls you've made, and, if you can, photographs. Let's say someone put sod in your yard and the sod didn't take. Take pictures of it and bring the pictures to court. Or, if you had repairs done to your house and the repairs were done poorly, take pictures that illustrate the sloppy work.

If the judge finds in your favor, be prepared for the hard part—collecting on your judgment. If you're dealing with an honest individual or business, you'll get a check right on the spot. If the other guy is going to fight tooth and nail not to pay you, your ability to collect the money will depend on your persistence. A judgment means you have a license to search for money or other assets. If you can't find any, the judgment is worthless.

Depending on the state, you may have the right to take money from the person's paycheck or checking account, put a lien on his or her house, or seize the person's automobiles. Mississippi even provides help in collecting on your judgment. Check with the clerk of the court to see what the rules are in your area.

It's possible that you won't be able to collect, particularly if someone is unemployed or self-employed, or if the person skips town. The only way you'll ever have a chance to get your money is to try. If you're trying to locate someone's checking account, try to remember whether or not you've ever written the person a check, or the person has ever written a check to you. If so, you can find the person's bank name and account number either on the back of your cancelled check, or, if you deposited the check written to you, on your bank's microfilm copy of the check. If you've never exchanged checks, have a friend write the person a small check. You'll get the account information when the check clears and is returned in your friend's bank statement. With your judgment, you'll be able to garnish the person's bank account before he or she knows it.

The clerk of the court will be able to provide the forms and tell you how to garnish someone's wages or checking account. It's easiest to garnish someone who works for a large employer or the government.

Collections attorney Gary Jackson tells some great stories of the lengths he's gone to collect on a judgment. One of Gary's clients took his car into a mechanic for a major repair, then became ill and couldn't immediately come back for the car or call the mechanic. Three weeks later, after he was feeling better, the fellow came back in to settle his bill and pick up the car. But the mechanic, having neither seen nor heard from the car owner, had sold the car to pay the repair bill. Under local law, he couldn't do that without filing a lawsuit, so the car owner took the mechanic to small claims court and won a $5,000 judgment.

The mechanic refused to pay, and because the garage didn't take checks, Gary couldn't locate his checking account. He did find out through a records check that the mechanic owned a camper, so he had the sheriff seize the camper and it was auctioned off for $1,000. That didn't come close to covering the judgment, so the sheriff went back and seized some engine hoists, a cash register, and a set of golf clubs. On the third trip, the mechanic refused to let the sheriff onto the premises. Gary protested to the judge, but local law at the time allowed the mechanic to keep the sheriff off his property. Gary solved the problem by contacting his state legislator and getting a new law passed that allowed the sheriff to enter. A year later, Gary presented the judge with a copy of the new law and the judge ordered the mechanic, who was in the courtroom, to let the sheriff take anything he wanted from his garage. The mechanic immediately stood up and paid the car owner a portion of what he owed—$500. He eventually paid the full amount.

In another case, a woman went in for breast reduction surgery and the insurance company mistakenly sent the benefits check to her instead of the doctor. She cashed it and refused to pay the bill, so the doctor sued and won a judgment. She refused to disclose information about herself and was called before the judge. She walked into court wearing a neck brace from an auto accident in which she was hit by another driver. Gary Jackson asked the judge to force her to disclose who had hit her, then garnished both drivers and both insurance companies. Because she wouldn't pay directly, Jackson intercepted the money due her from the auto accident and collected on the judgment.

Returning Merchandise —

Few things inspire confidence and loyalty among customers more than a retailer's willingness to pay refunds or exchange merchandise cheerfully. If you buy something and it's the wrong size or color, or you just don't like it as much as you thought you would, it's great to know you can bring it back. It's also very disturbing if you can't.

In many states, retailers are permitted to adopt any return or exchange policy they desire, as long as they announce the policy to customers. A retailer may refuse any refund or exchange and post a notice that all sales are final. It can provide refunds under certain conditions, such as requiring you to return a television in its original packaging. Or it can provide exchanges or in-store credit but refuse cash refunds. Notice can be provided in any of several ways. The refund/exchange policy can be printed on the sales slip or the clothing tag or posted on a sign at the cash registers.

It's a good idea to find out a store's policy on returns and exchanges before you buy there. Be aware, too, that return policies are different from refund policies. A store may be very liberal about allowing you to bring merchandise back and exchange it for other merchandise or receive an in-store credit. But it may be inflexible about giving your money back. Many items that you purchase cannot be returned for cash and you're simply expected to know that policy. The best example is an airline ticket, which is almost always nonrefundable.

You have to make your own decision about whether to patronize a store with a rigid refund or exchange policy. If you are willing to take your chances in return for a better price, then go in with your eyes open. If you often buy something and change your mind, then be selective in where you shop. If you're buying a gift, be fair to the recipient. You may believe it's the best gift ever, but he or she may disagree, or may already have something exactly like it. Buy gifts only from stores that have liberal return policies.

- Tips on - Returning Merchandise

● In most states, retailers are permitted to adopt any return or exchange policy, as long as they announce the policy to customers. That includes refusing any refund or exchange.

● The refund/exchange policy can be printed on the sales slip or the clothing tag or posted on a sign at the cash registers.

● It's a good idea to find out the store's policy on returns and exchanges before you shop there. Be aware, too, that return policies are different from refund policies.

● You have to make your own decision about whether to patronize a store with a rigid refund or exchange policy. If you are willing to take your chances in return for a better price, then go in with your eyes open.

● If you're buying a gift or shopping by catalog, make sure the item can be returned for a full refund.

I don't recommend buying floor samples or clearance merchandise marked "all sales final," where the item is not packed in its original factory carton. Then you really are at risk if you've spent money and, when you get the item home, it's damaged or doesn't work.

When you buy from catalogs, be certain you understand the company's return policy. There's a big difference when you buy from a catalog, when you've only seen a picture of an item, versus buying in a store, when you've had an opportunity to see and evaluate the merchandise. You buy from a catalog at your own risk if you don't have the right to return it for a full refund.

The fastest-growing retailers in the nation all have very customer-friendly return/refund policies, and I don't think that's a coincidence. Treating customers fairly is just good business. It's a shame that some stores are so unbending with customers, and it's sadder still that those policies are adopted because of a few who abuse return privileges. Think about how harshly you're often treated when you write a check. Blame it on the very few people who write most of the bad checks.

Dry Cleaning —

As much as I love a bargain, I have to tell you that price is not the most important factor in every consumer decision. It's more important, for instance, to choose a dry cleaner that will do a good job of cleaning your clothes, and will be fair to you if problems ever develop, than it is to find the absolute lowest price for this service.

Get this clear before you bring your first garments in to be cleaned. Tell the dry cleaner you don't ever expect to have a problem, but you're curious, because you've heard so many horror stories, what the cleaner will do if a piece of clothing is lost or damaged. The answer will help you decide if you should take your clothes to this particular dry cleaner.

If there's a change in ownership, talk to the new owner and see what his or her attitude is about service. If you don't like what you hear, you may want to switch cleaners. It's a good idea to get to know the owner or manager in any case. If a problem ever develops, it's easier to resolve if you already know someone in charge. If the only person you ever speak with is a clerk, you may have trouble getting satisfaction.

Just as with a doctor, lawyer, or accountant,

one of the best ways to find a dry cleaner is to ask friends and neighbors whom they use and whether they're happy with the service. I prefer to use a cleaner that does the work on their premises. They'll have immediate access to spot-removing chemicals and will be able to test a stain immediately. If the work is done on-site, the clothes don't go anywhere, so there's less of a chance an item will be lost.

If clothes are cleaned on the premises, ask how often the cleaning fluid is distilled. You have no way to know if they're being truthful, but it's a good idea to ask anyway. A good cleaner should distill the solvent daily, because clothes cleaned in dirty solvent can become dingy and discolored. You wouldn't wash clothes in dirty water and a dry cleaner shouldn't use dirty solvent.

Most of the calls I get about dry cleaning problems concern white or off-white garments that become dingy after being cleaned. One caller won a $263 judgment in small claims court because a dry cleaner refused to make good on a white suit that was discolored. Once a garment is cleaned in dirty solvent, it's ruined. The original color can't be restored.

If you notice that an item you've had cleaned has been damaged, go back as soon as possible and show it to the manager on duty. A lot of times they'll ask to clean or press it again or to repair a button or zipper. Or a manager may want to show it to the owner. That's fine. But if the item is still bad after that second cleaning, it's time for the cleaner to take responsibility and come up with some money.

If an item has been destroyed in the cleaning process, the cleaner does not owe you the amount of money needed to replace the garment. The company owes you a depreciated value based on the expected life span of that item. If it's a shirt you would normally keep for five years and you've owned it for two years before it is destroyed, you deserve 60 percent of the value of the shirt. If you normally keep

an item for two years and it's damaged in the second year, you may not be entitled to any money at all, since it was near the end of the useful life of that garment. You'll have to negotiate with the cleaner over how much you deserve as compensation for a ruined item.

Sometimes, you might have a cleaner that has been doing a good job up to that point and takes responsibility for the damage, but doesn't seem able to cough up any money. You could cut a deal for some free cleaning service in exchange for the loss suffered on that item. A number of Better Business Bureaus offer dry cleaning arbitration programs.

If the cleaner claims that an item has been damaged due to improper manufacturing and you believe the cleaner has damaged it, you may want to turn to a third party. If the cleaner is a member of the International Fabricare Institute (IFI), you can have an evaluation done of that item by the IFI testing laboratory in Silver Spring, Maryland, which will issue a report on the cause of the damage. The fee may be paid by the cleaner or customer, or both may agree to split the cost. According to IFI, manufacturers are responsible for the damage in 47 percent of the items the lab tests, consumers for 37.5 percent, and dry cleaners for 15.5 percent. The dry cleaners' share is low because dry cleaners send problems to the lab only when they believe they are not responsible, IFI says.

If it turns out to be the manufacturer's fault, most retailers will look at the report and either give you a credit or put you in touch with the manufacturer, who will generally reach some form of accommodation with you. I once had a suit that bunched up after being cleaned. The cleaner said it was due to a specific defect in a manufacturing process called fusing. I went back to the store, which was a retail outlet for a manufacturer. They recognized the defect, knew it was their responsibility, and immediately offered to give me a new suit.

- Tips on - Dry Cleaning

● Choose a dry cleaner that will do a good job of cleaning your clothes and will be fair to you if problems ever develop. Price is less important.

● If an item is destroyed in the cleaning process, the cleaner does not owe you the amount of money needed to replace the garment. The company owes you a depreciated value based on the number of years the item is expected to last.

● If there's a dispute over how a garment was damaged, the customer or cleaner can submit the item to the International Fabricare Institute for testing.

● If it turns out to be the manufacturer's fault, most retailers will look at the report and either give you a credit or put you in touch with the manufacturer, who will generally reach some form of accommodation with you.

Contact:
IFI Garment Analysis Laboratory
12251 Tech Road
Silver Spring, MD 20904

Chargebacks —

When you pay for something in advance, such as an airline ticket or a custom-made sofa, you're taking on some risk. What if the airline or furniture store goes bust, as so many have over the past few years? What if you order from a catalog and the merchandise never arrives? If you prepay and you don't get the merchandise or service, you could lose your money.

If you write a check or pay cash to a merchant who fails to deliver, the only way to get your money back is to sue. If the merchant goes out of business, you become a claimant in bankruptcy court, where you'll wait forever and, if you're lucky, collect a few cents on the dollar for what you're owed.

There's a simple way to protect yourself from the risk of prepaying—use a major credit card. That way you offer yourself the privilege of a chargeback, a refund paid by your credit card company.

Banks, credit unions, and other credit card issuers are deluged with chargebacks and in many cases refuse to honor them. But the limited rights you have to receive a chargeback from your card issuer are bolstered by broader protections provided by VISA International and MasterCard International. Contact VISA or MasterCard if you have a chargeback denied by your bank, credit union, or other card issuer.

If you pay a deposit to order furniture and the store shuts down before you receive it, VISA or MasterCard will refund your deposit. Some credit card issuers incorrectly reject a chargeback in this circumstance if the claim isn't made within 60 days. But the time limit applies only to disputes over products or services, not to failure of the company to deliver. Even so, if you don't receive the merchandise from a mail order house within 60 days, notify your credit card company via certified mail and initiate a chargeback. Do that even if you're being assured by the catalog company that you'll get what you ordered. If you do get the merchandise, just notify your bank and release your chargeback.

If you dispute something on your bill within the first 60 days, you have a very clear right to a temporary chargeback. Whether the chargeback is permanent or whether the amount is re-posted to your bill should be determined by the facts of your case, but that

- Tips on - Chargebacks

● When you pay for something in advance, such as an airline ticket or a custom-made sofa, you're taking on some risk. If you prepay and you don't get the merchandise or service, you could lose your money.

● If you use a credit card when you prepay, you give yourself the privilege of a chargeback, a refund paid by your credit card company.

● In some cases, there's a 60-day time limit for disputes regarding purchases, but there's no time limit if the company fails to deliver products or services.

Contact:
VISA International Customer Service
P.O. Box 8999
San Francisco, CA 94128
415-570-3200

MasterCard International
Public Affairs Department
888 7th Avenue
New York, NY 10106
212-649-5476

depends on the fairness of your card issuer. You find out about your credit card company's loyalties when you do a chargeback. Some consider the merchant their most important customer, not the consumer.

Infrequent Purchases —

It's easy to sympathize with a young couple buying a new sofa. Buying items such as furniture, jewelry, and carpet can be daunting, indeed; we buy them so infrequently that it's difficult to know how to shop. Here are some special tips.

Furniture

When buying furniture, you should deal only with reputable retailers—healthy businesses with knowledgeable salespeople. You also need to think through how a piece of furniture will fit into your home. If you're considering a sofa with an unusual pattern or color, ask if you may take home a cushion for a few hours and look at it with the rest of your furniture. Many times something that looks like a perfect match in the store will look like a sore thumb in your home.

Don't ever feel you need to make a snap decision, even if an item is on sale. Furniture sales scream at you every week in the newspaper.

There are a few things you can look for to determine if a piece of furniture is well made. For wood pieces, such as a desk or dresser, the top should have a very smooth finish, ideally hand rubbed. If you see tiny bumps and craters, like the surface of an orange peel, it's a poor-quality finish. Solid wood is great, but veneer, a thin piece of wood applied to another piece of wood or particle board, is good, too. Many fancy pieces with intricate inlays in the top are veneer. What you don't want is a plastic top with a wood-grain finish that's photo-applied to particle board. It's basically plastic with a picture of wood on it.

Next, open a drawer and look at the connection between the front of the drawer and the side. You want something that's dovetailed, that is, connected firmly by a series of stubby, interlocking fingers seen on both the front and side. In a cheap piece, the drawer fronts may be stapled or nailed to the side and eventually will pull right off. The inside of the drawer should be smooth enough that you can rub a piece of gauze on it and the gauze won't snag. Also, the drawer should be deep when measured from front to back. Sometimes manufacturers cut corners by using shorter drawers.

It's harder to judge the quality of upholstered furniture. You could place a $399 sofa next to a $1,399 sofa and not see much difference. One thing to look for is whether the patterns line up correctly. Just as the stripes on a shirt pocket should match up with the rest of the shirt, so should the patterns on furniture. It costs more to have the pattern on the back match up with the rest of the piece, because that takes more fabric. Ask the salesperson about the springs. "Eight-way hand tied"—in which the springs are tied together with twine in eight directions—is a classic way to put furniture together. Another spring design, an independent Marshall unit, is okay, too.

If you're buying furniture and taking it home with you immediately, it doesn't matter how you pay. But if you're paying a deposit or waiting for it to be delivered, pay only by credit card. In the last few years, a lot of furniture stores have closed up shop without filling orders or delivering goods. I've had to tell too many callers who prepaid by cash or check that they will not be getting any money back.

It's not uncommon for furniture stores to shut down suddenly and leave stunned consumers without their furniture or their money. Some eventually get their merchandise or partial refunds, but they are lucky. Many others learn an expensive but important lesson. If you pay by check or cash, you could lose your money. If you buy with a credit card and the furniture store fails to deliver the merchandise, you are protected by your chargeback rights.

Furniture sales depend on expansion of the housing market, and the slower housing growth of the 1990s has cost furniture retailers mightily. Unfortunately, some have responded by using customer deposits to pay the rent or utility bills, instead of ordering merchandise. That's why it's smart to shop at financially healthy retailers.

Another reason for the problems of many traditional furniture retailers is the growth of newer, high-volume, no-frills furniture stores, which have steadily taken market share. One of the most popular and fastest-growing furniture retailers in the nation is IKEA, a warehouse-type operation that sells discount furniture, much of it to be assembled by the consumer.

Mattresses

I've had a number of questions in the past few years about how to buy a bed. My own solution is pretty low-tech. I go to my favorite warehouse discount store with a book or magazine and read for awhile, in different positions, to see if I'm comfortable on the bed. If I am, I buy it. If I'm not, I don't. The most recent mattress I bought, a Sealy, has been the best one I've ever owned. And I've never had a problem with a bed I've purchased in this manner.

The book answer is somewhat more complex and probably will end up being somewhat more expensive. But the experts say spending a bit more for a bed is pretty reasonable when you consider that you spend one-third of your life in bed, and that a good set of bedding should last 10 to 15 years.

It's recommended that you look primarily at mattresses and boxsprings made by one of the four major bedding manufacturers, Simmons, Sealy, Serta, and Stearns & Foster. Look for a mattress that's priced in the middle of the manufacturer's product line. The most expensive mattresses will be loaded with bells and whistles you don't need. The cheapest won't be of adequate quality.

The most important characteristic a mattress should have is the proper firmness. A soft mattress won't give your body the support it needs, and you'll wake up feeling achy, like you slept in a hammock. A mattress that doesn't give at all will make you feel like you slept on the floor.

The right mattress should give enough to

accommodate the contours of your body, yet provide good support. A 200-pound man will need more support than a 90-pound woman, so it's absolutely necessary to try a mattress out before you buy it. Wear comfortable clothes and see how each mattress feels. If you're married, go shopping with your spouse. Any reputable store is fine.

You'll hear a lot about mattress construction when you talk to salespeople or read product materials. The most important parts of all that gibberish are the coils and the upholstery, which determine the firmness of the mattress and its ability to react to your body. A good quality full-size mattress will have 400 to 800 separate coils. Queen- or king-size mattresses will have more coils than their full-size counterpart of the same brand and model, and twin-size mattresses will have fewer. Ask the salesperson how many coils the full-size version has, and use that figure to help evaluate quality. Don't buy a full-size mattress with fewer than 312 coils.

At least one top-of-the-line mattress has coils that are individually wrapped in a cloth pocket, which I'm told enables it to better adjust to shoulders and hips. That's great, but there are plenty of excellent mattresses with the more standard, open-coil design.

The surface layer of a mattress isn't just cosmetic. Manufacturers use materials from horse hair to high-density foam, in combination with cotton batting, to help adjust the level of firmness. But don't worry too much about the content or design of the upholstery fabric. A silk surface will cost a lot more, and you'll have it covered most of the time with sheets and blankets. Another worthless extra is a spun Dacron filler some manufacturers use to give the surface 7 to 10 inches of extra puffiness. It isn't worth the extra cost.

It's also strongly recommended that you buy a new boxspring at the same time you buy a new mattress. Some people try to save money by buying just the mattress. But experts say boxsprings wear out just like mattresses, although not as visibly. Putting a new mattress on an old boxspring may cause the new mattress to sag. Some new boxsprings have metal frames, rather than wood. That adds weight, but it may add strength as well.

Any bed frame will do, as long as it has a center support bar or enough horizontal slats to support the bed.

Carpet

When you buy carpet, it's important to buy from a good dealer, to get a good-quality carpet yarn, and to make sure it is properly installed. It doesn't matter if you buy from a carpet store or a department store, just don't buy over the phone. Generally someone who tries to sell carpet over the phone is trying to rip you off, selling cheap-quality carpet at inflated prices.

When you buy from a carpet store, make sure the showroom is neat and well kept, not a sloppy warehouse. An owner who takes care of his showroom is more likely to insist his installers do a good job in your home.

Choosing the carpet itself is relatively easy. Buy a carpet made from a premium carpet yarn, such as Du Pont's Stainmaster, Monsanto's Wear-Dated, or Allied Fibers' Worry-Free. Zeftron from BASF and XPS from Hoechst Celanese Corp. are two more good yarns. It's less important which mill turns those yarns into carpet, but you should look for a finished product whose yarn has a good twist to it. If you look closely at the carpet fibers, the tips should have a sharp, pencil-point appearance. That means it's been properly twisted. Poorly made carpet will have very little twist and the tips will have a frayed look. Quality carpet should look good for five to ten years, but cheap carpet can look ugly in as little as six months.

Installation is critical to the way the carpet will look in your home. Most carpet dealers use contractors to do the installation, rather than their own employees, and most contractors are poorly trained and use sloppy procedures. Ask the dealer what kind of guarantee is offered on installation. Ninety days to one year is normal. More than one year is a plus.

For proper installation, carpet should be power stretched into place so it is drum tight. Most installers use a knee-kicker to stretch carpet, a technique that won't achieve the right tautness. Loose carpet looks terrible and wears unevenly. When you buy, get it in writing that the carpet will be power stretched. As for padding, the best kind is half-inch, six-pound rebond, a dense padding made from chopped, pressed foam.

Expect to pay $18 or more a square yard, including installation and good padding. Figure the yardage you'll need by dividing the square footage by nine, then add 10 percent to account for waste. You should pay about $550 to carpet a bedroom that measures 12 feet by 21 feet, or just under $4,000 for an entire 1,800-square-foot house. But make sure to get a few quotes on the amount of yards that will be needed. Telephone salespeople and other unethical installers commonly mislead customers by quoting a cheap price but overestimating the yardage. It's no bargain to pay $15.99 for 195 yards (total price: $3,118) when another dealer, charging $18.99, says you need only 150 yards (total price: $2,848) to do the job.

One company no longer in business quoted its prices in "units" that were actually equal to half a yard. A buyer who needed only 27 square yards wound up paying for 54 "units" at $12.99 a unit. In other words, she bought cheap, builders' grade carpet at the outrageous price of $25.98 a yard, paying more than $700 for cheap carpet when she could have bought good carpet for less than $500.

Ask the installer how much carpet he's brought and make sure it's the amount you've purchased. Also check the manufacturer's name on the carpet and look at the padding. Some dealers will pull a fast one by giving you cheaper carpet or padding than what you bought, or selling you one quantity of carpet and sending the installer out with less.

Jewelry and Other Collectibles

When it comes to jewelry, some consumers see a purchase as an investment that could increase in value. But buying jewelry with that goal should be done only by someone who is an expert in the industry. If you're buying jewelry as a gift for yourself or a loved one, it will be very difficult for you to know the true value of the item. Plus, jewelry bought at retail loses a large amount of its value as soon as you purchase it.

I recommend buying jewelry only from a store that allows you 72 hours to inspect it and, if you choose, to return it for a full refund. This gives you the power to buy a piece that you like and then have its value estimated by other jewelry appraisers.

Jewelry generally is an emotional purchase, not a financial one. It's possible to buy jewelry now in warehouse clubs with concrete floors, but you might not want to tell an admiring friend that your diamond ring came from a warehouse. On the other hand, if you consider money more important than love or emotion, consider buying jewelry from a warehouse club or, perish the thought, buying a used piece, perhaps from a pawn shop.

The Better Business Bureau publishes an excellent booklet on how to understand the various quality and grades of diamonds, gold, and other jewelry. I recommend you read it before making a major jewelry purchase.

It's also quite difficult to buy or sell coins, stamps, and other collectibles. I don't expect you to become an expert in the field just to sell a collection you may have inherited, but a good way to protect yourself is to visit the stamp and coin shows that come to town. Go

- Tips on -
Infrequent
Purchases

● When buying furniture, you should deal only with reputable retailers—healthy businesses with knowledgeable salespeople.

● If you're considering a sofa with an unusual pattern or color, ask to take home a cushion and look at it with the rest of your furniture.

● Wood furniture should have a very smooth finish. With upholstered furniture, make sure the patterns line up.

● If you're paying a deposit for furniture or waiting for it to be delivered, pay only by credit card. With your credit card chargeback rights, you are protected if the furniture doesn't arrive.

● Always try out a bed before you buy it, even if you shop as I do, at warehouse discount stores.

● Experts recommend that you look primarily at mattresses and boxsprings made by one of the four major bedding manufacturers, Simmons, Sealy, Serta, and Stearns & Foster.

● It is important to buy a mattress with the proper firmness. A decent full-size mattress needs to have at least 312 coils to provide good support.

● When you buy carpet, it's important to buy from a good dealer, to get a good-quality carpet yarn, and to make sure it is properly installed.

● It doesn't matter if you buy from a carpet store or a department store, just don't buy over the phone.

● Buy a carpet made from a premium carpet yarn, such as Du Pont's Stainmaster, Monsanto's Wear-Dated, or Allied Fibers' Worry-Free.

● When you buy, get it in writing that the carpet will be power stretched for proper installation.

● Buy jewelry because you like it, not because you hope it will increase in value.

● Buy jewelry only from a store that allows you 72 hours to inspect it and, if you choose, to return it for a full refund.

● To buy or sell coins or other collectibles, visit dealer shows and get a number of quotes.

to the show, talk to several dealers, and see what kind of prices you're quoted. Some trends will quickly emerge. Then you can either settle for the price you're offered or advertise the collection for sale in the newspaper. Ask for a price 20 percent to 30 percent higher than the dealer quotes. If you want to buy something from an ad in the paper, offer the seller 20 to 30 percent less than what you see dealers selling similar goods for at a show.

When you're buying or selling collectibles, prices vary widely, due either to someone's knowledge of the business or their perception of the condition of the item. The more people you talk to, and the more dealers you visit, the better a feel you'll have for the value of merchandise.

Contracts —

Most people don't bother to read the contracts they're asked to sign when they buy a car or rent an apartment. But you do yourself a disservice when you sign one without knowing all its contents. Ask for time to take the contract home and read it.

If the party trying to get you to sign a contract refuses to let you leave with it, or pressures you to make a decision right then, don't sign the contract and don't do business with that organization. That happens a lot in health clubs, which often try to press you into signing expensive, long-term deals.

It's important to remember that a contract is a negotiated document, not a unilateral declaration. Many standard prewritten contracts are very one-sided, with the consumer having all the responsibilities and the other side having all the rights and privileges. But you can insist on changes. If an organization says the terms and conditions of a contract aren't negotiable, think about doing business with somebody else.

If you read a contract and something sounds unfair, or you don't understand something, mark it out with a pen and put your initials by that item. Don't agree to any clause in a contract you don't understand or you don't like. Once you sign the contract, you have to live with that provision.

Franchises —

People see franchises as a quick way to go into business for themselves, without having to build the reputation of a business from nothing. Buying a franchise isn't necessarily bad or good in itself, but it requires planning.

- Tips on - CONTRACTS

- A contract is a negotiated document, not a unilateral declaration. Always ask for time to take a contract home and read it.

- If the party trying to get you to sign a contract refuses to let you leave with it, or pressures you to make a decision right then, don't sign the contract and don't do business with that organization.

- If you read a contract and something sounds unfair, or you don't understand something, mark it out with a pen and put your initials by that item.

Any time you're thinking of going into a business or industry you know little about, don't immediately go set up shop or buy a franchise.

The best approach is to go to work in the industry, either for an independent operator or the franchise you're evaluating. Work in it for at least six months, preferably one year. I don't care if it means you're taking out the trash. Go in with your eyes and ears open so you can learn as much as possible. By doing this you'll learn two things. First and most important, you'll find out if it's a business you like. Second, you'll learn enough as an insider to know if promises made by a franchise are genuine. You'd be amazed how many people do this and then completely drop any thoughts of getting involved in the business.

Before I went into the travel business, I went to work in an agency for six months. I did everything you do as a lower-level employee in a travel agency, including writing and delivering tickets. The only mistake I made was doing it for only six months. A year would have

- Tips on - Franchises

● Before buying a franchise, go to work in the industry, either for an independent operator or the franchise you're thinking about buying. You'll learn plenty about the business and may decide it's not for you.

● Find out the answers to these questions: Is the franchise name readily recognizable in your area? Does that name brand have a good reputation in the general community and in that trade? Does the franchisor provide strong support?

● Call franchisees in the next town and ask them what they like and don't like.

● Evaluate your territory and make sure the company won't put another location close to you.

been better. But because I did that, we started turning a profit in my fourth month of business. It was terrific to start making money that quickly.

If you find after working in an industry that you like it and want to buy a franchise, think about these questions: Is the name readily recognizable in your area? Does the name brand have a good reputation in the general community and in that trade? Does the franchisor truly provide the support its glossy literature promises?

The best way to find out about franchise support is to call franchisees in another town. People in your own town may not be truthful because they may see you as a potential buyer for their business. You also need to evaluate the cost you pay for that support, including the up-front fees and the percent of your sales you'll

pay the franchisor. Make sure your business will be able to support that level of royalties.

Another thing to evaluate is territory. Some franchisees, just as they become successful, are stunned to find out that the franchisor is placing another franchise right down the street from their business. A famous sandwich shop chain has made many of its franchise holders unhappy by opening too many of its stores close to others, making it difficult for them to be profitable.

Other franchises have been criticized for spending too much effort to open new stores and thus generate up-front fees, or letting corporate leadership lapse because a founder sells out or becomes less involved. Some say the Wendy's hamburger chain has enjoyed a resurgence because founder Dave Thomas has become a more visible leader.

One of the big advantages of a well-recognized franchise name is that your company is easier to sell if you decide to leave the business. It's much harder to sell an independent, non-branded location. However, the fact that a franchise remains on one street corner for years does not mean it's successful. I know of one print shop in my neighborhood that appears to be a rock of stability but has had five owners in six years.

Often a franchisor will buy back a troubled franchise and run it until a new owner is found, rather than let anyone know it has failed. The industry rule of thumb is that 90 percent of franchises succeed. But one franchise consultant I've spoken with believes a third of franchises at any given time are successful, a third are getting by, and a third are failing.

Multilevel Marketing —

If you're thinking of going to work for a multilevel marketing organization, beware of all the hoopla and be on guard for possible illegalities.

Multilevel marketing organizations recruit

individuals to sell a variety of products, including household cleaners and diet aids.

You make money in two ways in a multilevel marketing organization. The first is by serving as a combination retailer and sales representative—you buy products from the company and resell them to customers. The second way is by recruiting people into the organization and earning a commission off their sales. That's where the term multilevel comes in. If I recruit you and you recruit a friend, I get commissions off both your sales and your friend's sales.

Multilevel marketing organizations want you to believe that, with a very limited expense on your part, but a great desire to win, you can become wealthy.

A multilevel marketing presentation is something like a high school pep rally. You'll hear testimonials from people who say they were near the financial abyss and found the ticket selling purple oranges. Now they're rolling in money and have a fancy car and a retirement home at the beach.

If you're thinking of joining such an organization, consider whether you have any sales skills, whether you believe in the product, and whether the product is priced fairly. You should be confident you will be able to go up to a stranger or an acquaintance—because you're going to exhaust your friends and relatives very quickly—convince them of the virtues of the product, and get them to buy. A lot of people can't or don't want to do that.

If you're going to sell a product, it should represent a fair value. It's no fun to justify why you sold someone, particularly a friend, a product that's more expensive than a similar product they could buy at the store. As consumers, they won't want to and shouldn't buy something that's overpriced.

I don't recommend joining any multilevel marketing organization that requires you to pay a substantial up-front fee to participate.

It's also very important to determine if the emphasis of a multilevel marketing company is on selling its products or on recruiting other people into the organization. If you hear a lot on the virtues of the products, the organization is on a sound footing. However, if the main purpose of the organization is rounding up new recruits, it may be an illegal pyramid. One caller told me about a meeting she went to in which the product was never mentioned. All they ever talked about was recruiting.

A pyramid organization can succeed only as long as it recruits new members, but as it does so it requires more and more members to support its ever-expanding base. Normally, it will just collapse. But let's say, hypothetically, it is remarkably skilled at recruiting and has no difficulty signing members. Eventually it would run out of people in the United States or on the earth and would then collapse. Pyramids are illegal because only the scam artists who start them make any money.

One more word of caution about multilevel marketing. If you're an outstanding salesperson, you would probably do better by selling through a traditional sales channel, where you don't have to split your commissions with others in the organization.

One advantage of multilevel marketing, though, may be that it helps you discover a talent you didn't know you had, and you can then graduate to a true, full-time selling position. One thing you don't want to do is quit your regular job to join a multilevel organization. I've heard horror stories of people who've quit jobs only to find that either they weren't successful, or the multilevel organization left town and left them unemployed.

Too often when I get questions about cars, people are looking for remedies to problems. A new or used car turns out to be trouble-prone, a lease turns out to be a bad idea, or a minor accident turns out to be a major headache. I believe you're better off avoiding problems in the first place than trying to fix them later on.

With most purchases, we know enough, or can quickly learn enough, to control the process. But when it comes to cars, many of us never gain control. Too few buyers do any research on their favorite model, despite the fact that uncovering a poor repair record on a car could save a lot of hardship later on.

When you're buying a car, whom can you trust? Contrary to what most people think, the vast majority of car dealers are decent, honest people. Unfortunately, a dishonest person can take your money so many ways in a car transaction that it magnifies the harm you can suffer when you're not well informed.

Most of us simply cannot become an expert in the complexities of car repair. With the diversity of car models and shortage of well-trained labor, it's difficult enough for mechanics to do the work properly. The best way to handle an expensive car repair is by taking the time to get opinions and estimates from several repair shops.

In this section, I'll give you the information and resources you'll need to help you buy a new or used car, finance it, and get it fixed if something goes wrong.

Buying a New Car —

Few things make people feel so excited and so awful at the same time as the prospect of buying a new car. A lot of people would sooner have a cavity filled than shop for a new car, because they despise the process of negotiating the purchase price.

Yet who doesn't love driving off a dealer's lot with a new car? Many buyers are so thrilled with the idea of buying a new car that they act too quickly. They get a disease called new car fever, which forces them to buy a car right away, instead of taking a reasoned approach that will save them a lot of money.

It's not at all unusual for someone to buy a car within seventy-two hours of the moment they first decide to shop. Many people will visit a new car dealer just to see a particular model of car and, believe it or not, will leave the dealership a few hours later as the owner of that car. If money matters to you, that's not the way to buy a car.

Buying a car should be a deliberate process. Yes, it does take some of the thrill out of it. But how much of a thrill is it to write a larger monthly check, year after year? My formula for buying a car is rather simple. First, go to your bank or credit union and prequalify for a car loan. Once you prequalify, you'll know how much car you can afford and what type of monthly payment you will have to budget. It also means your purchase won't collapse because you can't get financing.

Once your financing is set up, it's time to decide what kind of car you want. That's when you go look at cars and test-drive them. One of the best times to go look at cars is when a dealership is closed. During off hours, there's no salesperson to pressure you. You're free to look around the lot at vehicles.

I recommend that people become familiar with the various versions of a car. Nowadays, one model name is actually an umbrella for several different versions of the car. The Honda Accord, for example, might come in a DX, LX, EX, and SE version. Each version comes with a different package of options and standard equipment. You'll find that the most expensive version of the car will cost several thousand dollars more than the least expensive version. It's to your advantage to buy the least expensive version of the model that meets your needs. That's because, over time, the value of those two vehicles converges. An initial gap of $8,000 between the cheapest and most expensive versions might dwindle to $1,000 in the resale value of the two cars after a few years of ownership. If you buy the most expensive version, you pay a higher price both up front and at resale time.

I don't recommend test-driving the car at the dealership. You'll only have a short time to check out the car, and the salesperson will be right there. The best way to test-drive a car is to rent that model for a day or two. Car rental companies make most of their money on business rentals, so they offer great specials on the weekends, when volume is light. I actually check out cars this way on business, since I travel so much. I've rented cars I thought I might want to buy and changed my mind after driving them for a few days. It's the ultimate test drive and it's not expensive. After all, considering that you might spend $15,000 to buy a car, spending $25 to $40 to rent it is rather inexpensive.

Start your research with at least two different vehicles in mind. Then check out the price, reliability, and cost to insure each of the cars you're considering. Everyone wants a car that will run dependably and stay out of the repair shop. The best way to improve your odds of getting a trouble-free car is to check out the repair records of the models you've selected. *Consumer Reports* magazine is the best place to find repair data on cars. Each year, the magazine's April issue is devoted to car buying, and it contains detailed ratings and data on a variety of models for several model years. Consumers Union, which publishes *Consumer Reports*, also publishes a car-buying guide that is available year-round in bookstores.

Of course no repair data is available on newly introduced car models. I don't recommend buying a new or radically redesigned model, because if you do, you are the guinea pig for any problems the vehicle might have. After a few model years, you have a better idea if a car is well made and worth purchasing.

If you've narrowed your search to a couple of different models, it's helpful to call your insurance agent to find out how much it would cost to insure those vehicles. There may be a significant difference between your choices, even between two versions of the same model. The size of the cars' engines, for example, could be one reason for a cost difference.

The next task is to figure out what the car actually costs, disregarding the make-believe list price printed on the window sticker. There are a number of ways to get this information. If you're a member of a credit union, the dealer's cost of a car may be available to you for free. You can also go to a bookstore and buy *Edmund's New Car Prices*. Finally, *Consumer Reports* has a service that will provide you with the dealer's base cost and the cost of various options. But *Consumer Reports'* service is quite expensive—$11 for a price printout on one model, $20 for two models, and $27 for three models.

These sources will give you a breakdown of the car's base cost and the cost of options such as automatic transmission and air conditioning. You'll get the dealer's actual cost and the suggested retail price. Ignore the suggested retail price. Just add up the dealer's base price, the dealer cost of any options you want, and other necessary charges, such as transportation. In most states, you'll also have to pay sales tax.

When you negotiate to buy a car, you should work from the actual dealer cost. Most dealers will sell a car for a few hundred dollars above their cost. In some very rare cases, you can actually buy a car for less than dealer cost. But buyers regularly pay sticker prices that contain markups of several thousand dollars. What you ultimately pay for the car is strictly a matter

- Tips on -
Buying a New Car

● Take your time in buying a new car. A reasoned approach will save you a lot of money.

● First, go to your bank or credit union and prequalify for a car loan. That tells you how much car you can afford and what type of monthly payment you will have to budget.

● Look at cars when a dealership is closed, so there's no salesperson to pressure you.

● Become familiar with the various versions of a car. Typically now, one model name is an umbrella for several different versions of the car.

● The best way to test-drive a car is to rent it for a day or two. It's the ultimate test drive and it's not expensive.

● Start your research with at least two different vehicles in mind. Then check out the price, reliability, and cost to insure each of the cars you're considering.

● Find out the dealer costs of the vehicle and options you want and begin negotiating from that cost, not the make-believe retail price.

● When you've narrowed the search to one or two vehicles and have the actual dealer cost for each, call a few dealers and ask for their best price on the vehicle. Do not go to the dealership, because if you do, the balance of power shifts to the dealer.

● The success of a particular model in the marketplace is a critical factor in how much you'll pay. If a vehicle is selling very poorly, a smart shopper may end up paying below dealer cost. You'll pay much more for a hot seller.

● When you go into the dealer to sign the paperwork, make sure what is on the purchase agreement is what you've agreed to previously by phone or fax. If it's not the same, do not agree to go through with the deal.

● The best way to protect yourself in a dealership is to be willing to walk out.

Reference:
Consumer Reports' April Auto Issue or
Car Buying Guide
Edmund's car guides, by Edmund
Publications Corp.

of supply and demand and your own ability to shop.

When you've narrowed the search to one or two vehicles and have the actual dealer cost for those vehicles, call a few dealers and ask for their best price on the vehicle. Tell them what options you want and what colors you will accept. Do not go to the dealership, because if you do, the balance of power shifts to the dealer and you are in a weakened position.

Most dealers will be happy to quote you a price on the phone. Some dealers will offer to beat whatever deal you come up with, or give you a very low price, which they don't intend to honor later. Don't do business with anyone who won't play it straight with you.

One method that eliminates any potential for misunderstanding is using a fax machine to send information back and forth to dealers. I've had calls from people who have been very successful using the fax to make a low-pressure, no-pain transaction. The idea here is not to prevent the dealer from making a profit. It's for you to get a deal you believe is fair, without being subjected to the high-pressure sales tactics employed by some car dealers.

There's no formula that says you should pay $300 or $500 above dealer cost. Some people like to buy at the end of the month, the end of a model year, or the end of the calendar year, when sales goals, the influx of new models, or inventory taxes may cause a dealer to be more motivated to negotiate. But there are drawbacks. If you buy a car at the end of a model year, you have, as soon as you drive it out of the dealership, a one-year-old car. You should look at an end-of-year closeout only if you keep a car a long time. The depreciation hit of that lost year doesn't matter once you have owned the car for several years. But it matters a great deal if you buy a car every few years.

More important than calendar cycles is the success of a particular model in the marketplace. If a vehicle is selling very poorly, a smart shopper may end up paying below dealer cost, because all the dealer's trying to do is move the vehicle. The dealer may be hurting because the vehicle is just sitting on the lot (that's called flooring) or the manufacturer may be offering incentives to sell slow-moving models.

When small cars aren't selling well, the manufacturers offer huge incentives to their dealers to move them. Because of CAFE, the Corporate Average Fuel Economy standards, manufacturers have to sell a certain number of small cars to balance the number of large cars they've sold, so that their average fuel economy will meet federal standards. If they don't meet the standard, manufacturers face huge fines. Usually your most aggressive negotiating with a domestic manufacturer, whatever that means now, is on smaller, entry-level vehicles they must sell.

At the other end of the spectrum is the "hot" car, the one everyone wants to buy. The sky's the limit on that car as far as price goes. A good example is the Mazda Miata, which was so trendy a few years ago that dealers were getting $1,000 above sticker price for them and customers were lined up to buy. If you want to pay a premium for a hot car, that's fine—just as long as you know the cost, both up front and at resale time, when the heavy demand likely will have waned.

The demand for most cars is average, so the price you pay will depend mostly on your knowledge of actual dealer cost. The more you know and the less emotional you are about the purchase, the better off you'll be. As you contact dealer after dealer, you're quickly going to get a feel for the market. You may have one quote that's very high, but most will be in a narrow range and the marketplace will establish the fair value of the car. I recommend calling at least six dealers. Some people get obsessed with this and call many more. Just call until you feel comfortable with the quotes.

When you go into the dealer to sign the paperwork, make sure that what is on the purchase agreement is what you've agreed to previously by phone or fax. If it's not the same, do not agree to go through with the deal. Remember, you've been shopping. If finalist A pulls a con job, you can go to finalist B. I've used this method for buying a car for years, and only once has a dealer tried to cheat me. Every other time the dealers treated me with complete dignity and honesty.

If you choose to buy a car the traditional way—by walking into a dealership and talking with a salesperson—be prepared for a difficult process. Some dealers—by no means all—will use a variety of tactics to snare you. They know you're excited about buying a new car and will use that to their advantage. One strategy they'll employ is delay. Dealers know that the longer they can keep you at the dealership, the more likely you are to buy a car. So they'll try to keep you there for several hours.

One common tactic to delay you is to make your car unavailable. When you show up at a dealership, they ask to have the used-car manager check out your car, to evaluate its trade-in value. While you're test-driving a new car, they send somebody to look over your car and make sure you don't get it back too quickly.

I recommend that you discuss any trade-in only after you've negotiated the purchase of the new car. I'll talk more about why in the next section. But if you keep the transactions separate and stay close to your car, you won't be kept in the dealership any longer than you want to be there.

One of the most despicable practices in the industry is "roofing," in which the used-car people literally throw the keys to your car onto the dealership roof, then report that they somehow can't find the keys. The purpose is to get you to drive home in the new car while they look for the keys. The best way to protect yourself in a dealership is to be willing to walk out. Only those who are willing to get up and leave are able negotiators.

One problem many Americans have in negotiations is our politeness. We might think that it's rude, when a salesperson is being too aggressive, to say, "I'm sorry but I need to leave." But sometimes that is the only answer.

Trade-ins, Financing, and Extended Warranties —

If you have a trade-in, the time to discuss it with the dealer is after you've negotiated the purchase of the car. Do it as a completely separate transaction; otherwise, if you mix the trade-in with the purchase, you'll never know whether a dealer is offering you a great price on the new car and making up for it by giving you a poor value for your trade-in.

Once you've shopped around and the dealers realize you're a good shopper, their prices will be similar. You can help decide which dealer to buy from by seeing how much they'll give you for the trade-in. Take the car to each dealer for a trade-in quote and use that as the decision maker.

I always skip the trade-in process and sell my cars myself. A large number of people do sell privately, and they are able to get a better price. But most prefer to trade their car to the dealer because they don't want to deal with the hassle of a private sale—classified ads, phone calls, and test drives. Your bank or credit union can help you find out what your trade-in is worth. They can tell you the average retail price of your used vehicle, plus its average trade-in value, by looking in the National Automobile Dealers Association (NADA) *Used Car Guide*. By selling the vehicle yourself, you'll get a price about halfway between average trade-in and average retail. A dealer will give you the trade-in price. Once you've measured that gap, you can figure out whether it's worth the bother of selling the car yourself.

You also should keep the financing of the car separate from the actual purchase. When you allow the dealer to arrange financing, all kinds of terrible things can happen. The dealer's business strategy is to close the deal quickly and send you away in the new car. They want to finance the car so they can close the deal. But if you drive home the new car and give the dealer your trade-in, you're in trouble if the financing later collapses.

Days to weeks later, the dealer may call you with the sad information that your loan didn't go through. Then you either have to come up with a lot more money for a down payment, or pay a much higher rate of interest, so that a lender will accept the loan. The other choice is undoing the sale. By prequalifying with your bank or credit union, you eliminate all three of those possibilities.

It's best to finance a car for 48 months or less. The 60-month loan, which has become so common, is a poor financial choice because under it, the value of the car declines much faster than the loan balance. So, for much of the five-year period, you're "upside down" in the loan—you owe more than the vehicle is worth.

Being "upside down" in the loan can be a major problem. Let's say you decide after a couple of years that you can't stand your car. Selling it won't generate nearly enough money to pay off the loan. Unless you can come up with several thousand dollars to pay off the balance of the loan, you're stuck in the vehicle. If the vehicle is totaled in an accident, you can end up owing the lender thousands of dollars. You have to cover the gap between the amount the insurance company pays and what you owe.

The beauty of a shorter loan, particularly 42 months or less, is that the loan amount tracks the value of the vehicle. For most people, 48 months is a good compromise. I know this sounds harsh, but if you go in for a car loan and the payments for a 48-month loan are too high, you're trying to buy too much car. Stretching it to 60 months is the wrong response.

I don't like service contracts or extended warranties. But if you're terribly afraid of the risk of having a car that does not work and want to buy an extended warranty, at least shop for the best price. The price on extended warranties is highly negotiable. One of the manufacturer's contracts that retails at $795 costs the dealer $180. The dealer may make little profit on the sale of a car, but on an extended warranty the markup may be 400 percent to 1,000 percent, depending on the type of warranty.

You can buy an extended warranty from three different sources: an extended warranty company, an insurance company, or an automobile manufacturer. Never buy a service contract that is not provided by the manufacturer or backed by an insurance company. I've had case after case of extended warranty companies selling cheap contracts to dealers and then going out of business without paying claims.

These ripoff companies sell service contracts to dealers for $90, and the dealers resell them to car buyers for $1,100. The pitch is that the dealer will make a fortune even if they sell the warranty for $600. After a few years, claims start coming in and there's not enough money in the pool to pay the claims. The company collapses or vanishes, and the consumer ends up with a worthless service contract.

If you buy an extended warranty, make sure you know who is behind it. If you buy a General Motors car, ask if the service contract is a General Motors—branded product. If it's an insurance company product, ask what insurance company it is from and what is its rating from A. M. Best Co., a rating company. If the company is not rated A + +, do not buy the product. If the salesperson tells you it's rated A + +, make sure the rating is stated in your purchase contract.

You can negotiate the price on a warranty from the dealer. One place to go for a quote is the company that writes your auto insurance. Many times your agent will be able to give you a quote on an extended warranty. Another

- Tips on -
Trade-ins, Financing, and Extended Warranties

● If you have a trade-in, the time to discuss it with the dealer is after you've negotiated the purchase of the car.

● After you've negotiated a price for a new car, you can decide which dealer to buy from by seeing how much they'll give you for the trade-in.

● Your bank or credit union can tell you the average retail price of your used vehicle, as well as the average trade-in value, by looking in the National Automobile Dealers Association (NADA) *Used Car Guide*. By selling the vehicle yourself, you'll get a price about halfway between average trade-in and average retail. A dealer will give you the trade-in price.

● Finance a car for 48 months or less. With a 60-month loan, the value of the car declines much faster than the loan balance. So for much of the five-year period, you owe more than the vehicle is worth.

● Keep the financing separate from the car-price negotiation, too. When you allow the dealer to arrange financing, all kinds of terrible things can happen.

● Don't buy an extended service contract from an automobile dealer or anyone else until you've had time to think about it and shop prices. You do not have to make this decision at the moment you're buying your vehicle.

Contact:
GEICO (For extended warranties)
One Geico Blvd.
Fredericksburg, VA 22412-3004
1-800-841-1003
In Texas: 1-800-841-5432

way is to call a company that writes service contracts, such as GEICO, and compare their costs and coverages to those offered under the dealer contract. The GEICO contract— which is available to those who have GEICO auto insurance—will cost about 40 percent of the suggested retail price of a manufacturer's extended warranty.

It's important not to make a decision on an extended warranty from the dealer or anyone else until you've had time to think about it. This is not a decision that has to be made at the moment you're buying your vehicle. In fact, that's the worst time to decide because you're not thinking clearly. You're excited about buying a new car and you want to be done with the paperwork.

With most extended warranty providers,

you have at least twelve months from the date you purchase the car to make the decision. One of the advantages to waiting is if the car turns out to be a lemon and you're always having problems with it, then you know you should buy an extended warranty. During the first year, the manufacturer's warranty protects you.

Leasing —

It's almost impossible to talk to an auto salesperson today without hearing a pitch for you to lease, rather than buy, a vehicle. That's because leasing is a very profitable method of selling vehicles for dealers. It can be harder for the consumer to compare prices on a lease, and the financing costs built into a lease are very high.

The biggest pitfall of a lease is when you use it to get more car than you can afford. The monthly payment for two similar cars will be cheaper for someone who leases than for someone who buys, so people will lease, foolishly, so they can have a more expensive car. Let's say you buy a $15,000 vehicle with no down payment. Over four years, you'll pay $15,000 plus interest, and your monthly payment will be based on the cost of financing $15,000. If you lease a vehicle, you may finance $9,000 and have a residual value of $6,000. Your monthly payments will be based on the $9,000 being financed, so the payments will be much lower. You'll have the option of paying $6,000 to buy that car at the end of the four-year lease.

But you're mortgaging your future when you lease. If you buy a vehicle and pay it off in four years, you own a vehicle that still has value. You can keep it and avoid making car payments for a while, or sell it and use the money to help buy a newer vehicle. But after four years of leasing a vehicle and making payments, you own nothing. You can turn the vehicle in and, four years of inflation later, you can lease or buy another car.

You may also owe sizable mileage penalties. Most leases allow you to drive an average of 15,000 miles per year. If you exceed the limit, you have to pay a penalty of 8 to 15 cents per mile. If you lease a car for four years and drive a total of 80,000 miles, you might owe as much as $3,000.

Many times people are not realistic about how many miles they're going to drive each year. Or they may end up changing jobs and find themselves driving much farther than they originally intended. Before they know it, they're near the end of the lease and tens of thousands of miles over the limit. If you owe a big mileage penalty, the best thing to do is buy the vehicle at the predetermined price specified in the lease. Then you won't have to pay the penalty.

I had a call from one fellow who turned in his Mercedes-Benz at the end of his lease, not realizing he was way over the mileage limit. He wasn't asked to pay any penalty. But two years later, he was told that he owed $8,000 in excess mileage costs. It would have cost him just $2,000 more, a total of $10,000, to buy the car outright. But the car had been sold long before and he no longer had the option to buy it.

If you're going to pay a mileage penalty or buy the car, you'd better have some cash on hand. If the car has a lot of miles on it, a bank won't lend you the money to pay off its residual value. You avoid all these problems if you just buy the vehicle in the first place.

Short-term leases can be bad enough, but a five-year lease is a recipe for disaster. Many customers end up married to a vehicle they hate. Even if they like the car, most don't keep it the full five years. Instead, they frequently end up paying severe early termination penalties.

If you lease for five years and your car is totaled in an accident, you may have big problems. You could be responsible for a giant gap between the amount the insurance company will pay and the stated residual in the lease. It's not at all unusual in these cases for the gap to be as much as $8,000. Some leases contain an automatic gap clause which states that, if the

- Tips on - Leasing

● It's harder to compare prices on a lease, and the financing costs built into a lease are very high.

● Leasing may seem cheaper than buying, but you're mortgaging your future when you lease. After four years of leasing a vehicle and making payments, you own nothing.

● Most leases allow you to drive an average of 15,000 miles per year. If you exceed the limit, you have to pay a penalty of 8 to 15 cents per mile.

● A five-year lease is a recipe for disaster. Many customers end up married to a vehicle they hate or end up paying severe early termination penalties.

● If you lease for five years and your car is totaled in an accident, you could be responsible for a giant gap between the amount the insurance company will pay and the stated residual in the lease.

● There are some circumstances when a short-term lease makes sense.

vehicle is totaled in an accident, the manufacturer's financing arm accepts the insurance company payment and releases you from any further responsibility. Be certain any lease you sign covers this gap provision. Some car dealers, if you raise this issue, will offer you a separate insurance product called gap insurance. You should require them to provide gap insurance for free as part of the deal.

There are two circumstances in which leasing a vehicle makes sense. The first is when someone likes to have a new car every two to three years. If that's your goal, to always have a new car and get rid of it before the warranty is up, you're a candidate for a short-term lease. You won't have to deal with getting rid of the car.

The other circumstance in which leasing can be okay is when there's factory-subsidized financing on the lease. If the manufacturer offers no-interest financing, your total cost to lease for four years and then buy the vehicle might be lower than if you bought it outright. But you have to have the discipline to put aside your savings each month so that you have the money to buy at the end of the lease. If you're not a disciplined saver, even with the prospect of factory-subsidized leasing, buy the car.

If the manufacturer subsidizes the lease by stating an unrealistically high residual value on the vehicle, you can lease for three or four years at a great price, but then you should walk away. In any case, don't lease for more than four years. My preference is for no more than three.

Buying a Used Car —

If people bought a car simply as transportation, they would always buy a used car. That's because used cars are a better value than new cars, if you buy wisely.

For many of us, buying a used car is a matter of economic necessity, even though we would prefer to have a new car. Others prefer buying a new car so they don't have to deal with the hassles of used-car ownership.

There are several different used-car markets. One is for nearly new cars—cars that are one or two years old. These cars have been returned from rental fleets, turned in from two-year auto leases, repossessed from buyers who couldn't afford them, or traded in by buyers who bought new vehicles. Two years is a key trigger point in buying a car, because a vehicle takes its worst depreciation hits in its first two years.

If you're interested in buying a car but can't

afford a new one, a one- or two-year-old car is a good compromise. In many cases it will come with a portion of the manufacturer's warranty still in effect, and you'll buy it at a fraction of what it would have cost brand new. A while back, I priced a brand new Ford Taurus at $18,600 retail. A two-year-old version of the same model, with 30,000 miles on it, would have cost $11,000 if you paid the sticker price. That's a savings of $7,600, or more than 40 percent, for buying a two-year-old car. Prices change, and I hope you'll pay less than the sticker price, but the price spread should hold.

With any used car, knowing the repair record becomes critical. Look only at car models that have performed well. *Consumer Reports* publishes a list every year in its April issue of recommended used cars, price ranges, and used cars to avoid. Don't buy a car if it's on the list of cars to avoid. Buying a used car is a risky proposition, and you don't want to do anything that worsens your odds.

With an older used car, you're better off buying one that has no gadgets on it, such as power windows or door locks. Those items can break over time, and you don't want to have to pay an expensive repair bill for something you don't need in the first place. A hand window crank probably will work forever.

Before you buy a used car, find out what the vehicle is worth. You can go to a bookstore and get a guide to used-car prices or go to your bank or credit union with the list of vehicles in which you're most interested. The bank officer can look up the average retail price and average trade-in price in the NADA *Used Car Guide* and give you a good idea of a fair purchase price for a particular car. With a new car, you negotiate from dealer cost. With a used car, you negotiate from average trade-in.

Whether you buy from a dealer or a private individual, make your deal with the seller contingent upon having the vehicle inspected by an independent mechanic.

Only a handful of states provides any protection for used-car buyers. New York State has one of the best. Its Used Car Lemon Law allows buyers to get a refund or replacement if a used car is defect-ridden or unsafe. And it requires dealers to provide minimum warranties of 30 to 90 days, depending on the vehicle's mileage. In many other states, you own the car as soon as you sign the papers. It doesn't matter if the car won't start and you can't drive it off the dealer's lot.

Some dealers have taken to selling worthless cars salvaged from wrecks. I got a call from a couple who spent $2,800 on a used 1985 Honda Civic, only to find that they couldn't get a title for it. The car had been wrecked in another state and shabbily repaired. The frame was bent in the crash and a plate was welded to the undercarriage in a half-hearted attempt to fix it. When my staff and I interceded, the dealer offered to buy the car back, but they wanted a $600 fee for eight months of use. The couple was considering a lawsuit.

Another car ploy is "program" cars, supposedly well-maintained, quality used cars owned for a year by an executive. Some of these are abused cars that may never have had the oil changed. You have no way of knowing the condition of these or any other used cars unless you have them inspected.

There are several services that do nothing but diagnostic inspections of cars and trucks. For $70 to $80, they will do a full test on the vehicle, often right on the dealer's lot. In most areas, you can find services like these in the Yellow Pages under the heading Diagnostic Services. If a seller refuses to allow the vehicle to be inspected, don't buy it. That's a deal killer.

Having the car inspected isn't foolproof, but it improves your odds tremendously of avoiding a lemon. It's funny, but when a buyer insists on having the car inspected, the seller often remembers some defect or repair work

- Tips on - Buying a Used Car

- If you're interested in buying a car but can't afford a new one, a one- or two-year-old car is a good compromise. In many cases it will come with a portion of the manufacturer's warranty still in effect, and you'll buy it at a fraction of what it would have cost brand new.

- With any used car, knowing the repair record is critical. Look only at car models that have performed well.

- With an older used car, you're better off buying one that has no gadgets on it, such as power windows or door locks. Those items can break over time, and you don't want to have to pay an expensive repair bill for something you don't need in the first place.

- Before you buy a used car, find out what the vehicle is worth. Go to a bookstore and get a guide to used-car prices or to your bank or credit union with the list of vehicles in which you're most interested.

- Whether you buy from a dealer or a private individual, make your deal with the seller contingent upon having the vehicle inspected by an independent mechanic. If a seller refuses to allow the vehicle to be inspected, don't buy it.

- When you buy a used car, buy it privately or at the used-car lot of a new-car dealer. Do not buy vehicles from dealers who sell only used cars.

- Buy from a dealer only if he provides a warranty of at least 30 days.

that was done recently. Suddenly, his memory returns, because he knows he's going to be caught.

It's important to have a nearly new car inspected, even though it's still under warranty, because quite often the car has been in an accident. A wreck can cause a car to have tremendous operating problems as well as suffer a huge loss in value. The only way to know whether it's been in an accident is to have it inspected by a diagnostic service.

The diagnostic tests aren't pass or fail. Sometimes, the mechanic will report that a part is worn, and you'll have to make the decision whether to buy the car. You can also use the disclosure of certain problems as leverage to lower the price. Then you can use the savings to pay for repairs.

The hardest calls I take on my radio show involve cars. A typical call involves someone who's recently purchased a used car, sometimes for several thousand dollars, only to discover it to be ridden with problems. She's faced with impossible choices. The vehicle often can't be properly repaired, and the dealer won't take it back. That could mean scrapping it, absorbing an expensive loss, and trying again. It's even worse if the buyer is making car payments on a useless vehicle. These situations are very sad, because in many cases nothing can be done to help the caller. Most people who find themselves in this situation have been ripped off by an unethical used-car dealer.

To protect yourself when you buy a used car, buy it from a private citizen, or at the used-car lot of a new-car dealer. Do not buy vehicles from dealers who sell only used cars. When a new-car dealer takes a trade or a return from a rental company, it keeps the best vehicles on its lot and sells the rest through auction. The most problem-ridden cars end up at used-car lots.

The worst used-car lots are the "Buy Here, Pay Here" lots. Almost always, the cars are incidental to the purpose of these places. They make their money on the loans they extend to you on your vehicle. They're in the loan business, not the car business.

Most states don't require the dealer to provide any warranty on used cars, but some new-car dealers do provide limited warranties on their used cars. When you buy a used car from a dealer, you're paying a substantial markup, and I believe you pay for satisfaction after the sale. You should agree to buy only if the dealer provides some kind of warranty, from 30 to 90 days.

Car Repairs —

Unless you have a relative who's a mechanic, there's no easy way to find someone who has the skill and integrity to fix your car correctly and for a fair price. Car repair has become much more difficult because of the proliferation of models, the advancement of technology in cars, and a lack of people who are properly trained to repair those vehicles.

There have been so many stories over the years about auto repair ripoffs. One of the most memorable is a landmark piece "60 Minutes" did in the 1970s, about mechanics who set up shop near an interstate highway, and conned customers into paying for unneeded repairs. The truth is, most of the time car repair isn't a question of fraud and dishonesty. So often when I hear complaints, the problem is a lack of competence on the part of the mechanics, not fraud. But if you overpay, the cause isn't that important.

There are some basic rules you should follow when you take your car in for service. First, every time you take a car to the mechanic— and especially if you have to return a car for the same problem—you should control what is written on the work ticket. Don't let the mechanic list a cure on the ticket, but rather a description of the symptoms. If the car is stalling out at 30 miles per hour, that's what should be on the ticket. You don't want the tick-

et to say, "Do a tune-up," because if the problem isn't corrected, they will be able to say correctly that they did a tune-up.

How you prepare the service ticket is a key strategy if you want to assert your rights under your state's Lemon Law (see also the Lemon Law section). To claim benefits under most of these laws, you have to produce service tickets that show you attempted to repair the vehicle. Make sure the shop writes a service ticket and make sure you keep a copy. If the service tickets you receive do not show clearly the vehicle was brought in several times to repair the same problem, you may not be able to provide the proper documentation in order to force the manufacturer to buy back or exchange your vehicle.

If you're going to have an estimate done on the car, make sure the work ticket says it has been authorized only for an estimate. If you're authorizing specific work, write down the exact dollar limit you are authorizing and don't permit any work to be done beyond that dollar limit.

If the estimate is large, don't accept it as the final word. Even if your car is not driveable, it would be wise to have it towed to another repair shop for another estimate of what is wrong and how much it would cost to repair. If the repair is $2,000 or more, it would not be overkill to bring it to three places for repair estimates.

Obviously the best circumstance is when the vehicle is still driveable. You'll feel like the worst kind of sitting duck when the car isn't driveable and you think you're married to the first repair shop to which it is towed. But a $50 tow charge is money well spent when the alternative might be hundreds of dollars in unneeded repairs.

Many times the estimates vary because two different mechanics can come up with two different explanations for what is wrong, or different ways to fix it. One summer, my air conditioning went out when a $550 computer module failed. I could have paid for a new module, but my car was four years old at the time with 60,000 miles on it and that sounded like an expensive answer. But the mechanic had a great idea. The module's job was to turn off the air conditioning compressor temporarily when the car was started. The mechanic suggested a simple re-wiring of the air-conditioning to bypass the module. I just had to remember to turn off the air conditioner before I started the car. Getting a second opinion in that case saved me hundreds of dollars.

If your car is towed to a mechanic, don't allow the tow-truck driver to choose the repair shop. Quite often, he or she will be paid to steer your vehicle to a particular shop. You have no way of knowing if that shop is legitimate, honest, or competent. Make your own decision about where to take the car.

Don't rely on a nationally famous name when you go for a car repair. Too often at a franchise location, the parent company fails to accept responsibility for a problem. A common response is, "We're not responsible, but we'll see if we can talk to them about an accommodation." That doesn't mean the national company is behind you. Make sure you know who backs the warranty. If the warranty is good only at that location, then taking your car to a chain or franchise means nothing.

No matter which repair shop you use, always ask for the return of parts being replaced. That's one of the best ways you can prove later that a repair shop didn't make a repair it was supposed to make. At the very least, it gives you peace of mind that the shop made the promised repair. There's always the risk they can dig out some old parts. If you're dealing with true crooks, these precautions don't really matter. That's why word of mouth is so important in car repair. If you know someone who has been thrilled with a certain service facility, you may want to consider taking your car there.

I've taken my cars to an independent shop that works on nothing but my brand of car. They've seen all these problems hundreds of times, so it's easier for them to make the correct diagnosis. Even if a specialty shop charges more for a repair, it's valuable to know the repairs are done right. My mechanics knew about a potential engine failure on my car that could be avoided by replacing a belt. They recommended this preventative maintenance to make sure there was no catastrophe.

That's a real benefit of using an independent shop. A dealer knows your make and model of car, but may side with the manufacturer and not disclose those kinds of problems. However, using an independent mechanic is no fail-safe method. You still have to make sure you're happy with the work the shop does.

Another problem with dealer repairs is that you often don't get to speak with the mechanic who works on your car. You speak to a service writer, who writes a note describing the problem to the mechanic. If you need to go to the dealer because your car is under warranty, or if you like going to that particular dealer, insist upon speaking personally to the mechanic if a repair is unsatisfactory. If you can talk to him directly, you can often explain the problem more completely.

I once had a Chevy Nova that was stalling out at any speed and the dealership couldn't repair it after two tries. On the third trip, I demanded to speak to the mechanic and explained what was wrong. He hadn't been able to understand the scope of the problem from a few perfunctory notes on the service ticket. But after I explained it to him, he realized what was wrong and fixed it in fifteen minutes.

There are two schools of thought on the shops that specialize in particular components of a vehicle. Some like to go to a quick-lube place for oil changes, a tune-up shop for tune-ups or a brake repair place for brake work. Others like to go to one mechanic for all repairs. I tend to do the routine things like oil changes at a place that does just those, but have anything significant done by a shop that specializes in my brand of vehicle.

I have a built-in skepticism about general repair centers that claim to be able to repair all components of all vehicles. You're asking a lot from a mechanic if you throw any number of different vehicles at him or her and say, "Fix this." I don't think that's possible; specializing by component or by vehicle are the two wisest methods.

Most car owners have only rare encounters with an auto body shop, so they have no idea what to expect when they need body work. First, get an estimate of the cost to repair the vehicle. Many insurers require two estimates, so they can be sure the estimate is accurate. Some use their own adjuster.

Most insurers figure into their estimate the cost of new, brand-name parts. Unless you insist upon new parts, some body shops will sneak in a used or generic door panel or fender, and charge you the same amount. If you have an older car, you may not mind used parts. But if you're paying for new parts, you ought to get new parts.

The insurance company check may be sent to you or the body shop you select. If you have a collision deductible, usually $250 or $500, you may have to pay that as well. Some body shops will agree to do the repairs for the amount paid by the insurer, so you won't have to pay the deductible. Check with a few body shops and see what kind of deal you can cut. If you don't mind generic or used parts, you can agree to let the body shop install used parts to reduce the cost.

You can have repairs done by any body shop you choose, even if the other driver's insurer is paying for them. Ask friends or your insurer for a referral, or try a new-car dealer's body shop. Since the dealer is likely to be a stable business, you know its body shop won't be a fly-by-night operation.

- Tips on -
Car Repairs

● Every time you take a car to the mechanic—and especially if you have to return a car for the same problem—you should control what is written on the work ticket.

● If you're going to have an estimate done on the car, make sure the work ticket says it has been authorized only for an estimate. If you're authorizing specific work, write down the exact dollar limit you are authorizing and don't permit any work to be done beyond that dollar limit.

● If the estimate is large, don't accept it as the final word. If your car is not driveable, have it towed to another repair shop for a second estimate.

● If your car is towed to a mechanic, don't allow the tow-truck driver to choose the repair shop. Quite often, he or she will be paid to steer your vehicle to a particular shop.

● Don't rely on a nationally famous name when you go for a car repair. Too often at a franchise location, the parent company fails to accept responsibility for a problem.

● No matter which repair shop you use, always ask for the return of parts being replaced.

Recalls —

If your brakes don't work or your ignition system fails, it's possible the trouble is due to a design or manufacturing error. Other car owners may have had the same trouble, perhaps prompting the manufacturer to issue a general recall or send a service bulletin to dealers detailing the defect. Unfortunately, the public usually receives no such notification.

In many cases, the dealer either won't know if a service bulletin has been issued or won't disclose it to you. That's where the Center for Auto Safety, a nonprofit consumer organization, becomes a great resource. Write to the center and list the make, model, and year of your car and the exact symptoms. If you enclose a self-addressed, stamped envelope, they will tell you if there's any known defect in your vehicle. It takes about four weeks to get a reply, but even after a repair has been made, information about a recall or a service bulletin can help you get a full or partial refund from the dealer or manufacturer. It is more difficult to get a refund if the work was done at an independent repair shop, but you can do it if you're persistent.

Even if a manufacturer does its job well, many consumers are going to be unhappy. After all, things do break and need to be repaired. The manufacturer's representative talks to unhappy people all day long. To get satisfaction, you have to stand out from the pack and justify what you want. You don't want to be viewed as just another complainer who doesn't like having to spend money.

You also help others by letting the Center for Auto Safety know about your car's problem, because the data on your vehicle can help establish trends. If you have trouble with your brakes and other car owners have the same complaint, the center knows there may be a broad failure in the brake system of that vehicle.

A number of callers have told me about a tendency for the paint to flake on some car models. If you know the paint has flaked in certain paint colors on specific vehicles, you'll have a lot more leverage if the same thing happens to your car. You might be able to convince the deal-

- Tips on - Recalls

● A breakdown in your vehicle may be part of a defect in the model that affects other car owners. You may be able to negotiate a lower repair price or receive a reimbursement for repair work if the vehicle has been cited in a recall or in a service bulletin.

● The Center for Auto Safety, a nonprofit consumer group, can tell you of any known defect in your vehicle.

● You can't count on the government or the manufacturer to disclose defects.

Contact:
Center for Auto Safety
2001 S Street NW, Suite 410
Washington, DC 20009
202-328-7700
(Send a self-addressed, stamped envelope with two stamps on it and a letter with the make, model, and year of your car and the problem it's having.)

National Highway Traffic Safety Administration
Auto Safety Hotline
(touch-tone phones only)
1-800-424-9393

er to repaint the car for free, or for less than $100. If you don't know about the paint defect, you may have to pay the full cost of a paint job, several hundred dollars. Or you may be able to negotiate some sort of cost-splitting deal with the manufacturer. Knowledge here is so important. If you know a particular vehicle has had a problem, you're going to win.

You can't count on the government or the manufacturer to disclose defects. Reports for several years have indicated that General Motors pickup trucks built from 1973 to 1987 may explode in collisions because of an alleged design defect in the placement of the gas tank. In 1993 a jury awarded $100 million in damages to the family of a man who died in such a collision. But the award was later overturned. In October 1994, the U.S. Department of Transportation issued an initial finding that the trucks were defective, a preliminary step to a potential recall of six million vehicles. GM, which declined a voluntary recall and vigorously contested the safety claims, settled the matter two months later by agreeing to spend $51 million on safety and research. However, that settlement also was overturned.

The only way vehicle defects become widely known is because consumers are willing to stand up and complain, by contacting the Center for Auto Safety and the National Highway Traffic Safety Administration.

The Lemon Law —

A lemon is a new car that breaks down repeatedly for the same reason and cannot be repaired. Every state except South Dakota has enacted a Lemon Law to protect consumers by allowing the car buyer to exchange the flawed vehicle for a new one or have the manufacturer buy it back.

Lemon Laws vary widely by state, but in most, if the defect involves the major safety systems of steering and braking, the dealer will have one chance to fix the vehicle. If the dealer cannot fix it, the manufacturer will have one chance to make the needed repairs. In other safety-related systems, the laws will allow two repair attempts for the dealer and one for the manufacturer. With any other component of the vehicle, it will be three repair attempts for the dealer, one for the manufacturer.

In most states, the Lemon Law applies to problems that arise during the first year or 12,000 miles of ownership. If you have a new vehicle with a serious problem, your best bet is to document everything. Keep records of every phone call, every repair attempt. That's why it's so important that the repair work tickets are written correctly. If they don't show a persistent defect, you may have a hard time invoking your rights under your state's Lemon Law.

You must follow other specific procedures in order to make a Lemon Law claim. For example, you might have to notify the manufacturer by certified mail. You can obtain the specific procedure in your state by calling the administrator of the state's Lemon Law. Ask for a copy of the rules governing the law.

One of the big battles you will have with the manufacturer, once you've established that it's going to buy back the car, is over the value of your vehicle. The scariest part of the negotiation is the amount you're charged for each mile you've driven. You want the per-mile charge to be as little as possible and the manufacturer wants it to be as much as possible.

Let's say the car cost $15,000 and you've driven 15,000 miles when they agree to buy the vehicle back. If the manufacturer charges you 30 cents per mile, $4,500 will be deducted from the purchase price and you'll get $10,500. If you're willing to pay 10 cents a mile, that's $1,500 and you would get back $13,500. There's a lot of money on the table even after the manufacturer has agreed to buy back the vehicle.

You'll have to pay the manufacturer to exchange your lemon for a newer model of your car. To figure a fair amount, take the dealer cost for the new model and subtract the dealer cost for the model you have. Generally the manufacturer will ask for the difference between the suggested retail price of each vehicle, which will be a larger sum.

One of my callers had serious problems with a sport utility vehicle he bought in April

1991. A month later, the vehicle started having a multitude of symptoms, including poor braking, vibration at high speeds, and pulling during steering and braking. After $3,500 worth of covered warranty work, the problems still weren't fixed. When the dealership tried to fix the alignment, the vehicle would pull in the other direction.

The manufacturer agreed to buy back the vehicle, but there was some negotiation over the mileage penalty. The buyback occurred 11 months after the original purchase, and the vehicle had 22,000 miles on it. But it became clear at 14,000 miles that the problems could not be repaired. The caller successfully argued for the 14,000-mile figure to be used in figuring the penalty.

Because the vehicle cost $22,000, the manufacturer applied a per-mile charge of 22 cents, or one cent for every $1,000 of its retail price. For 14,000 miles, the penalty was $3,080.

The best way to guard against getting a lemon in the first place is to buy a car that has a good repair record. That won't always work, but it will certainly improve your odds.

Arbitration —

If you are unable to resolve a dispute with a car manufacturer, you have an option other than a lawsuit. Most manufacturers agree to participate in arbitration to help resolve disputes over cars still under warranty. The arbitration programs may be independent of state-sponsored Lemon Law programs or a provision of the laws. Call the Council of Better Business Bureaus' Autoline for details on how to file for arbitration in your area.

Arbitration in most cases is binding on the manufacturer but not the consumer. You still have the right to sue if you are unhappy with the arbitration decision. But you don't want to sue; you want to solve it either through negotiations with the manufacturer or through arbitration.

Interestingly, just filing for arbitration often is enough to get the manufacturer to make a settlement offer. For a time General Motors was fighting every single arbitration filed against the company in the state of Massachusetts. The state started publishing statistics on arbitration, which showed that GM was the only manufacturer making no attempts to settle. Ever since those statistics became public, General Motors has shifted gears, both in Massachusetts and

- Tips on -
Arbitration

● If you are unable to resolve a dispute with a car manufacturer, arbitration may be an option. Most manufacturers agree to participate in arbitration to help resolve disputes over cars still under warranty.

● Arbitration in most cases is binding on the manufacturer but not the consumer. You still have the right to sue if you are unhappy with the arbitration decision.

● Just filing for arbitration often is enough to get the manufacturer to make a settlement offer.

● *Lemon Law: A Manual for Consumers* is the guidebook for documenting claims both under state Lemon Laws and in arbitration cases outside of the Lemon Law.

Contact:
Council of Better Business Bureaus
Autoline
4200 Wilson Blvd., Suite 800
Arlington, VA 22203
1-800-955-5100

Toyota or Lexus Vehicles
AutoSolve Manufacturers Arbitration
Program
1000 AAA Drive
Heathrow, FL 32746
1-800-477-6583

Ford Consumer Assistance Center
300 Renaissance Center
P.O. Box 43360
Detroit, MI 48243
1-800-392-3673

around the nation, and now does attempt to negotiate with the consumer rather than fight to the last inch in arbitration.

As a consumer, you have to weigh what you might gain in arbitration versus what you might lose by not settling. If you believe your case is well documented, you might want to take your chances with the arbitration panel. If you think it could go either way, the best approach might be to file for arbitration, then cut the best deal you can before your case is heard. That's really no different from what lawyers do. *Lemon Law: A Manual for Consumers* is the guidebook for documenting claims both under state Lemon Laws and in arbitration cases outside of the Lemon Law.

You will not appear before the arbitrators. They will decide the case based on written arguments submitted by both you and the manufacturer. So you want to give a short, clear, and detailed explanation of what has gone wrong with your vehicle, what efforts you and the manufacturer have made to repair the problem, why you believe the problem has not been solved, and what remedy you believe is fair. You want to appear to be eminently reasonable and have strong documentation. It's a good idea to organize your presentation carefully and make it easy to read. Include a short summary and then an index, with tabs that guide the reader to each area of specific documentation, such as your work tickets. It's very frustrating to get a car problem fixed, but writing a novel won't get you anywhere with an arbitration panel.

Accidents —

I hope you're never in a car accident. But if you are, even if it seems to be the most minor fender bender, don't just drive away. Having the patience to take a few simple steps can save you some big headaches later.

First, wait for a police officer to write a report. It will be vital to you in case any claims are filed. Second, exchange information with the other driver about yourselves and your insurance companies. You'll have about a two-thirds chance that the other person will actually be insured. If the person is not, you'll file the claim with your insurer.

Third, as soon as possible after the accident, report it to your insurance company, even if you don't plan to make a claim. I realize this sounds like strange advice, particularly if the amount of damage is too small to make a claim. People rarely want to tell their insurance company about minor accidents, but you have to guard against the possibility of a lawsuit, even if the accident was only a fender bender. Many times drivers will consider an auto accident a chance to get rich. They'll see a TV commercial for a lawyer who claims they can get a lot of money for accident victims. A lawsuit may seem absurd, but that doesn't make it less serious. Normally, your insurer will defend you in a lawsuit. But if you failed to notify them, the company might not have to defend you or pay a claim if you lose.

Most commonly, accidents cause some damage to a vehicle but no injuries. When that happens, getting your car fixed and being reimbursed properly is a real trick. In most cases, insurers will maintain that their insured driver was not at fault and try to force you to make a claim against your own insurance company. The best way to avoid being wrongly blamed for an accident is to get the names and telephone numbers of as many witnesses as you can at the time of the accident. That's going to be very difficult in a highway accident. But most accidents occur on surface streets, and in many cases witnesses will be blocked temporarily by the accident and unable to scatter. While the accident is fresh in your mind and you're waiting for the police, draw a sketch of the accident scene. If you think it was the other guy's fault, it's essential to have a police report. If the officer gives the other driver a ticket, it's a very

strong piece of evidence in proving fault.

Establishing fault is even more important if you have an older vehicle and no longer find it worthwhile to carry collision coverage. If you're ruled at fault, you will have to pay for the repairs to your vehicle. Sadly, some insurers try to take advantage of drivers who don't have collision protection. Be prepared to document every single phone call you have with that insurance company. Write down the date and time, whom you talked with, and what was said. Be prepared to sue the company in small claims court, if necessary.

If you have no collision coverage and the other driver has no insurance at all, your only recourse is to sue the driver. But the odds are if the person doesn't have any insurance, he or she probably doesn't have anything worth getting. When you choose not to carry insurance, you agree to live with the risk.

Contact both your insurance company and the other driver's insurance company after an accident. Even in situations where there isn't a shadow of a doubt about who was at fault, some unethical insurance companies will attempt to avoid you or avoid responsibility for the accident. Be persistent and use your state insurance department as a resource when another insurer fails to act in good faith. The state insurance department may not want to get involved in questions of fact, but they can help push an insurer to discuss the accident and try to reach some accommodation. If there's a dispute about who is at fault, file the claim with your own company. The two companies will duke it out later over the amount each will pay.

I heard about one case in which a car was damaged in a collision and the other insurance company initially accepted responsibility for the claim. The car was fixed, but poorly, and the insurance company tried to duck out of its responsibility to pay for additional repairs. The victim was worried that she would have to pay for thousands of dollars in new repairs herself. But there was no reason at all to do that. Instead, she made a claim against her own insurance company and paid her deductible. Finally, her company went after the other company for the bill.

You pay premiums to your insurance company so you will have protection when you have a problem. When you buy insurance, it's important to see if your state insurance department can tell you which insurers do the best job of handling claims. You should expect your insurance company to provide speedy service and fair treatment, to make sure the body shop does the job correctly, to track down the other insurer if the company is eluding you, and to defend you if you are sued. You are their customer. I'm always disappointed when I hear callers say their insurer is treating them like the enemy, rather than as a valued customer.

A few years ago, *Consumer Reports* said the average household had paid $8,910 in premiums over the previous 10 years but had filed just one claim, typically for about $600. For that kind of money, a consumer wants and should expect great service. After surveying 83,000 readers around the nation, the magazine rated the following companies as the best at providing service:

1) Amica Mutual Insurance
2) Cincinnati Insurance
3) United Services Automobile Association
4) PEMCO Mutual Insurance
5) National General Insurance
6) Hartford Underwriters Insurance
7) Auto-Owners Insurance
8) New Jersey Manufacturers Insurance
9) Citizens Insurance Co. of America

If your vehicle is going to require some repair, ask your insurer if your coverage includes reimbursement for a rental car. If the accident is the fault of the other driver, insist that his or her insurer provide a rental car. Make sure the rental car is authorized for as long as it takes to repair your vehicle. Don't agree to release the body shop or the insurer of final responsibility until you're comfortable that the repairs are complete and the vehicle operates properly. It's typical with major body work that the first repair isn't the final one and that more work will be required to finish the job.

I receive a lot of questions about how much the insurance company is required to pay for a vehicle that has been totaled in an accident. No matter which insurance company you're dealing with, this is an area of great frustration. Insurers tend to offer approximately 70 percent of the amount it would cost to buy your vehicle on the used-car market. But the initial offer is negotiable. To improve your odds of getting the best price, go to your bank or credit union and ask an officer to tell you the retail value of the car in the NADA *Used Car Guide*.

If you don't know any better, you'll take too little money for your car. Once the company realizes you've done your research, the negotiating usually gets to be more fair and honest. If the insurance company won't budge, accuse them of failing to act in good faith and request a face-to-face meeting with the adjuster and the adjuster's supervisor. Your state insurance department won't get involved in determining fair market value of your car, but it will push the insurer to meet with you if the insurer refuses to do so.

If the insurer still won't budge, talk to them about "substitution of vehicle," under which your car loan or lease remains in force and the insurer finds you a similar vehicle as a replacement. If they think the car is worth so little, let them find you a replacement vehicle for that price.

Substitution of vehicle is critical for people who have a long-term lease or loan. It may be the only way to keep a lease in force without being subject to extremely large termination penalties. With a loan, it may prevent you

- Tips on -
Accidents

• Don't just drive away from an accident, even a minor fender bender. Wait for a police officer to write a report.

• Exchange information with the other driver. Get the names and telephone numbers of as many witnesses as you can.

• As soon as possible after the accident, report it to your insurance company, even if you don't plan to make a claim. If you believe the other driver was at fault, contact his or her insurance company also.

• If there's a dispute about who's at fault, file the claim with your own company. The two companies will duke it out later over the amount each will pay.

• If your vehicle is going to require some repair, insist upon being supplied with a rental car or reimbursement for a rental car.

• Don't agree to release the body shop or the insurer of final responsibility until you're comfortable that the repairs are complete and the vehicle operates properly.

• If your vehicle is totaled, don't accept your insurance company's first settlement offer. Go to your bank or credit union and ask an officer to tell you the retail value of the car in the NADA *Used Car Guide*.

• If you have a five-year lease or loan and owe more than the car is worth, ask for "substitution of vehicle," in which the loan or lease remains in force and the insurer finds you a similar vehicle as a replacement.

from being left with a sizable loan balance and no car, because you owed more than the vehicle was worth. It's very common for drivers with five-year loans to be "upside down" in a loan, because with relatively small monthly payments, the car's value drops much faster than the loan balance.

The cost of housing usually is the largest figure in the family budget. Knowing the right way to buy housing can make a big difference in your life, whether your goal is having a great home, accumulating wealth, or a combination of the two.

In this section, you'll learn how to make smart choices in buying, renting, and selling real estate, so that you can live where you want, or get what you want, out of your housing dollar.

Real Estate

Buying a New House —

Buying a house is a cornerstone of what many people want to accomplish as adults. It is a symbol of much more than simply finding a place to live. But making this major purchase is also a complex process with plenty of potential for costly mistakes.

Because of its symbolism, home ownership is as much an emotional matter as it is a practical one. There was a time when housing values increased so steadily that buying a house automatically was a smart financial decision. But that's not true anymore. It's important to decide whether you're buying a house for financial or personal reasons.

If you're buying a house strictly for financial reasons, look at each house you're considering just as you would evaluate a purchase of stocks or bonds. It just so happens that it's a living, breathing investment because it's where you will live.

To buy a house as an investment, it's best to look for one with "people problems," generally a used house that is selling for below the fair market value because of special circumstances such as a divorce, a death, a relocation, or a foreclosure. That's a wise purchase because you are likely to be able to increase its value.

You get a true bargain on a people-problem house only if you've done your homework first. Figure out the condition of the house and—by researching other homes for sale—its normal market price. Many times a house with people problems has been neglected for a while, so you may be facing extensive repairs that would negate any bargain price. You can prevent unforeseen expense by making a purchase offer contingent upon an inspection of the house. Even if the inspection reveals problems, it might be worthwhile to make the purchase.

More often, people want to buy a house as a place to live. They want something that they like and can afford, and they don't want to make any mistakes. One of the most important guidelines I can give is, don't buy one of the first houses in a subdivision. It's too risky, primarily because the developer could go bust and be unable to complete the subdivision. Early buyers can end up in a home surrounded by scarred and abandoned land. Even worse, these houses could be surrounded by partially built homes. There's also the danger that amenities promised by the developer, such as a pool or tennis courts, might not be built. If the developer fails, those promises disappear.

I think it's wise for new home buyers to find out a little about the builder of a house they're considering. When you buy a car, you look for a model made by a manufacturer with a reputation for quality. But few people think to ask about the builder of a house. If you're interested in a house, ask what other homes the builder has done. Then ask the owners how they like their houses. Most homeowners will be happy to tell you whether their house was well built or whether the builder did a shabby job.

Make any offer on a home contingent on its passing an inspection. Some people won't bother to inspect a new home, because they figure there shouldn't be anything wrong with a brand new house. But an inspector could discover shortcuts in materials used or necessary work that wasn't done. If that happens, a builder could be forced to make repairs. You can locate a certified inspector through the American Society of Home Inspectors.

Be sure also to include a financing contingency in your purchase offer. The purchase should be contingent not just on your ability to qualify for financing, but on your ability to get financing at or below a set interest rate. You might not be approved for financing at 8 percent, but you could be approved at 12 percent, even if you believe you can't afford to buy with a 12 percent mortgage.

As part of your loan, you'll be required to purchase a title insurance policy, the kind that protects the lender in the event your ownership of the property is ever challenged. I recommend a very low-cost addition—owner's title insurance. It protects you if anyone ever claims you are not the legal owner of the property. Owner's title insurance can cost as little as $100 if you buy it at the time you buy the house. Ask the closing attorney for a quote. If the quote seems high, see if you can negotiate down the fee.

There was a title case a few years ago in which residents of an entire community almost lost their homes. A woman claimed she was part-owner of a tract of land that later was divided to form a subdivision. She sued the homeowners in the community for a partial share of the land. The woman eventually agreed to a settlement, but the homeowners spent several thousand dollars in legal fees to defend their property rights. Owner's title insurance not only protects you from loss, but the title company must defend you if your ownership is ever challenged.

There are two kinds of "new" houses to consider. There's the off-the-shelf new house that a builder has recently completed. There's also the new house that is either custom-built

from scratch or custom-finished according to the wishes of the buyer. Some buyers like to buy a house while it's under construction, then dress it up with special features such as whirlpool tubs, skylights, or premium-grade carpet. Most of the problems I hear about from callers concern the second group—new homes being custom-finished. Two problems tend to come up: the builder either doesn't keep a promise or doesn't complete the job by the specified date.

If you're having a home custom-finished and the job isn't done by your closing date, you have to act to protect yourself. If you go through with the closing, you give up your leverage and run the risk the job never will be completed. If you decide to close with items unresolved, give a letter outlining these items to the closing attorney and the real estate agent or agents involved in the sale. That will prevent anybody from later getting amnesia about these issues. Get assurance from the real estate agent to help see that the work is completed.

When you're negotiating a contract for the purchase of a house, especially one that has not been completed yet, the contract should be reviewed by a real estate attorney. It's wise to spend some money up front to prevent problems that could be expensive and hard to resolve. A real estate attorney also will review the closing documents. You should require in your purchase contract that the closing documents be made available to you at least two days prior to closing for review by your attorney. Real estate closings are incredibly confusing. You have no idea what documents are being put in front of you—the language is so unfamiliar and the forms are so complex—and it's easy to make an expensive mistake. The lender and seller both will have representatives at the closing. That's why you have your lawyer check everything.

If you choose to shop for homes with a real estate agent, there's something you need to know. The agent who takes you around to look for homes actually is not "your" agent, although he or she may be very friendly and helpful. In most cases (unless you have a specific agreement that states otherwise), the agent represents the home seller. It's similar to the way a salesperson at a department store represents the retailer. The sales agent is required by law to tell the seller about anything you say. So if you offer $78,000 for a house, but let it slip to the real estate agent that you can afford to pay $83,000, the agent has to disclose that to the seller. The agent also will pass on information about you, such as your income, which may weaken your negotiating status. It's doubtful, too, that a real estate agent will show you any "For Sale by Owner" houses, because an agent receives no commission on such a sale.

Most home sales today involve two sales agents. One is the listing agent, who is hired by the seller to market and sell his or her house. The other is the selling agent, the person who shows you different houses for sale. Because agents split commissions, the selling agent may try to get you to buy a house he or she has been directly hired to sell. In that case, the sale involves only one agent. But whether there's one agent or two, the agents work on behalf of the seller.

You do have an alternative to using a traditional real estate agent. A buyer's broker, also known as a buyer's agent, works for you, in much the same way as a lawyer or accountant. He or she will prevent home sellers from learning personal facts about you and allow you to see any home in which you're interested. The buyer's broker will help you decide how much to offer and negotiate on your behalf.

Buyer's brokers are paid in much the same way as a traditional agent. They receive a percentage of the sales price. Because of that, a buyer's broker does get more if the house sells for a higher price. But buyer's brokers tell me it's worth far more to them to negotiate the lowest price possible for the buyer—and get referrals from a satisfied buyer—than to get a nominally higher commission from a higher sales price.

Buyer's brokers are very popular in many parts of the country, and I'm certain they will continue to grow in popularity. Many traditional agents will work as buyer's brokers, as long as you don't buy properties whose owners they already represent. Just ask the agent for a buyer's broker agreement. A few years ago, most sales agents were hostile to buyer's brokers, simply because of a reluctance to change the way houses were sold. But because the change hasn't hurt traditional agents, the hostility is gone.

When you're giving an agent a price range for your house shopping, always quote less than you're willing to spend. If you tell an agent you're looking for a $90,000 house, the agent inevitably will use that figure as a floor, not a ceiling, and will show you houses priced at $90,000, $95,000, and $99,000.

Before you buy a house, try your commute to work during rush hour. When you make a long drive from a house to your workplace on a weekend, you don't get a true idea of the travel time. It's also important to learn about the area surrounding a potential new house. You need to know what potential there is for new roads or new development. Is there a chance your backyard someday will look out on a new shopping center? Are there any vacant lots that might be the site of undesirable government or commercial projects? Make sure your real estate agent discloses any easements there may be for a property you're considering. An easement allows a power company or a city to run a power line or sewer line across your property. I know of someone who found out on the day of closing that there was a sewer easement running right under the house, making it possible the house could be

- Tips on -
Buying a New House

- If you're buying a house strictly for financial reasons, look at each house you're considering as you would evaluate a purchase of stocks or bonds.

- To buy a house as an investment, look for one that is selling far below the fair market value, because of special circumstances such as a divorce, a relocation, or a foreclosure.

- Don't buy one of the first houses in a subdivision. The developer may go bust and be unable to complete the development.

- Check out the reputation of the builder by talking with people who live in some of the builder's houses.

- Make any offer on a home contingent on its passing an inspection. The purchase also should be contingent on your ability to get financing at or below a set interest rate.

- Get an owner's title insurance policy that covers you, not the lender, if your ownership is successfully challenged.

- Hire a real estate attorney to review the closing papers and, if you're buying a house still under construction, to draft or review the purchase contract.

- Consider using a buyer's broker, a real estate agent who, unlike the traditional real estate agent, represents your interests, not the seller's.

- Before you buy a house, try your commute to work during rush hour.

- Learn about the area surrounding a potential purchase, including the potential for new roads or new development.

- Look at a property while it's raining to see how water flows across it. Look for signs of poor drainage and danger of flooding.

Contact:
American Society of Home Inspectors
1735 North Lynn Street
Suite 950
Arlington, VA 22209
1-800-743-2744

torn down at any time. That scrapped the whole deal.

Look for potential problems such as high-voltage power lines that run near the property. There's no clear opinion as to whether high-voltage power lines are dangerous to human health, but being adjacent to power lines has become less desirable and therefore made houses harder to sell.

It's also a good idea to look at a property while it's raining, to see how water flows across it. Look for signs of poor drainage and danger of flooding. It helps, if you can, to look in the basement of a home during or just after a rainfall.

Drainage problems are quite common these days and can be very costly. One of my callers bought a $121,000 house in a very nice neighborhood, then discovered that during a rainfall, water cascaded across his patio like a river. He spent $1,300 to install an underground drain, but the system still backed up during heavy rains. A civil engineer told him it would cost another $2,000 to design a plan to solve the problem. State laws provide minimal protection for homeowners in these cases, sometimes requiring the builder or developer to make repairs. The best solution is to examine a new house while it's raining before you buy it.

Home Warranties —

A home warranty is not a substitute for choosing a responsible builder or for having a home inspected. But a warranty can provide assistance and is a good selling tool when it's time to move. It's a confidence builder for the buyer.

A home warranty that comes with a new house offers a fair amount of protection in the first two years and minimal basic protection for three to ten years after you purchase the house. Pay close attention to how your warranty works. Usually your builder is fully responsible in the first year, and the warranty company is responsible in the second year.

The home warranty company generally will be responsible for problems in the second year only if you've followed its procedures correctly. Let's say you have a plumbing problem in the first year and you've asked the builder to fix it, but you never notified the warranty company. By not notifying the warranty company, you may have waived your rights to getting help. So it's important to notify both the builder and the warranty company as soon as a problem develops and at the address and in the manner they require. They may require notice by certified mail, or you may prefer to send it by certified mail so you have proof it was sent. You also gain leverage by contacting the warranty company, as officials there usually tell the builder to fix the problem.

If, during the first year of warranty protection, you notify both the builder and the warranty company, and the builder attempts a repair but is unsuccessful, immediately send another letter. Document. Document. Document.

The other kind of warranty concerns a used home. I bought a home in 1991 that came with a third-party warranty designed to assure me that the basic systems of the home were working. I never had to claim against the warranty and I let it expire after one year. For about $150 a year, I could have renewed it each year forever. This kind of warranty is really like extended warranties on appliances, which cost too much and rarely pay claims. Mainly what it covers is heating, air conditioning, and other major systems of the home.

Termites are another concern for buyers in many parts of the country. In some states, the seller is required by law or by the mortgage lender to have the house inspected for possible termite damage. Even if it is not required, if termites or other wood-destroying insects are a problem in your region, you should ask that an inspection be performed.

Within the first 90 days of ownership, you should interview and select a pest-control company, so that you can protect the property against any future infestation. Check with the Department of Agriculture, entomology division, or the structural pest control board in your state to find out its policy. Or call the National Pest Control Network to locate the appropriate agency in your area. These agencies often will conduct an inspection for you if you suspect a pest-control company has given your house an inadequate termite-control treatment.

There are two principal types of termite-protection policies provided by pest-control companies. Under a retreatment policy, the company simply promises to come back and retreat the property. There's no real risk to the termite company for its failure to spot termites. Your best bet is a repair guarantee, under which the termite company is responsible for repairing any damage caused by termites. With a repair guarantee, the termite company is your partner in making sure your house is well treated because the company is at financial risk if it doesn't do a good job locating infestations and treating them.

A comprehensive, initial termite treatment, including a repair guarantee, can cost several hundred dollars. And pest control companies often won't provide a repair guarantee unless their company has done the treatment. After that, expect to pay $85 to $100 for annual, follow-up termite inspections, with retreatment if needed. A good way to find a company is to ask a real estate agent.

Buying a Used House —

Just as with buying a used car, you often get a better value buying a used house. That's because part of the cost of a new house is the cost of new construction. As construction costs increase, new houses become more expensive.

An important advantage of a used home—and I prefer the term "used" to "resale" or "existing" home—is that the house, because it's located in an established neighborhood, has found its true value in the marketplace. With new construction, particularly in a new neighborhood or a new subdivision, you never have a real solid feel for a house's value.

Of course, buying a used house means taking on an added risk of breakdowns and repair costs. I've bought houses built during the Depression and just after World War II, and in both cases I bought trouble. But there are two different concerns here. It's a bad idea to buy a house that has major structural problems, such as with the roof or foundation. But there's nothing wrong with buying a house that has irritations.

I bought a house in 1983 from a seller who had already moved to another state. It was built in 1937 and needed so many repairs that my late father referred to the house as "The Howard Hovel." He couldn't imagine his son living in such squalor. It smelled terrible and had the worst paint job I have ever seen— deep dark reds, ugly greens, and rooms with absolutely bizarre color trims. The floor in the bathroom was sinking. The front steps were all beat up. The driveway had completely collapsed. It was overgrown with weeds and not usable, except by a four-wheel-drive vehicle. Nobody was going to go anywhere near this thing.

I had an inspector come out and carefully go over this place and he found no structural problems. So I brought in contractors and got estimates of the cost to bring the place up to speed. It cost $17,000, but the house was so cheap that even with repairs included, I still bought it for less than its market value. The key with this sort of work is to avoid moving walls or expanding rooms; otherwise, it can cost $17,000 just to renovate a bathroom. It's far cheaper to accept the layout the way it is and change cosmetic weaknesses.

I turned "The Howard Hovel" into a fine house and a good buy with renovations that were mostly cosmetic. I ripped out all the carpet, which completely eliminated the foul odor, and had the hardwood floors underneath stripped and restained. A good paint job and some attractive wallpaper took care of all those weird colors, and some new sheetrock made peeling ceilings look great. I had a great time showing people the house and then bringing out my before-and-after pictures.

In fact, because the house came with a vacant lot next door, it turned out to be the most profitable real estate transaction I've ever made. The lot was considered worthless by everyone because a giant storm sewer ran through the middle of it. A few years after I bought the house, I hired an engineering company to determine if it would be possible to move the storm sewer and build a new house on the lot. It worked. I relocated the storm system for $8,800 and ended up with a lot that was worth more than $100,000. It just never occurred to anybody that you could do that.

Look for hidden values and undervalued property. This house turned out to be a grand slam because I got both in the same purchase. Just be careful not to fall in love with a house you're considering. To get the best deal in any negotiation, you have to be willing to walk away.

Use good judgment to pick a used house. If you see potential, a place that can look good with some cosmetic changes, you may have something that will work. But if you would have to pay for expensive renovations to be happy, it's not going to be a good purchase.

It is critical when looking at used houses to make a purchase offer contingent on an inspection. That's the only way to get a good feel for possible repair expenses.

One unexpected expense that can pop up when you're buying a used home is the cost of removing a dead tree. It's not something you think about when you're looking at a house, but the cost of removing a tree can be substantial. To protect yourself, ask the seller if there are any dead trees on the property. If there are, ask him to remove the trees as a condition of the sale. Also, look around the grounds yourself to see if you can find any problem trees. A dead, leafless tree can be pretty easy to spot in spring or summer, but it may blend into the background in fall or winter.

When you buy a used house, it's important to put at least $50 a month into a repair fund. In an old home, you never know what can break—pipes, the heating and air conditioning

- Tips on -
Buying a
Used House

● You often get a better value buying a used home, because rising construction costs make new houses more expensive.

● A used home often is located in an established neighborhood and has found its true value in the marketplace. With new construction, particularly in a new subdivision, you never have a solid feel for a house's value.

● Buying a used house means taking on an added risk of breakdowns and repair costs. Just make sure the purchase is contingent on an inspection, and don't buy a house with major structural problems.

● When you buy a used house, it's important to put at least $50 a month into a repair fund. You never know what can break.

● If you buy wisely, you can get a good home in an attractive neighborhood and not be overrun by the myriad problems of a booming new area. With a new house, there's a danger of crowded schools, poor drainage, and an abundance of new construction that can make it hard for you to resell your house.

or live with them as is until they die. It's fairly expensive to refinish an appliance, and it can turn out to be a bad decision if the appliance gives out a year later.

As you probably can tell, my bias is toward buying used houses in established neighborhoods. If you buy wisely, you can get a good home in an attractive neighborhood and not be overrun by the myriad problems of a booming new area.

If you buy a new house in a new subdivision in a growing section of town, there are so many factors beyond your control. You have no way to know if the rest of the houses in the subdivision are going to be of the quality and character of your home. The next street over could be developed with houses a third less expensive than yours, which ultimately reduces the value of your home.

I get a lot of complaints from owners of new houses about drainage problems. In the typical case, there's no problem for the first year or two of ownership. But that changes after more houses are built and more trees are cut down. Suddenly, every time it rains, the yard is flooded.

In an established neighborhood, you know the schools aren't overcrowded. You don't have to worry about so many new homes being built that your children will have to attend classes in a portable trailer. An abundance of new construction can also cause your house to lose value. Let's say you buy a new house in a new subdivision and two years later, you're forced to relocate. Because the subdivision is growing, there are brand new houses all around your house. That's trouble, because buyers usually prefer a brand new house to a house that's two years old.

I also prefer the sense of character in an older neighborhood that comes with lots of big trees. Often when you go into a new neighborhood, the only trees you'll see are stick trees. Because of the methods of construction, there may be just a few small trees left between houses.

system, or an appliance.

Sometimes when you buy a used house, you get with it an ugly 1970s-era avocado or gold refrigerator and stove. As part of your cosmetic changes, you can pay to refinish the appliances in white or some other color. But I've learned that it's better to replace old appliances

One advantage to buying a new house is that most tend to have large and attractive bathrooms and kitchens, which people have come to desire over the years. That's a sacrifice I've made in buying older houses.

Remodeling —

With the huge bloc of baby boomers now mostly in their thirties and forties, America is in a remodeling boom. A lot of homeowners would rather add onto or fix up a house than move into a more expensive house in a new neighborhood.

You have to be very, very careful picking somebody to remodel your home. Do not hire people who drop fliers off in your mailbox, or who ring your doorbell and tell you your roof or gutters need fixing. Phony remodelers are one of the oldest scams around, typically preying on older people. Almost always, they take the homeowner's money and disappear.

Your house is the most valuable investment you have. Do some legwork first, before you hire someone. Believe me, that will be far easier than dealing with the problems you'll have if you hire an incompetent or crooked contractor. For a minor renovation job, take recommendations for a remodeler from friends and neighbors. For a major renovation job, which I consider anything above $5,000, you need to be much more scientific about the hiring process. Get recommendations from the National Association of the Remodeling Industry or the Remodelors Council of the National Association of Home Builders.

After you've had a few remodelers come out to your home and narrowed the field, it's time to start checking references. Ask for a list of the last ten homes they've worked on, a description of what they did, the dates they started and completed those jobs, and how to contact each owner. The dates are important because it will allow you to see gaps in work. Perhaps they couldn't find any work for several months or perhaps they blew a job and got sued. You'll also get a feel for how many jobs a contractor takes on at one time.

Ask what kind of insurance each contractor carries. For example, does he carry workers compensation insurance and his own liability insurance policy? Some experts might tell you not to hire anybody who doesn't have proper insurance. That's the book answer. But you're going to have some difficulty finding people who have kept their insurance current. If you pick someone who has no insurance, make sure you have enough liability coverage in your homeowner's policy in case the contractor or an employee gets hurt on your property. Be prepared to be sued if any worker gets hurt in or around your house.

Once you decide which contractor is going to do the work, the next task is drawing up a contract. Most contractors will present you with a standard builders supply house contract. Don't sign this under any circumstances. Instead, consider using a contract from the American Institute of Architects (AIA) or from the American Homeowners Foundation. The AIA has dozens of sample contracts that have stood the test of time.

The American Homeowners Foundation has a fill-in-the-blanks prototype contract that's very user friendly. If it's a renovation costing more than $10,000, have the contract reviewed by a lawyer prior to signing it.

In a few states, you'll need to obtain lien releases as part of the renovation process. A lien release or waiver is a document the contractor can give you that you will ask materials suppliers and subcontractors who work on your site to sign. In a few states, subcontractors and suppliers can place a lien on your home if the contractor doesn't pay them, even if you've paid the contractor in full. So you could be forced to pay twice. With a lien waiver, subcontractors and suppliers give up their right to come after you for payment. If you're buying a house or refinancing one, you can ask the general contractor to sign an affidavit swearing he has paid the subcontractors. To be extra safe, you could still get a lien waiver from the subcontractors.

Never agree to any remodeling contract that calls for a large payment up front. If the contractor is short of cash and says he or she needs money to buy materials for the job, you should buy the materials. Go with the contractor to make the purchases. I've heard sad story after sad story from individuals who gave the contractor a large sum up front and never saw the contractor again.

Devise with the contractor a reasonable timeline and pay schedule under which the contractor is paid as work is completed. Don't frontload the money to the point that the contractor has most of the money while just a portion of the work has been completed. My feeling is you shouldn't pay anything up front. For a small job, you might pay half the money halfway through the job, 40 percent of the money at completion, and the final 10 percent once you're satisfied everything has been done correctly and nothing further must be done. For bigger jobs, pay 10 percent of the cost after each 10 percent of the job is done, with a 10 percent holdback at the end to protect against problems that crop up. You and the contractor should decide in advance how to determine when the 10 percent levels are met.

All this may sound petty, but if you're having remodeling work done, it matters. If you set out the schedule for payment ahead of time, you keep problems from occurring while the work is going on. You don't want to be in a financial dispute with your contractor in the middle of the project, no matter who thinks the other is being unfair. That doesn't create a spirit of cooperation and communication.

It's possible you could suffer if the job isn't completed on time. For example, if you're renting a place while your house is undergoing renovation, you would have to pay extra rent if the job takes too long. If that's the case, the contract should include penalties against the contractor for failing to complete the job on time. If you have to pay an additional $250 a week to live in another house or apartment, the penalty for late completion of the job should be at least $250 a week.

Besides losing your money by foolishly paying up front, the worst thing that can happen in a remodeling case is getting incompetent work. If you've been damaged in this way, you have a tough road to walk. You're going to have to bring someone else in to finish or redo the job, and many times it will cost more to redo it than it would have cost to do it correctly the first time. Then you have to go to court to try to get your money back from the contractor who botched the job. If the contractor has no assets, there's nothing to go after. If you can't prove your case or if you win but can't collect, you don't get anything back. It's tough.

Then there's the distress you endure. People take a messed-up home renovation job very personally; it upsets them and disrupts their lives. They are so excited about adding a room or fixing up a kitchen, and when things don't go right they have an emotional crash.

One more caution about remodeling: be very wary of contractors who not only brag about their workmanship but also say they can arrange for financing. Home-improvement loans or second-mortgage loans arranged by the contractor tend to be extremely costly, with interest rates usually far above market rates. If you need to borrow money to renovate, repair, or add to your home, go to your bank or credit union and stay away from contractor-supplied referrals.

- Tips on -
Remodeling

● Be very, very careful picking somebody to remodel your home. Do not hire people who drop fliers off in your mailbox, or who ring your doorbell and tell you your roof or gutters need fixing.

● For a minor renovation job, take recommendations for a remodeler from friends and neighbors. For a major renovation job—anything above $5,000—get recommendations from the National Association of Professional Remodeling Contractors or the Remodelors Council of the National Association of Home Builders.

● Ask candidates for your remodeling job for the last ten homes they've worked on, a description of what they did, the dates they started and completed those jobs, and how to contact each owner.

● Ask what kind of insurance each contractor carries. Protect yourself by hiring people who have a current certificate of insurance or by making sure you have enough liability coverage in your homeowner's policy in case someone who's uninsured is hurt on your property.

● Don't sign a standard builders supply house contract for a remodeling job. Instead, consider using a contract from the American Institute of Architects (AIA) or from the American Homeowners Foundation.

● In a few states, it's important to get subcontractors to waive their right to place a lien on your home if they aren't paid by the contractor.

● Never agree to any contract that calls for a large payment up front. Devise with the contractor a reasonable timeline and pay schedule under which the contractor is paid as work is completed. In the contract, include penalties against the contractor for failing to complete the job on time.

Contact:
The Remodelors Council
of the National
Association of Home Builders
1201 15th Street, NW
Washington, DC 20005
1-800-368-5242 ext. 212

American Institute of Architects
AIA Orders
2 Winter Sport Lane
P.O. Box 60
Williston, VT 05495
1-800-365-2724
(For a remodeling contract, ask for the standard form of agreement between owner and contractor:
A101, A111 or A201)

American Homeowner's Foundation
1724 South Quincy Street
Arlington, VA 22204
703-536-7776

National Association of Professional
Remodeling Contractors
4301 North Fairfax Drive
Suite 310
Arlington, VA 22203-1627
1-800-966-7601

Selling Your House —

Selling a house has become much more frustrating for people as values for houses have flattened out in the last several years, compared to the rapid increase in values from the 1970s through about 1985.

People are in a much more difficult fix when they try to sell a home, especially if they've purchased it since 1985, because their house, minus the real estate agent's commission, might actually be worth less than what they paid for it.

That's led to a mass migration of people to FSBOs, or "For Sale by Owner." They try to market and sell their home themselves, to avoid the commission, so they can sell without losing any money on that home. But I want you to know a FSBO is not a panacea. Many people find it very hard to sell their own home, primarily because they have no training or experience in selling. They may not price the house correctly and may be offended when buyers criticize the house. Owners who sell their own houses also have to be incredibly patient, because they have to deal with unqualified buyers and with people who make appointments to see the house but don't show up.

When you sell your own home, always specify on the sign that brokers or agents are welcome. That way you will protect yourself from "steering," in which agents avoid your street and don't show buyers your home because you're not paying commission. If you indicate that brokers or agents are welcome, you're agreeing to split the commission with a selling agent who brings you a buyer. Generally you should offer 3 1/2 percent. Don't get greedy. If that 3 1/2 percent brings you a willing buyer at a reasonable price, that's a smart decision on your part. You've still saved 3 1/2 percent.

The hardest part of selling by owner is negotiating the selling price. There's a tendency among people who don't do this often to play their cards badly and let the buyer know too much. You may end up costing yourself more money than if you'd had an experienced hand at the wheel helping with the negotiating. If you want to try a by-owner sale anyway, set a reasonable time limit. If you're going to give a real estate agent a three-month listing on a home, give yourself three months to try to sell it. If you find you're miserable doing it, then stop and go hire a real estate agent.

Be aware that when you are trying to sell your house FSBO, you will be approached by a lot of agents trying to get that listing. Some agents will be greedy and will try anything to get you to give them the listing. Others will be helpful to you, giving you advice and information, with the thought that later, if you're not successful in selling the house yourself, you'll select them to be the listing agent on your property. I call that enlightened self-interest; it is in both parties' interest.

Interview a number of real estate agents before you hire one to sell your home. Ride around the neighborhood first and see which names keep popping up on lawn signs. When you see the same agent's name several times within your area, you know that agent is "farming" your area. You want to deal with a farmer. They know the agents who traffic that area, they know the true value of your home, and, if they have multiple listings, they probably have good strategies for selling homes in your area. If you still know how to get in touch with former neighbors, call them and ask their experiences with the listing agent they had on their home.

When you interview an agent, ask for a written sales plan of how the agent would market your home, with specifics. Limit the listing time with that agent to three months. Agents will always present you with a six-month contract, but my attitude is that this gives them all the rights and privileges and you all the responsibilities. If an agent balks at doing a three-month listing because of the expenses they have, then reach an agreement with them that you can back out of the listing after 90 days in return for paying a fee to them. If you're miserable with that agent, it's worth paying the fee.

Real estate commissions by law are negotiable. However, in many real estate markets, there is de facto price setting where, by tradition or design, commissions in that area are set. It may be known as a 7 percent market or a 6 percent market or a 5 percent market. You can try to negotiate a commission, but you'll probably have to live with the de facto fixed commission in the marketplace.

Give serious consideration to any offer for your house, and never be insulted by it. Always make a counteroffer. So often when I've sought to purchase a house, agents have told me the seller would be insulted by my offer. I've always told them to pass along my offer. This is a negotiating situation and you as the potential buyer should not make a ridiculously low offer. However, you shouldn't make an offer that's too high; then you narrow the range within which you and the seller can negotiate. Make a reasonable offer but one that is a little on the low side.

As the seller, you must first price your house reasonably, not far above the market, and be willing to enter into a good give-and-take with the buyer. Let's say you have a house listed at $115,000 and the potential buyer comes back with an offer at $90,000 and you're angry they've offered so little money. You know in your heart and mind that your house is worth more than that. Put your anger aside and come back with a counteroffer with which you'll be happy. If you and the buyer can't reach agreement, fine. At least go through the process of offer, counter, offer, counter. The first buyer is very important. It may sound trite, but it's generally true that the first offer you receive on a house will be the best offer. I've bought two houses in which the sellers accepted less

than they earlier rejected.

If you think your house is worth $109,000, you should probably price it at $115,000, or about 5 percent above what you'd like to get. But if you list at $125,000, you may be so high that you don't get any offers at all. A real estate agent will help you price your house, but remember that real estate agents face a constant battle to get a listing for a home. Sometimes we make the mistake of choosing one agent over another because one gives a higher estimate of the selling price. That's speculation. More important is the person's sales plan for your house.

When you're asked about your house, tell the truth. If you're asked about the condition of your roof and you don't know what it is, don't say it's in great shape. Say you don't know. If you're asked about the air conditioning and you had to have it fixed last summer, say it. Don't lie. Generally you'll be asked to fill out a seller's disclosure statement. These forms are required by law in only a few states, or it's your choice. But I recommend that you do it. I think disclosing the condition of the house creates a sense of trust that helps make the sale. You won't be able to deceive them anyway, because most buyers will have the house inspected and the inspection may disclose things you've tried to hide. You're better off being honest and telling the buyer up front about problems. If the buyer finds out about a defect just before closing, it could kill the sale or force you to lower the price or pay for repairs.

If you were selling your car, you would probably clean and wax it, vacuum the interior, and fix any minor flaws, like a broken tail light. The same holds true for your house. You want it to be clean, bright, uncluttered, and uncrowded. Areas of the home need to be well lit. If you furnish your house to the max, get rid of some the furniture. Closets need to be clean. If you have both winter and summer wardrobes in your closets and they're stuffed, take out the opposite-season clothes and store

- Tips on - Selling Your House

● Many people try but find it very hard to sell their own home. They may not price the house correctly and may be offended when buyers criticize the home.

● When you sell your own home, always specify on the sign that brokers or agents are welcome. That way you will protect yourself from "steering," in which agents avoid your street and don't show buyers your home because you're not paying commission.

● Interview a number of real estate agents before you hire one to sell your home. It's good to deal with someone who sells a lot of houses in your neighborhood.

● When you interview an agent, ask for a detailed, written sales plan of how the agent would market your home. Limit the listing time with that agent to three months or negotiate a fee you can pay to get out of the listing after three months.

● Listen to every offer for your house and always make a counteroffer.

● Prepare your house for sale. It should be clean, bright, uncluttered, and uncrowded.

them. People are buying a fantasy and they don't want it ruined by a crowded closet. They're also looking to see if their furniture and possessions will fit, so you need to make the house seem like it's at less than capacity when people walk in.

Some sellers are having their own inspection done to check out the house before they sell it. If you don't want to go that far, go through the house yourself and make sure things work. Check the heating and air conditioning system and fix minor problems such as loose doorknobs or railings. Clean, paint, patch, or replace anything that isn't up to speed, and pay special attention to the kitchen and bathrooms.

Buyers also want a house to seem fresh and inviting. Having fresh flowers in the house and decorating the front walkway is a good idea. Some agents recommend putting a saucepan on the stove with some cinnamon or potpourri to put a fresh scent in the air. Sometimes little things can give people the feeling of warmth they want to have when they buy a home.

Moving —

Whether you buy a house or rent an apartment, changing residences means packing up your possessions and moving. If you're moving from state to state, you're going to be extremely disappointed about the total lack of concern expressed or help provided by the Interstate Commerce Commission (ICC), which is responsible for regulating movers. This agency does absolutely nothing to help the consumer, and its employees are virtually contemptuous if you call with a complaint about a mover.

With no regulatory relief available, it's very important to do a good job up front in selecting a mover. First, you want to know that the price estimate given to you is solid. Is it a soft estimate or a firm price for the move? Second, you want to thoroughly understand what protection or insurance coverage you have coming with the move or that you can buy as optional coverage to protect your belongings. Third, you need to know the record of quality of the mover you're considering. The only survey I've seen on this is one conducted several years ago by *Consumer Reports* magazine rating movers based on customer satisfaction. If you're planning a major move, I recommend you get a copy of it from your local library.

The survey gave good marks to a few movers—Paul Arpin, Wheaton, United, Atlas, and Graebel—but found widespread dissatisfaction with movers. The survey found 1 in 5 respondents was unhappy with the way the moving company handled the job. Movers arrived late 5 percent of the time, and 12 percent of the time they were late to drop off and unload. Nearly half of the survey respondents said some of their possessions were lost or broken during their move. The typical customer lost $300.

When there are complaints, they can be most difficult to deal with. In all the years I've been doing radio, the problems my staff and I have had trying to resolve problems with movers have ranked among the most difficult. I'll talk to a caller who has done everything one should do to solve a problem—she's called, written, sent follow-ups, sent certified mail, sent complaints to the ICC—and the movers don't seem to care and don't budge. Not every mover, but many. We had one situation in which a major moving company hung up on my producer, Kim Curley, for no other reason than she was inquiring on behalf of one of our callers. We were able to get help at that point by going to the American Movers Conference, a trade association.

The best way to protect yourself is simply to find a mover who does a good job. If, after the move, you find yourself with lost, stolen, or damaged merchandise and you can't get the mover to do anything about it, you can turn to the American Movers Conference, which has an arbitration program. It applies to movers that are members of the association, primarily large national companies. For some reason, we receive far more complaints about the large movers than the local movers who generally handle shorter trips.

The *Consumer Reports* survey found customers spent $700 to move 100 miles or less and $3,000 for a move of more than 1,000 miles. Those numbers probably would be higher today. Movers generally charge for the weight of your possessions and the distance traveled, then add charges for special circumstances, such as having to climb stairs or move special items, such as a piano.

Many people prefer to do their own packing when they move. In the *Consumer Reports* survey, 55 percent of the respondents who let the movers pack their merchandise reported damage. But of those who did their own packing, just 32 percent reported damage. Before you choose a moving company, get a clear understanding from that mover of what happens if something is broken that you've packed yourself. Most movers will accept and insure delivery of boxes you pack yourself, but make sure you do it right. If something breaks, you'll have to show it to the company, along with the packing materials, to prove you did a good job.

When the mover drops off your furniture at your new residence, do not sign the release form until you've examined your furniture piece by piece. Use a flashlight if your house isn't well lit yet. Sit in each chair and bounce on your sofa to make sure all the legs are still solid. I know this sounds silly—it's the last thing you want to do on the day you're moving in to a new place—but actually it gets your adrenaline flowing to bounce on your furniture, so do it. Check the exterior of cartons for signs of damage and open boxes marked fragile. It's much easier to document a claim while the moving

- Tips on - Moving

● It's very important that you do a good job up front in selecting a mover. Ask if the price estimate is firm. Ask the mover and your own insurance agent what insurance protection is provided or is available.

● Before you choose a moving company, get a clear understanding from that mover what happens if something is broken that you've packed yourself.

● When the mover drops off your furniture at your new residence, do not sign the release form until you've examined your furniture piece by piece.

● The best way to protect crystal, china, and any other extremely valuable and delicate possessions is to move them yourself in your own car.

● If you want to risk your back and move yourself, be careful about what packing materials you buy for the move. You'll generally do better renting the truck from the rental company and buying your boxes and other materials somewhere else.

● Get a written confirmation ahead of time on the price per day for the truck, cost per mile if there is one, and any additional charges that may apply. On the day of rental, examine the contract carefully to make sure the prices and information on it match up with your written confirmation.

Contact:
American Movers Conference
Dispute Settlement Program (Applies to movers that are members of the organization)
1611 Duke Street
Alexandria, VA 22314
703-683-7410

people are still there, before you sign to receive your possessions. You can ask for a damage claim form or make a note on the acceptance that some merchandise was damaged.

Some homeowners insurance policies cover damage during moving. It's best to check first. If your policy doesn't cover moves, you can buy coverage from your insurance company or the mover. The ICC requires that movers provide free limited liability coverage. But the reimbursement is extremely limited. Added valuation coverage reimburses you at replacement cost minus depreciation. It costs about 50 cents per $100 of declared value. Full-value coverage reimburses you at replacement cost with no charge for depreciation. It can cost as much as 80 cents per $100 of value, but adding a deductible can sharply cut the cost.

A lot of families suffer damage in a move. In the *Consumer Reports* survey, 46 percent of the respondents incurred damage and 11 percent had damage of more than $1,050. The best way to protect crystal, china, and any other extremely valuable and delicate possessions is to move them yourself in your own car, if you're driving. You're going to handle those items more carefully than a mover will.

If you decide to move yourself using a rental truck, think about your back first. If you have items that are extremely heavy, the hundreds of dollars you save in the short term can be easily eaten up by the cost of medical care or by the unmeasurable cost of pain and suffering from a damaged back. This is another one of the few times when my bias toward thriftiness is overwhelmed by other concerns.

If you want to take the chance and move your household yourself, be careful about what you buy for the move. One of the big profit centers for truck rental companies is renting and selling the accessories that go along with moving. You pay a convenience charge when you buy or rent those items from the truck rental company. You'll generally do better renting the truck from them and getting your packing materials somewhere else. Some people like to get moving boxes for free from a supermarket or discount store. If you want to do that, make sure you get there before they're crushed for recycling.

Try to get a written confirmation ahead of time on the price per day for the rental truck, the cost per mile if there is one, and any additional charges that may apply. On the day of rental, examine the contract carefully to make sure the prices and information match up with your written confirmation. Although I've heard allegations in the past about truck renters who will suddenly change the rates when you show up—because it's moving day and you don't have other options—I don't believe that's the normal method of operation for movers. I think that more often, it's a matter of misunderstanding or a simple mistake on the part of

the truck renter. That's why having a written confirmation is an important protection.

Home Security Systems —

Many people buy a home security system after suffering a break-in or seeing a crime story on the news. So they're not in the best state of mind to buy a burglar alarm. That makes them easy prey for aggressive salespeople.

Regardless of the reason you might want a burglar alarm, it's important to divorce yourself emotionally from the decision so you can shop wisely. The first thing to do is make a drawing of your home, or a checklist, and figure out how many doors and windows you need to protect. Next, call your insurance agent and ask what discounts are available on your homeowners insurance and what requirements a security system must meet for you to qualify. Generally you'll have to get a system that's monitored by an outside service, not just a noise-maker alarm that is intended to frighten the burglar into fleeing. There may be other requirements for you to get the insurance discount.

Always get smoke and fire monitoring as part of the system. People get a security system in their home because they fear an intruder, but the bigger danger is the potential for fire. Usually it costs very little more to get fire protection.

After you complete your list and talk to your agent, call burglar alarm companies for tentative quotes. Don't consider any company that won't give you a quote on the telephone and instead wants to send a salesperson to your home to give you an estimate. That's a strategy they use to close a deal. They know if the salesperson is in your home, the odds are greater that you'll agree to buy an alarm from their company, regardless of whether it's the best buy. So get at least six quotes and then decide who may come to your house.

Many companies will offer supposedly fantastic lease deals, but I don't advise you to

- Tips on -
Home Security Systems

● Even if you've recently had a break-in, try to stay calm when you buy a burglar alarm so you can shop wisely. The first thing to do is make a drawing of your home, or a checklist, and figure out how many doors and windows you need to protect.

● Call your insurance agent and ask what discounts are available on your homeowners insurance and what requirements a security system must meet for you to qualify.

● Always get monitoring for smoke and fire as part of the system.

● After you complete your list and talk to your agent, call burglar alarm companies for tentative quotes. Don't consider any company that won't give you a quote on the telephone. I also don't advise you to lease a burglar alarm.

● Watch out for the monthly monitoring cost. Some companies will quote a very low price on the equipment and its installation and then have an extremely high monthly monitoring fee.

● Make sure you get a long-term commitment for the monitoring fee.

lease a burglar alarm. If you need the security of an alarm system, you're going to want it for the long term and not for the length of a short lease. A burglar alarm can also be a confidence builder for a buyer when it's time to sell your house.

The next trap to watch out for is the monthly monitoring cost. Some companies will quote a very low price on the equipment and its installation and then have an extremely high monthly monitoring fee. Paying $17.95 a month for monitoring instead of $22.95 may not seem like much, but it will save you $120 over two years. That's why it's very important to find a good price for monitoring and often less important how much you pay for the security system itself. For a truer comparison of quotes, figure the total cost of the system and monitoring for two or three years.

Make sure you get a long-term commitment for monitoring. The contract I have guarantees the monthly monitoring charge of $16 won't increase as long as I maintain the service. That's an unusually solid price guarantee. If you can get a commitment of a few years, that's great. It's also a good idea to have an escape clause that will allow you to terminate the agreement if the monitoring service is terrible. Unfortunately, it's very hard to determine the quality of monitoring in advance.

Sometimes the price quote you get over the phone disappears when a salesperson comes to your house. If that happens, don't give in. Try the next bidder or call around for more quotes. I've seen some terrible abuses in the sale of home security systems, mostly from companies trying to justify an unusually high price by claiming their system is far superior to others. Some of my callers have paid as much as $4,000 for a security system that should have cost well below $1,000. By getting multiple quotes and comparison shopping, you'll get an accurate reading of a fair price.

Technology changes. The burglar alarm systems I bought ten years ago are much less sophisticated than the one I put in a year ago. But I don't buy state-of-the-art technology. I buy current technology. That's a very important distinction. The latest, greatest gadget may be unproven and usually is overpriced. With current technology, competition has reduced the price and time has allowed the system to prove its reliability.

There's no specific technology you need to buy. You'll want monitoring, smoke and fire detection, some form of perimeter security to protect the entrances to your house, and some form of motion sensor. Actually, the motion sensor is usually a heat-sensing device so the alarm isn't set off by some object falling in your home. If you have a dog, the motion sensor can be set to register movement a few feet above the ground, allowing your pet to roam around. Cats are a bigger problem, because they like to climb and jump. If you have a cat, you can keep it in one room while you're out, or use an alarm that's triggered when someone breaks a window to get inside.

One drawback of home security systems is false alarms. If you have a lot of them, you may be fined by your police department. That's a choice you'll have to make in deciding whether you want a security system. I've been close to being fined, and had to decide to risk the fine or discontinue monitoring and go with a noise-maker alarm.

Refinancing —

When mortgage interest rates fall, homeowners start to think about refinancing. Very simply, refinancing means taking out a new mortgage with a lower interest rate to pay off your existing mortgage. Through refinancing, homeowners can often cut their monthly payments, shorten their loan term, or combine a home equity loan and a mortgage into one lower payment.

But because it's expensive to refinance, you can wind up paying more than you'll save. Let's say it would cost $3,000 to refinance and you plan to sell your house in three years. That means you'd have to lower your monthly payments by at least $84 to make refinancing worthwhile. Just determine the savings per month at the lower interest rate, multiply by the number of months you expect to stay in the

house, and compare the savings to the cost of refinancing.

On the other hand, the savings from refinancing can be substantial. The monthly payment on a $90,000 loan at 10 percent interest is $790, while the same loan at 8 percent costs $660 a month. Traditionally, experts have recommended that you refinance if current mortgage rates are 2 percentage points lower than your mortgage and you plan to stay in the house a while. So if you have an 11 percent mortgage and the current rate is 9 percent, you would be wise to refinance.

Refinancing also can be worthwhile if you plan on staying in the house for a long time, or if the new mortgage has a shorter loan term. Let's say you have a 30-year mortgage at 9 percent and you can go to a 15-year mortgage at 7 1/2 percent. That 1 1/2-point difference may be enough to justify the cost of a refinance if you plan on staying in the home for several years.

Before you decide to refinance, think about how long you want to remain in the house and what length loan you want. If you have a 30-year mortgage with 26 years left, you do yourself a disservice refinancing into a new 30-year mortgage, because you're adding four years to the amount of time you'll be in debt. Approximately half of all people who refinance choose a shorter term for their new loan and that's usually a smart decision.

Refinancing may make sense even if you don't plan to stay in the house a very long time. If you have a fixed-rate mortgage that has a moderate or high interest rate, it could be worthwhile to refinance if you could cut your monthly payments sharply by refinancing into an adjustable rate mortgage.

Be careful with an adjustable rate mortgage. Studies have shown that ARMs almost always are a better deal than fixed-rate mortgages, but you trade peace of mind for savings when you take an ARM. When I bought a

- Tips on -
Refinancing

- Refinancing means taking out a new mortgage with a lower interest rate to pay off your existing mortgage.

- To figure out if refinancing is worth the cost, calculate your savings per month in lower payments, multiply by the number of months you expect to stay in the house, and compare the savings to the cost of refinancing.

- Insist on a good-faith estimate of the costs up front, before you give the lender a penny.

- Traditionally, experts have recommended that you refinance if current mortgage rates are 2 percentage points lower than your mortgage and you plan to stay in the house a while. But it really depends on your specific situation. It can also be worthwhile if you plan on staying in the house for a long time, or if the new mortgage has a shorter loan term.

- Think about refinancing into an adjustable rate mortgage, or ARM, that allows you to convert to a fixed rate.

- Another option is a low- or no-cost refinance. With these, you agree to accept a mortgage rate that's above the current market rate but lower than you're paying.

- Before you refinance, check your credit report for anything that could foul up a refinance. You don't want to lay out the money if a credit problem is going to keep you from refinancing.

Contact:
Mortgage Bankers Association of America
1125 15th Street
Washington, DC 20005
202-861-6500

house in 1991, I knew intellectually I would have been better off with an ARM, but I couldn't jump that psychological hurdle. I went for the sure thing and chose a fixed-rate mortgage, because fixed-rate mortgages were the lowest they had been in decades. But the sure thing and that peace of mind cost me money.

The danger with an ARM is the possibility that the interest rate can rise, often as much as 6 points over the lifetime of the loan. If it does, your monthly payment can soar. A fixed rate doesn't change, even in a period of high inflation and high interest rates. A good com-

promise is to get an ARM with a conversion feature, which gives you the right to convert to a fixed rate during the loan for a modest fee—usually less than $500.

Another option is a low- or no-cost refinance. With these, you agree to accept a mortgage rate that's above the current market rate, but lower than you're paying. In return, the lender charges a very small refinancing fee. This is a wise choice if you've recently refinanced but rates have fallen further, or if you really are uncertain about how long you're going to stay in the house. But it's a bad deal if you're going to be in the house for several years. Those with FHA loans may be eligible for a "streamline" refinance, which is a no-cost refinance that gets you a slightly above-market rate of interest. Streamlines are permitted only if you don't change the amount left to be paid.

Another mortgage option that's become increasingly popular is the 5/25 or 7/23 hybrid mortgages. This is a 30-year fixed loan in which the rate of interest resets after five or seven years. If you choose a 5/25, you pay a set interest rate for the first five years and then, based on an index, the rate resets for the last 25 years. The lender is willing to give you a lower rate of interest for the first five years because, instead of having to gamble on where interest rates are going to be in 30 years, the lender only has to accept a five- or seven-year gamble. I don't like these. If you plan to stay in the house a very short time, up to five years, you're better off with a convertible ARM. If you plan to be in the house for a long time, you're better off going with the fixed rate. The 5/25 and 7/23 are really marketing gimmicks, because the lender is able to lure you in with lower rates.

It's very important with a refinance to insist on a good-faith estimate of the costs up front, before you give the lender a penny. If you don't, you shift all the power to the lender and take unnecessary chances. You may find that a refinance doesn't make sense for you. If you find out too late, you could lose any money you've paid toward the refinancing costs. Another protection you have is the option of locking in the interest rate you're offered. That protects you in case rates rise after you've agreed to refinance.

Before you refinance, get a copy of your credit report to see if there's anything on it that could foul up a refinance. You don't want to lay out the money if a credit problem is going to keep you from refinancing. Get all documentation ready for the lender immediately. You need to document your employment, income, debt, and assets. When you provide the proper documentation, give the lender a dated, signed memo showing that you have given them the needed information. Make sure to keep a copy. This is to protect you later if the lender is slow to close the loan and causes you to miss a good interest rate. Lenders often can wiggle out of a commitment they don't like because the consumer was sloppy about handing over the required documentation.

Mortgage Servicing —

When you first get a mortgage, you might think you'll be doing business with the same lender for 30 years. But that's rarely the case. Mortgage lenders often sell your loan to investors as soon as the ink is dry, take a fee for originating the loan, and use the money they get from selling the loan to make another loan. A single mortgage might be owned by a dozen companies during its life.

A lender has to disclose to you what percentage of its loans are sold and what percentage are kept in the lender's own portfolio. If the lender sells nearly 100 percent of its loans, you know you're dealing with a loan retailer.

Investors and lenders use mortgage servicing companies to handle the everyday business of collecting your payments, keeping track of your loan balance, and letting you know if you're late with a payment. So in addition to having several owners over its life, a loan also might be handled by several different servicing bureaus. That creates a large potential for mistakes, such as unapplied payments or errors in calculating your balance.

Mortgage servicing is a very profitable business and an area that causes a lot of consumer complaints. To add to the confusion, lenders don't do the best job at handling loan problems when they do occur. The most important thing I can tell you about your mortgage is to keep a copy of every check you ever write for your loan. I know that sounds like overkill, but if you have a loan for 5 or 10 years and there's a dispute about whether a particular payment was made, your best defense is to be able to produce the canceled check. Even if you pay on a mortgage for 30 years, you write only 360 checks. That doesn't take up much room.

All mortgage servicers must have an 800 number you can call for customer service. I've had quite a bit of experience calling these numbers, and I find it quite distressing how long I'm left on hold before I reach a human being. When you do reach a person, make sure you get his or her full name and write it down. You'll find a page in the Workbook chapter of this book to help you document mortgage and other consumer problems. If a promise is made to you by a lender and the promise isn't kept, you'll have someone you can call back and hold accountable.

If you find yourself in a dispute with a lender about a payment or another issue, don't send correspondence to the same address you send your payment. In most cases, that will be a separate bill-processing center, and clerks there will throw your letter away. Find out from the mortgage servicer where you should send correspondence. Start by sending your letters with a regular postage stamp. But if the lender ignores the letters, start sending them by certified mail.

You can also get help by contacting the Mortgage Bankers Association office in your state. This trade association has a strong interest in seeing that your complaints are dealt with properly, because if they aren't, the state or federal governments may decide to regulate mortgage lending activities.

The biggest dispute in mortgage lending is escrow practices. Escrow is the process whereby your lender collects a monthly fee from you to cover the cost of taxes and insurance on the property. The lender needs this protection, because if you were to let your homeowners insurance lapse and your home burned to the ground, the lender would lose its collateral on the loan. The same thing would happen if you failed to pay your property taxes and lost your house. While the lender has a legitimate need for escrow, many lenders have proven themselves to be extremely greedy by overcollecting escrow. In most states, lenders are not required to pay interest on escrow, creating an incentive to overcollect.

Lenders are allowed to keep in reserve an amount equal to one-sixth your annual escrow needs. Let's say your annual bill for taxes and insurance is $1,200. The lender would be able to collect $1,200 annually, plus a $200 reserve. Many lenders play fast and loose with the numbers and collect far more money each year. I believe the most effective way to solve the abuses of escrow would be to require that lenders pay interest on these accounts. If your lender ignores your requests for an accounting of how escrow totals have been determined, tell them you're going to contact your congressman. Lending institutions fear congressional action more than anything else.

General Motors is one of the largest lenders in the country. In a court case in 1992, its financing arm, GMAC, settled out of court without admitting guilt and agreed to change its practices for escrow. The case originated with allegations the company was charging way in excess of the proper amount for escrow. General Motors was a target because of its size. It's difficult to police the mortgage lending industry because it has many small players who feel protected by their relative anonymity.

To give you an idea of how complex things can get, let me tell you about a loan I originated in 1978 with a small mortgage lender in Ohio. The loan servicing was handled by SunTrust Banks. The loan was sold repeatedly and moved around through a series of transactions and bank mergers and got all fouled up.

After paying SunTrust every month for 14 years, I decided to do a refinance with a bank on another property. The whole process came to a halt because, to my horror, a company known as Society Mortgage was showing me in default on my credit report. They said I hadn't made a payment in five months. I had never even heard of Society Mortgage and I certainly didn't know they owned the loan.

It took four weeks to get this straightened out. Eventually I got an apology from Society Mortgage acknowledging that the company had been in error when it reported my loan in default. Even more maddening was the fact that Society Mortgage wasn't supposed to report my loan at all, because it was not the loan servicer. Only SunTrust Banks should have reported the loan to the credit bureau. My credit report showed the same loan with both lenders and different balances.

The loan officer with whom I was doing the refinance told me something I find extremely interesting. She said her colleagues find so many inaccuracies on credit reports that they routinely call the customer and ask for an explanation, instead of automatically rejecting the loan. Then, the financial institution calls the other financial institution directly and tries to verify the information, bypassing the credit bureau entirely. It's taking so long to get errors corrected on credit reports, she said, that the lender loses business. So they're having to take the credit-reporting business into their own hands. It's too bad the credit-reporting industry is losing such credibility, because that slows down the whole system.

One of the smartest things someone can do with a mortgage is to prepay on the loan. That's a lot simpler than it sounds. All you need to do is contact your lender and ask for its prepayment procedure. Generally on your payment coupons there'll be a box for prepayment. Just fill out the box and increase the amount of your check by whatever amount you choose.

Some people prefer to write a second check and write on it "prepayment of principal." Once a year, check the loan balance sent to you by the lender to make sure the payments have been applied properly. Instead of throwing several hundred dollars at your mortgage one month and nothing another month, I recommend prepaying your principal by a set amount each month. Try to pay $50 or $100 extra each month, or whatever you can afford.

It's remarkable what impact you can have on your mortgage by making prepayments. There are books and software programs—one is called *The Banker's Secret*—that contain amortization tables and explain this in great detail. You plug in your loan balance and interest rate and you can see how much you can reduce the length of your loan, and the total amount of interest you pay, by adding something to each mortgage payment. For example, if you have a 30-year, $90,000 loan at 9 percent interest, adding $50 a month to your $724 payment would cut seven years off the length of the loan and save you more than $47,000 in interest over the life of the loan. Prepaying by $100 per month would cut nearly 11 years off the loan and reduce the total interest paid by more than $72,000.

I don't like fee-based plans that allow you to prepay your principal. They charge $300 to $500 for administering a prepayment system you can do better by yourself. The typical plan collects half your regular mortgage payment every two weeks, which for the full year would amount to 26 half-payments, the equivalent of 13 regular monthly payments. These organizations forward a regular payment to the bank at the end of each month, then add a 13th payment at the end of the year. Since you can do this yourself, there's no reason to pay a set-up fee to someone else. Just take your mortgage payment, divide it by 12, and add that amount to your regular payment each month. You'll be making one additional monthly payment each

- Tips on -
Mortgage
Servicing

● Mortgages typically have many different owners over the years and many different servicing bureaus, so it's not difficult for a mixup to occur over your loan balance. To protect yourself, keep a copy of every check you ever write for your loan.

● If you call a mortgage servicing bureau about your loan, make sure you get the full name of the person with whom you speak.

● If you find yourself in a dispute with a lender, about a payment or another issue, don't send correspondence to the same address you send your payment.

● Keep an eye on how much money your bank collects to cover your annual property taxes and insurance. Lenders are allowed to collect your annual escrow needs plus one-sixth this figure, but many overcollect.

● One of the smartest things someone can do with a mortgage is to prepay on the loan. All you need to do is contact your lender and ask for its prepayment procedure. Then, once a year, check the loan balance the lender sends you to make sure the additional payments have been applied properly.

● Fee-based plans that charge $300 to $500 for administering a prepayment system are not so helpful; you can do it better and cheaper by yourself.

Reference:
The Banker's Secret
(1-800-255-0899; $14.95 for the book, $39.95 for the book and software)

year. If you do that early in a loan, it will cut seven to eight years off the length of a 30-year loan.

There are other reasons I don't like fee-based prepayment plans. What happens if the company you're paying doesn't forward the payment to your lender, or doesn't pay on time? You could lose your money or suffer penalties. Finally, they're holding your money during the year and earning interest. If you prepay, those dollars should benefit you immediately, not up to a year later.

There's a philosophy among some financial planners that it's foolish to prepay on a loan and that you're better off putting the money in the stock market or some other investment. But most of us will spend the money, rather than invest it. Prepayment of principal is a very clever method of forced savings and truly an investment in your future, because you reduce the length of your loan and the amount of money you pay on it.

Some people are trimming the length of their mortgage at the start, rather than after the fact. Some people are doing mortgages as short as 10 years. For most of us, that's not practical financially, and we're frightened off by the monthly payment on a 15-year mortgage. If you can't swing a 15-year mortgage, look at a 20-year loan. A loan for 20 years represents only a marginally higher payment per month than one for 30 years, and it dramatically decreases the amount of money you would pay over the life of the loan. For example, a 30-year, $90,000 loan at 8.5 percent carries a monthly payment of $692. You get a lower interest rate for a shorter term, so you could borrow the same amount on a 15-year loan at 8 percent, with a monthly payment of $860. That $168 difference may be too much for many people to try the 15-year loan. But a 20-year loan on the same amount, at 8 percent, would be $781 a month, just $89 more than for the 30-year loan. By choosing a 20-year term instead of a 30-year term on this loan, you'd pay $187,446 in total interest instead of $249,117. A 15- or 20-year term lets you pay off the loan quicker, with a lower rate of interest and a lower total cost.

Being a Landlord ——

Many people end up being a landlord because they have a condominium or a house they can't sell. Because they go into renting property reluctantly, it's easy for them to get frustrated.

If you rent property, manage it as a business. First, set a rent that's fair for your market, not one that's based on your mortgage payment. People aren't going to rent your house or condo for $950 a month if they could rent something similar for $700, even if $950 or $1,000 is your mortgage payment. By the same token, if your mortgage payment is $500 and the market rent is $700, don't set your rent too low.

As prospective tenants come through your property, require those who are interested to fill out an application. Get a standard financial application from an office supply or bookstore. If you have friends at an apartment complex, ask if you can see one of theirs. You need to check a potential tenant's historical record. Does the person move constantly? Are there gaps in employment? You're entering into a financial partnership with your tenant and you need to know if he or she will honor an obligation to you. Ask potential tenants to provide a copy of their credit report, so you can see if they've behaved responsibly in their other financial relationships. If someone has a lot of debt or a recent bankruptcy, you may prefer a different tenant.

Choosing the wrong tenant can be a big mistake. I know of one case in which a landlord was left with a huge bill because a tenant failed to report a water leak. Under the lease, it was the tenant's responsibility to pay the water bill. But the tenant moved out without paying the bill and without telling the landlord about the water leak. The damage to the property was significant, but the leak also increased water usage. The water bill itself cost the landlord more than $1,000.

If a prospective tenant passes your screening, set a realistic security deposit, but don't make it exactly the same as a month's rent. Make it a little higher or a little lower, so the tenant doesn't interpret it as in lieu of the last month's rent on a lease. Get a standard lease and then include any special protections that are particularly important to you.

For landlords with just one or two properties, I recommend you include a repair clause that makes the tenant responsible for the first $50 cost of any repair. Tenants who used to live in apartment complexes are conditioned to calling the management office to fix any problem. That's expensive for you because unlike those complexes, you don't have a maintenance person on staff. You have to hire a contractor to do the work. Many little problems could be fixed by the tenant with a $3 part from a hardware store, but might cost you $100 to have someone come in to make the repair. If you have a repair clause, you may have to charge a little less in rent. But reducing the hassle and irritation for you makes that worth it.

Another thing you should do is discount rent for early payment. You give somebody a discount, say $20 or $50, if the rent is paid prior to the first of the month. This is very important for landlords who are new to the business, since most tend to be very slack about collecting overdue rent. The penalties and the process for eviction are such a pain that you're much better off giving the tenant an incentive to get the money in early.

Do a move-in inspection and move-out inspection of the property to protect yourself in case you have to keep part or all of the security deposit to cover damage. Be clear up front what condition you expect the unit to be in when the tenant moves out.

- Tips on -
Being a Landlord

● If you rent property, manage it as if it were a business. Set a rent that's fair for your market, not one that's based on your mortgage payment.

● Require prospective tenants to fill out an application, and ask them to supply a copy of their credit report.

● Make the security deposit a little higher or lower than, but not the same as, a month's rent.

● For landlords with just one or two properties, include a repair clause that makes the tenant responsible for the first $50 cost of any repair. To do this, you may have to charge a little less in rent.

● Provide a discount for early rent payment.

● Do a move-in inspection and move-out inspection of the property to protect yourself in case you have to keep part or all of the security deposit to cover damage.

● If your tenants do not pay the rent, be prepared to evict them.

● If you're relocating far away from your property, ask a friend or relative to handle the rental, in return for some compensation, or consider professional management.

Contact:

Housing & Urban Development
Washington, DC
202-708-0547
(Questions regarding landlord/tenant disputes; ask to speak with the desk officer representing your state)

Or:
The clerk of the court in your county

If your tenants do not pay the rent, be prepared to evict them. Don't accept excuses. Don't be soft-hearted, because you're being walked on if you allow them to occupy a rental unit for free. To evict tenants in most states, you have to send them a letter demanding they pay the rent or turn over the premises. If they don't do either, you can't just go in and set their stuff out on the street. You must go to the county courthouse and begin an eviction action, and the clerk of the court will help you. The tenants will be served with an eviction notice and normally will have five to seven days to answer. If they answer and give a reason why they're not paying, a hearing before a judge will give each party a chance to explain their side. In most cases, the tenants never answer, so the court authorizes the eviction. Then the county marshal or sheriff will go to the property with you, or with people you hire, permit you to enter the premises, and put the tenants' possessions on the street. If you are speedy about an eviction, you can have it done within 30 days. Some landlords let tenants slide for months.

Others start eviction proceedings by the fifth of the month if they don't have the money. Do what you are comfortable with. If you've requested the money twice and don't have it by the middle of the month, I recommend you start the eviction process.

If you're relocating far away from your property, don't try to manage it by remote control. If you do, you're asking for trouble. Instead, ask a friend or relative to handle the rental of the property, in return for some compensation. Don't ask for it as a favor. Professional management is another option for people who are relocating out of state or who don't want to be landlords. Many real estate companies have divisions that will manage a property for you. The typical fee for a rental management firm is half the first month's rent and a 10 percent commission each month. So the fee for a $600 condo would be $300 up front and $60 a month. That's well worth it if you're in Chicago and the house is in St. Louis. Rates may vary in your community. Examine closely the agreement with the rental management company to see if you're protected if the company fails to do a good job collecting rent or securing tenants. And keep an eye on the quality of tenants the management company chooses. The company may not be as careful as you would be.

Being a Tenant —

The biggest mistake people make when hunting for an apartment is not asking enough questions. Before you write a check for an application fee or a deposit, get the specifics on the basic three—the length of the lease, the amount of rent, and the amount of deposit. If you have a pet, find out about the pet deposit. If you have any special needs, make sure they are met before you hand over any money or make any agreement to rent the apartment.

Never sign an apartment lease on the spot. Take it home with you and read it. If you don't understand something, put question marks next to the item and get an explanation. Always add a clause to an apartment lease giving you the right to terminate the contract before its normal expiration if your circumstances change. You should have the right to terminate early, by paying a fee of perhaps one month's rent, because of a job transfer or if you decide to relocate to another city. In return for a greater fee, perhaps two months' rent, your lease should permit you to terminate for any reason.

It's important to have early termination rights to avoid a potentially huge penalty. In most states, if you leave an apartment before the end of the lease, you remain responsible for the rent for as many months as it takes the landlord to re-rent the property. If you're three months into a one-year lease, you could be on the hook for nine months' rent. You need this protection even if your intent is to stay the full year, because circumstances change and you should be prepared.

Most states have their own rules for people who occupy an apartment without a lease. Usually, the state has the equivalent of its own lease that governs these "tenant-at-will" cases. Generally under these rules, you can terminate at any time by giving the landlord 30 days' written notice. The landlord can raise the rent at any time, or demand the premises back, by giving you 30 or 60 days' written notice.

Many leases renew automatically unless you notify the landlord that you are leaving. Let's say you sign a year's lease that ends March 31. In many cases, you'll have to notify the landlord in writing by March 1, or pay rent for April. Sometimes the lease will renew for another 12 months.

In most cases, your landlord will conduct a move-in inspection before you move into an apartment. Make sure to be present for it, and note everything you can find wrong with the apartment. Whatever you don't note will be held against you at the time you move out.

At the end of the lease, there will be a move-out inspection. Be present for that as well, so you can dispute anything the landlord says that isn't valid. This is vital in order for you to get back your security deposit. In fairness, the landlord may notice something you didn't. Maybe the bathroom isn't terribly clean and the landlord wants to bring in a cleaning crew. If you're present at the inspection, you can offer to clean it.

Before you sign, ask what condition the landlord expects the apartment to be in when you move out. That should be pretty revealing. If he hems and haws, you might have trouble getting back your security deposit. Some landlords, due to cash-flow problems, look for any excuse to keep your security deposit. Others use it only for a legitimate purpose.

If a landlord doesn't give you back a security deposit, you have specific rights, which vary by state, to go after him. In many states, you have the right to sue for two or three times the amount of the security deposit. Act quickly. If you don't have the deposit within 30 days of when you move out, send the landlord a letter demanding your security deposit. If you don't receive it within 10 more days, sue the landlord in small claims court. Usually in these cases, the landlord will dispute the condition of the unit. If you have any reason to suspect the landlord is going to try to cheat you on the security deposit, take pictures that prove the apartment is in good condition. A roll of film costs just a few dollars. You don't even have to get the film developed if you get the security deposit back. If you want to prove you shot the pictures after you moved out, rather than when you moved in, photograph the front page of the local newspaper early on the roll of film.

Some people like the idea of renting a condominium or a house, rather than a unit at an apartment complex, because they prefer a true residential neighborhood to a transient one. The drawback to renting from a nonprofessional owner is that management tends to be haphazard and inattentive. Maintenance requests go unanswered more often with a nonprofessional landlord. The biggest risk is the possibility the property owner will be foreclosed upon for nonpayment of the mortgage. In many states, if that happens, you can be evicted on very short notice. Another danger with a private owner, condominium, or house is not being able to live there year after year. A private owner could sell it and not renew your lease. An apartment complex is always going to be there.

Noisy neighbors are a headache for too many renters. If a neighbor is making your life miserable, try a friendly talk with him. If the neighbor doesn't respond, go to your apartment manager for help. If she doesn't do anything to solve the problem, call the police each time the noise level rises and have the neighbor cited for disturbing the peace. You have a right to live in peace and quiet.

On the other hand, people need to have some tolerance of normal noise levels. One of my callers moved into an apartment with her family and quickly learned that the people living beneath her thought her children were too noisy, even though she didn't think so. The neighbors kept complaining to management and banging on the ceiling with a broom handle, even though the noise wasn't out of the ordinary. The apartment complex eventually asked her to move to a different apartment in the complex. Because she had a lease, she didn't have to move. I recommended that she move only if she wanted to, and only if the apartment complex paid all her moving expenses, including the fees to reconnect the telephone and utilities.

Perhaps the most common complaint I hear from renters is slow or inadequate response on maintenance requests. I strongly recommend that you show some faith in your landlord. But as soon as your landlord fails to serve you, start documenting every maintenance request. If the landlord ignores your written requests, write "Request No. 2" and "Request No. 3" on subsequent letters, to reaffirm that you're having a continuing problem. If the landlord still ignores your requests, you may have to take the more drastic step of paying for the repair yourself and deducting it from your next month's rent. Do this only when the breakdown makes the apartment unlivable, such as for a burst pipe or a nonworking stove, refrigerator, or major appliance. Keep the repair receipt and enclose a copy of it with the rent check.

Your explicit rights to repair and deduct vary by state, but there's an implicit right for you to have a livable dwelling. Let's say your water heater explodes and your landlord won't do anything about it. Hit the landlord with a written notice and let her know that, if it's not replaced within 24 hours, you will use the right of repair and deduct. One thing you cannot do is completely withhold rent because you don't like something. That will get you evicted.

Some landlords can be extremely gracious in major repair situations. A friend of mine had a case a few years ago in which an upstairs neighbor inadvertently set off the sprinkler system, saturating his living room ceiling with water and causing the sheetrock to cave in. The apartment complex agreed to put him and his family in a hotel for four days while repairs were made, and they returned to find a bottle of champagne waiting in the apartment.

My friend's possessions weren't damaged, because there was enough time to cover the furniture with a tarpaulin. But that's a risk too many renters ignore. The landlord is almost never responsible for damage to your possessions, even from a burst pipe, unless you can prove gross negligence, which isn't easy. You thus need renter's insurance to protect against theft and damage. It's not that expensive, about $15 a month, and it will keep you from being wiped out. A few years ago, a friend of a friend lost all her possessions in a fire and had no insurance. She lived above a store and when the store caught fire, her apartment and all her possessions were destroyed. Losing photos and irreplaceable items was a given, but she was left with no clothes, except what she was wearing, and no furniture. It was terribly sad and unnecessary.

Your landlord should provide you with smoke detectors, although they are not required in many states. If the landlord doesn't, buy them yourself. The cost is just $5 to $20, a real bargain if it saves a life. Make sure yours work, and, if it's battery powered, check the batteries at least once a year—a good chore to do on New Year's Day. In a multiunit dwelling, there's a greater chance of fire than in a house, and smoke detectors are even more critical.

As I discuss in the chapter on credit problems, your mortgage or rent is the first and most important bill for you to pay, because eviction is a real danger. The eviction process is pretty standard in most states, although specific details vary. Some cities even have their own landlord/tenant laws. If you fear you may be evicted, check with the clerk of the court in your county to find out how the process works specifically in your area.

In most states, a notice will be delivered to you or tacked onto your door informing you of the eviction proceeding. You'll have a short time, approximately five to seven days, to pay the rent or explain why you should be allowed to remain. If you don't pay and don't respond, you'll have little chance to stay in the apartment or house. But even if you do appear in court, don't expect the judge to be very sympathetic to a sad story. Landlords are not charities and you have no right to live somewhere if you don't pay the rent.

Normally it takes about 30 days from the

- Tips on -
Being a Tenant

- Before you write a check for an application fee or a deposit on an apartment, ask about the length of the lease, the amount of rent, and the amount of deposit.

- Never sign an apartment lease on the spot. Take it home with you and read it. If you don't understand something, put question marks next to the item and get an explanation.

- Always add a clause to an apartment lease giving you the right to terminate the contract before its normal expiration if your circumstances change.

- Many leases renew automatically unless you notify the landlord that you are leaving.

- Make sure to be present for the move-in inspection, and note everything you can find wrong with the apartment. Be present for the move-out inspection, too.

- If a landlord doesn't give you back a security deposit, you have the right to sue in small claims court.

- Renting from a private owner is fine, but be aware of the danger of not being able to renew your lease, or of the owner being foreclosed upon.

- If your landlord fails to respond to maintenance requests, send written requests. If a landlord doesn't respond to a breakdown that makes the apartment unlivable, consider paying for the repair yourself and deducting the amount from your next month's rent.

- If you know you're going to be evicted, try to make some arrangements to move your possessions, either to a friend's house or into storage.

Contact:
Housing & Urban Development
Washington, DC
202-708-0547
(Questions regarding landlord/tenant disputes; ask to speak with the desk officer representing your state)

Or:
The clerk of the court in your county

day the landlord begins the eviction action until the sheriff puts you out of the residence. If you know you're going to be evicted, try to make some arrangements to move your possessions, either to a friend's house or into storage. A small, self-storage rental unit, for $60 or $70 a month, will give you a place to keep your things until you find a place to live. If your stuff is put out on the street, it could be stolen or ruined by foul weather.

You really have to be on your toes these days to avoid the ripoff artists, because they're all around and looking to take your money. Many of the calls I get each week on my radio show are from people who have been ripped off by a phony loan company or telemarketer, or who are suspicious that something they've heard about is not legitimate.

Most scams appeal to your dreams or your vanity. The common cons operate on the premise that you will make a decision quickly and emotionally, instead of doing the legwork to verify information or to develop your own basic knowledge. If you rely exclusively on what you're being told by someone else, you become a sitting duck. Often when you are taken you have no recourse, because the ripoff artists are clever enough to avoid committing a crime.

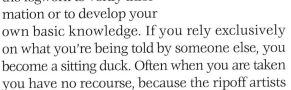

I hope especially that you beware of a sales technique called the "No Be Back," which you'll see often in high-pressure sales schemes. It turns up in health clubs, buying clubs, and timeshares—whenever a salesperson wants you to buy something that isn't a good value. In "No Be Back," the salesperson forces you to buy right then, because if you're able to leave the high-pressure sales environment, go home, and think about it, odds are you'll realize it's not a smart decision and you won't waste your money. The salesperson would rather have you say no than leave as a maybe.

In this chapter, I'll tell you about many of the most common ripoffs and help you to avoid being taken.

Health Clubs —

Most health clubs are interested more in your checkbook than your health. And signing a long-term contract with one can really hurt your financial fitness.

When you go into these high-pressure health clubs, you're greeted by a commission salesperson, not a health expert. Her job is to strong-arm you into signing a long-term membership, typically for three years.

Callers have told me they're not even shown the facilities during a sales presentation. If they do see the facility, it's a very limited tour. The salesperson concentrates on making oral promises that are not in the contract and doesn't bother to show you the contract until very late in the presentation.

Salespeople use all kinds of "closer" techniques, words and phrases designed to pressure you into signing. For example, a salesperson might say, "Don't you think today is the day you should start building a healthier body?"

People usually go to a health club with the best of intentions. Sometimes they go to get healthier, or, more often than not, to get thinner. People often sign a health club contract because they believe they're doing something to improve themselves. But signing the contract doesn't do anything except obligate you to a long-term commitment to pay a lot of money, usually with hefty finance charges attached.

The enthusiasm of a new health club member often wanes quickly. For the first few weeks after you join, you'll probably visit the club several times. Then you start going twice a week and then once a week. Suddenly, you're going every other week, and before you know it, usually within three months, you're not even setting foot there. You're feeling so guilty that you're driving a different route home so you don't have to see the place.

At that point, the deal starts to look very unfair. You're getting a bill every month from a health club that you're not visiting, and you don't want to pay any more. But if you don't pay, they're going to come after you, either with their own collectors or with a third-party collection agency. I often get calls from people who can't qualify for a mortgage because of something on their credit report. A major reason for that—No. 1 as far as my callers are concerned—is a past-due bill for a health club.

Once you enter into a health club membership, you own it—with one exception. Most states give you three business days from the day you sign the contract to cancel your membership with no consequences. You must follow the exact procedure in the contract for canceling. Don't telephone and tell the club you're canceling. Don't drop by and hand them a note. Usually you'll have to send a letter by certified mail, return receipt requested. Keep a copy of that letter and your certified mail slip forever. You never know when someone's going to get amnesia about the fact that you properly canceled. One day you may need to provide proof.

If you've waited beyond the allowed number of days to cancel, you have little choice but to keep paying. If you stop paying, the club will ruin your credit, making it difficult for you to buy a car or home, or obtain a credit card. Normally you'll get a notice from the club or their finance company. Later you'll be turned over to a collection agency. The collection efforts will continue, often sporadically, through the years. Eventually, when you try to establish new credit, the delinquent membership will jump off your credit report to bite you. At that point, you will have to come to an accommodation with the health club.

Ripoff health clubs often operate right on the edge of the law, and their goal is to get money out of you no matter what. I had one case involving a 17-year-old boy who signed a health club contract, then went home and realized that he was pressured into it by a salesperson. In his state, a contract signed by a 17-year-old is voidable, but it's not automatically void. He tried for months to cancel

his contract but the health club kept stalling. I got the call the day before his 18th birthday. Once he turned 18, he could no longer void the contract. So I had to walk his father through the steps to make sure the boy didn't get taken at midnight that night. It would have been an unfriendly birthday present.

Another thing to watch out for with a health club is "free membership" contests. Health clubs offer free memberships to gather names and addresses of possible new members. When you sign up at the yogurt store to win the one-year membership, and win a free 30-day membership instead, you know you're just being taken in for a sales presentation. Normally they won't give you your membership card until you've been on the sales presentation, and by then, they expect to have sold you a membership. Every single person who enters the contest at the yogurt store wins the 30-day membership. By winning, you're actually losing.

Reputable health clubs do exist, and if you're looking to join one, here's what I recommend. First, look for a club that allows you to pay as you go. Very few health clubs will tell you outright that you can sign up on a month-to-month basis, but if you're persistent and are willing to pay a little more per month, several clubs probably will cut you that kind of deal.

I heard of one club that charges $10 a month more for month-to-month membership, and it requires that you authorize a monthly draft from your checking or credit card account. That's not a great offer, but it's better than a three-year contract. Another had a no-pressure approach and a membership that included a $150 initiation fee and a $40 per month charge with a two-month minimum. A third asked for a $150 down payment and charged $37.98 per month. That was actually $4 a month less than their one-year contract. These are just some examples. Health clubs come and go and offers change. But you can find acceptable deals out there if you look.

It's okay to sign a three-year agreement with a health club if the agreement has a buyout clause, and as long as you don't pay in advance. With a buyout clause, you're protected if you move to a different area. A fair buyout is two months of membership fees. At least it gives you a way to get out early.

In some states, membership money isn't held in escrow or by bond. So if the club closes its doors and you've paid in advance for a full year, you lose all your money. It's a real danger because health clubs close all the time.

I remember one club that had been offering very inexpensive one- and two-year memberships. The club kept collecting cash from members right up to the day it closed its doors. All of those people got stuck without a membership and without refunds. When you pay in advance for a health club, you do so at your own risk.

Some states do provide greater protection. New York, for example, requires health clubs to post a bond of up to $150,000 if it signs members to long-term contracts. The money is used to reimburse the club's members.

If you finance your membership contract and the club closes, you no longer have to make any payments to the finance company. If your club has closed, send the finance company a certified letter telling them the club has closed and that you owe no more money on the contract. One caveat: some states may require you to attend another location of the club that remains open.

If your club does close, competing clubs nearby may take you as a member at little or no cost. They do it for good will, and they figure you may sign up with them when your original membership expires.

If you think a particular health club may suit you, call the local consumer agency in your state to see if there are any unsatisfied complaints about the club. If the club passes that test, go and take a look. Visit during the busiest time of the week—usually early in the week in the evening. Ask for a tour and look at the condition of the equipment and how crowded the facility is. If you wanted to use a stair step machine, is there one available, or do you have to wait in line to use one? Go into the locker room and see how clean it is. Watch an aerobics or other fitness class and see whether or not the instructor seems knowledgeable. Then, talk to some of the participants after the class. Interview a fitness trainer. See how long he has been there and ask what his training recommendations are for you. That will tell you how interested he is in you and how knowledgeable he is. Nobody in just a brief conversation can let you know exactly what your weight program will be, but you'll be able to tell how much he really knows.

If you like the club, ask for a copy of its contract that you can take home. Do not sign the contract while you're at the health club but ask for time to read it carefully. If there's anything you don't understand, put a question mark next to it. Then call the club—don't go back in—and get answers to those questions. The reason you don't go back in is you may not get any answers, or you may get false answers, and you'll feel pressure to sign when you're back in the club's environment. If you're calling, you maintain the balance of power.

Don't agree to anything you don't understand. If there's anything a club salesperson can't explain to you, put a slash through it, put your initials by it, and sign the contract without that clause included.

If the health club does not allow you to leave with a copy of the contract, do not sign and do not join that health club. Any reputable business will give you an unsigned contract for you to review. I don't care what you're buying.

Don't listen to what the salesperson says unless she includes it in writing. I had one caller who was thinking about moving to another state

- Tips on - Health Clubs

• Don't sign long-term contracts for health club membership or pay for more than 30 days in advance. Month-to-month deals are much safer.

• Don't fall for "free membership" contests that are really sales pitches.

• Take the contract home with you and read it thoroughly. Don't sign the contract at the club.

• Get any promises made by the salesperson included in the contract, or they don't mean a thing.

• In most states, you have three days from the day you sign a health club contract to cancel with no consequences.

• If you finance your membership and the club closes, you have no further obligation to pay.

• If you think a particular club may suit you, call the appropriate consumer agency in your state to check for outstanding complaints against the club. Tour the facility and ask questions.

and wondered what would happen to his membership if he moved. He was told that it would be no problem, that all he had to do was provide documentation—say, a copy of his new lease—and the club would let him out of the membership. Well, that wasn't true at all. The agreement he signed keeps him obligated no matter where he lives.

Another fellow was told he could either use his local health club or transfer his membership to another place. That was wonderful because he loves to play racquetball. But the membership was not truly transferable, because although he could play racquetball at facility No. 1, at facility No. 2, the membership was good only for general health club use. The racquetball portion was an extra $500 a year. Here he was obligated to a membership that was useless for what he wanted. Any promises that are made about facilities, terms and conditions of the agreement, or potential termination promises must be included in the language of the contract.

Timeshares —

Most people would love to own a vacation home or cabin, a place to get away for a week when life gets hectic. Trouble is, many of us can't afford a mountain or beach home. Ripoff artists who sell timeshares are able to make a killing by promising to put a vacation paradise within our reach.

When you buy a timeshare, you get the right to use a vacation property at a particular time each year, usually for one week. It seems as if you're buying real estate, but you're not.

Timeshares turn out to be a very poor deal. In addition to the cost of buying a timeshare, usually $8,000 to $10,000, you have to pay an annual association fee of about $400 a week.

I could stay somewhere for seven days for roughly the same amount, about $60 a night, that a timeshare owner has to pay for maintenance. That's a lot of money for a place you already own. And you can't simply decide later that you don't want it anymore, because nobody else will take it off your hands.

A timeshare is virtually impossible to sell because it has no real value. Even if the upfront cost was zero, the burden of paying the annual fee makes owning a timeshare a bad idea.

In fact, if you ever inherit a timeshare, I recommend that you disavow your inheritance of it. Otherwise, the obligations of the deceased become yours. Generally things you inherit are to your benefit. A timeshare is to your detriment.

I get calls every week from people who would gladly give their timeshares away. Nobody will take them, because they don't want the obligation, either. Remember when Super Glue first came out and they said it would stick to anything? Well, a timeshare is a new and improved version of Super Glue. Once you own it, it's with you forever.

When you buy a house, you know that in a few years you can sell that house to somebody else, often for a profit. You also can give up ownership through foreclosure. You can't do either with a timeshare. Developers won't take one of these things back because they know they ripped you off by selling it to you. If you don't pay, they'll send you to a collection agency and eventually sue you. Your obligation continues no matter what.

People are so desperate to sell timeshares that they get conned by timeshare brokers, people who say they can successfully market a timeshare. These folks will charge a listing fee of about $300. Once you write a check for that listing fee, you can kiss it goodbye. I have never heard of any caller who has ever been able to sell a timeshare through a broker.

Timeshare presentations are a very elaborate con game. First, you'll be called by a telemarketer, whose job is to convince you to come to the presentation. That person is paid based on how many people show up for the timeshare presentations, so he'll tell you anything to get you in the door.

The biggest lie he'll tell you is it's a short presentation; in reality it will last about three hours. The idea is to immerse you completely in a carefully orchestrated event. A timeshare presentation is theater.

The prizes you're offered as an incentive to attend a presentation are almost always overly glorified. For example, you'll be told you're going to receive two free tickets to Hawaii, with a retail value of $1,200. Later, it turns out that you've won a certificate allowing you to purchase a trip to Hawaii. You get the free tickets only if you agree to buy 10 nights at a specific hotel. Before you know it, the hotel and free tickets cost more than it would have cost to buy the air and hotel from someone else.

This certificate program is a common tactic in high-pressure sales schemes. The timeshare operator can obtain these "free airfare" certificates for $5 each. If a company is selling these certificates for $5, it's obviously not going to redeem them for free airline tickets to Hawaii.

When you show up for the timeshare presentation, the first thing they do is check to see if you're qualified to be a timeshare owner. If you have good credit, and aren't wealthy enough to buy your own beach house, you're probably a good target.

If you qualify, you're brought into a very impressive-looking reception area. A salesperson will then take you through an elaborate presentation, normally followed by a film. Next you'll be shown an actual model of the timeshare unit, fully built and beautifully decorated. This is another "No Be Back" sale. It isn't a sensible purchase, and they know that once you leave their high-pressure environment, you'll never buy.

There are three price levels for timeshares: peak, off-peak, and shoulder. Let's take the Caribbean as an example. December 15 to April 15 is peak season. May or early December would be shoulder, basically just before or after peak season, and summer would be off-peak. The prices vary tremendously. Obviously a week at a beach resort during Christmas is going to cost a lot more than a week during hurricane season. Whatever the price, expect a timeshare to lose 80 percent of its value the moment you sign the agreement. The money goes toward sales and marketing expenses, commissions, and endorsements.

During the film segment of the presentation, there will be a product endorsement of the timeshare by someone who appeals to the potential buyer. I went to a timeshare presentation for a property in Myrtle Beach, S.C., in which a stock-car driver made the pitch. The endorser could be any of a number of different people, depending on what market segment the timeshare is targeting.

The message is seductive. "Just imagine yourself once a year with us on this beautiful stretch of sand." They're selling an illusion, a piece of the American dream. A lot of people figure maybe they can't afford to have the whole dream, but these seven days they can have.

Most people have to stretch to come up with $8,000 to $10,000, and generally they have to finance it. Even with financing, people just don't have an extra $100 or more to throw away each month.

Sometimes, you buy a timeshare and don't even get to use it. A caller to my show bought a houseboat timeshare for $5,500. He purchased the right to use the houseboat for vacation one week a year. Then the operator went bust and none of the buyers were able to use their timeshare. But their obligations continued. My staff and I were able to help several of the timeshare owners form an organization to fight their case. Eventually, the boat was fixed up and the buyers were able to use the timeshares again.

Even though you pay a maintenance and association fee, you don't have control over what happens if a timeshare is not well maintained. You don't have the rights you would have with a condominium complex, where the owners of the condominium units run the association that takes care of maintenance. Timeshare agreements are always done so the timeshare operator has the power even when you have the ownership.

After the presentation and film, you're brought into another room, usually with a lot of tables and chairs, and all kinds of psycho-logical tricks are used to get you to buy. For example, every time somebody buys, they pop a champagne bottle. The sales reps stand up in unison and start applauding. There's a festive atmosphere. The buyers smile, their picture is taken, and champagne is poured. Then the sales rep will say something to you like, "Do you see the joy in their face? Don't you want to be able to experience that joy of ownership yourself?"

If you don't agree to buy, a closer is brought to your table, a professional who knows how to hit people where they're weakest. At the presentation I went to, the closer was alternately trying to humiliate me, trying to be charming, and trying to be threatening. They'll frighten you into thinking you're letting a wonderful opportunity get away. Or they'll put you down by saying you don't have the money to do it. The idea is to get you to prove you do have the money by signing the deal. Many people do buy the timeshare after the closer comes to the table.

When you finish and don't buy, just wait until you try to get your prizes. It's not easy. I had a call from someone who didn't buy and was told to walk down a hallway to get his prize. The fellow and his wife opened the door and started walking down the corridor, then realized it was the fire exit. They were locked out and the only way they could go was to the parking lot. They could have gone back in the entrance, but they didn't. They never got their prizes.

Whether or not you get a prize, I recommend you avoid going to timeshare presentations at all. There's too much of a chance that you might be tempted or intimidated into buying something that will turn out to be a very big mistake.

Don't underestimate how persuasive these people can be, even if their targets are highly educated. I have a friend who called from a resort area where she and her husband, both lawyers, had been looking at a timeshare. At the high end of the market, they sell the units by giving you a free weekend at the resort. They had been immersed in this weekend and had gone to see the presentation. They called me and asked if they should do it and I said absolutely not. I went through all the reasons why they shouldn't buy. They wanted to talk to another expert, so I told them to call Clinton Burr, president of the Resort Property Owners Association. He told them not to buy because they would lose all $18,000 of their money. Sure enough, they bought anyway. It doesn't matter what your income level is or what your level of education, you can fall for these false pitches.

Buying Clubs —

Nobody enjoys a bargain more than I do. I buy soft drinks by the case and keep them in a little refrigerator in my office because I won't pay 50 cents a can at the office vending machine. But the desire to save money can also get you into trouble.

One way to get burned is to join an illegitimate buying club, an organization that charges a big membership fee and promises to allow you to buy merchandise at wholesale prices. The initiation fee typically will be $900 to $1,200, plus an annual membership fee of $50 to $100.

These buying clubs are nothing but catalog distributors. They have a showroom, where they display a variety of merchandise, but they don't actually have merchandise in inventory.

Not having the merchandise on hand is one way these clubs differ from legitimate warehouse clubs, such as Sam's Club and Price Club. In the legitimate clubs, you pay a membership fee of up to $30 a year and the merchandise is right there on the shelves for you to purchase.

At the very least, the illegitimate buying clubs depend on an antiquated method of retailing. Nobody wants to have to get into a car and drive to a buying club for the privilege of looking through their catalog. People who buy via mail order like it because it's convenient to look through the catalog at home and order through an 800 number.

These clubs claim their merchandise is sold at cost and therefore is extremely cheap. But you have no way of knowing if that's true unless you comparison shop. Even if these buying clubs did have decent prices, you would have to buy quite a bit of merchandise to make back a $1,200 membership fee and $50 to $100 in annual fees. In all the years that I've been attacking ripoff buying clubs on the air, I've had only one consumer call and say it saved him money. He had just bought a house, then joined the club and bought every piece of furniture for his house through the club. The caller believed he had saved money and that it was a good thing for him.

Buying clubs use mailings and telemarketers

- Tips on - Buying Clubs

● Legitimate warehouse clubs such as Sam's Club often can provide excellent savings on merchandise.

● In the legitimate clubs, you pay a membership fee of up to $30 a year and the merchandise is right there on the shelves for you to purchase.

● Illegitimate buying clubs are nothing but catalog distributors. They have a showroom, but that's just a front, because they don't actually have merchandise in inventory.

● Illegitimate buying clubs charge an initiation fee typically of $900 to $1,200, plus an annual membership fee of $50 to $100.

● The ripoff clubs don't care if you ever buy anything from them, but they'll force you to pay the fees, to the point of suing you.

to lure you in to hear their presentation on "a great new way to buy products." Just for coming in, they promise to give you one or more great prizes. One caller to my show was offered eight sirloin steaks, a weekend at Epcot Center, and a car alarm to get him to listen to a buying club presentation. When you get there, a high-pressure salesperson will try to convince you to sign up for a lifetime membership.

Joining these clubs is a foolish decision that people regret the second they do it. Most people who join never walk in the place again, and the club doesn't care either way, as long as members pay the fees. If a member goes into default, the buying club goes to court and seeks a judgment against him.

Judges don't like to rule in favor of the clubs, but there's not much they can do. One caller told a judge the membership club had promised she could simply stop paying if she no longer wanted to be a member. But that's not what the contract said and she had signed it. The judge had no choice but to rule against her.

Most states give you three days after you sign to back out of a buying club membership. Unfortunately, most buyers don't cancel within that time. If they try, the club often will lie to them to keep them from canceling on time.

Any time you walk into a high-pressure sales presentation, whether it's for a buying club or a timeshare, and you're told you must make a decision right then, just say no and walk out the door.

Extended Warranties —

One of the things people worry about most when they buy a new TV or VCR is what to do if it breaks. Repairs can be costly and manufacturers' warranties are notoriously short. That's why service contracts, or extended warranties, have been such a successful ripoff.

Extended warranties are a bad deal for the consumer because they rarely pay off. Only 12 to 20 percent of the money paid for extended warranties is ever used to pay for repairs or claims, making this a remarkably profitable product. A typical insurance product pays out 70 cents of every premium dollar in claims.

There are several reasons the claims rate is so low on service contracts. People often lose the contracts, or they move, or they forget they purchased the contract in the first place. The usage rate is even lower than the breakdown rate of the appliance.

In any case, you are better off taking the money you would have spent on service contracts and putting it into a repair fund, although admittedly this takes quite a bit of discipline. However, over time you'll come out way ahead by not buying service contracts and self-insuring appliances this way.

When you make a purchase, the salesperson may heap on a lot of pressure to buy the extended warranty. Extended warranties are very profitable—often the most profitable part of the sale—and salespeople risk being fired if they fail to sell enough of them. In fact, many times the warranty is the only profit on the sale, because of the razor-thin margins in appliance retailing and the comparison shopping done by consumers.

Extended warranties are so profitable that when the Financial Accounting Standards Board changed the method by which retailers had to account for these contracts in their financial statements, retailers suffered losses in that quarter. The losses occurred because the board said retailers could no longer book profits from those contracts all in one quarter. They had to amortize the profits over a number of quarters. It became very clear to everyone outside the appliance and electronics industries how profitable these contracts were.

People are hit with extended warranties most often when they buy appliances, rather than cars, because they make these purchases more frequently. But a car is where the decision represents the greatest amount of money. Actually, it's more important to check out the reliability record of the car you're considering than to decide on whether to buy an extended service contract. For more on cars and extended warranties, read the sections on trade-ins, financing, and extended warranties in the Cars chapter of this book.

Inventors' Groups —

There's been an explosion of interest in the United States in inventing. People are tinkering in their basements and garages, hoping to hit it big with a new, commercially successful product. They want to be the next Apple Computer.

Enthusiastic would-be inventors have become perfect prey for a group of ripoff artists who promise to help take these inventions to the marketplace. Instead, they steal hundreds of dollars from each inventor, without ever providing any help.

The ripoff "invention services" attract folks by offering a free evaluation of inventions. Inventors call the 800 number, send in some application forms, and inevitably receive a call from a salesperson who raves about the invention and its potential. But to do further research, the salesperson says, the organization needs $500 from the inventor. Many of the people quickly send a check.

- Tips on -
Inventors' Groups

- Most ripoff invention services use a three-step program to steal money. They offer a free evaluation of the inventor's product through an 800 number, take $500 or so to fund "research," and later request another $5,000 to $6,000 for more extensive "market research."

- One such company was forced to disclose that less than 1 percent of the ideas people submit ever make it to market.

- Turn to the local bookstore or library for legitimate advice on how to bring inventions to market.

- It's important to create a working prototype of your idea, because companies won't buy ideas from sketches.

- Your best bet is to find an invention broker to propose your idea to a company.

- Nonprofit inventors clubs, which can be found in many cities, also are excellent for sharing ideas and providing encouragement.

Reference:
Patent It Yourself
by Nolo Press ($34.95)

The Inventing and Patenting Sourcebook: Desktop Companion
by Richard Levy ($24.95)

After a few more weeks, the company will start the second phase of the scam. They'll send a second, more complete information kit, and tell the inventor that his idea is now ready to be prepared for the marketplace. They'll ask for a larger amount, usually $5,000 or $6,000 "to conduct a thorough market analysis." Many inventors send in a second check, only to learn weeks or months later that the ripoff invention service did nothing but take their money.

One of these companies, Invention Submission Corporation, entered into a consent agreement with the federal government in which they agreed to disclose that less than 1 percent of the ideas people submit ever make it to market. These companies are not in the business of bringing ideas alive, they're in the business of getting rich off of you.

The reason these phony organizations continue to operate is that it's very hard for law enforcement authorities to prove that their actions are criminal. So authorities have taken civil action to try to win restitution for victims and, through greater disclosure, try to warn others to stay away. Unfortunately, con artists who have little fear of going to jail will continue what they're doing.

If you believe you have a good invention idea, there's legitimate help at the local bookstore or library. I like two books in particular, *Patent It Yourself*, by Nolo Press, and *The Inventing and Patenting Sourcebook: Desktop Companion*, by

Richard Levy. Not surprisingly, *Patent It Your-self* describes the process of patenting an idea. The Levy book addresses how companies select products to market and how inventors can increase their chances of getting an audience for their ideas.

To have any chance of success, inventors must have a working prototype, Levy says. Companies won't buy sketches; they have to see a working model of the product. So if you've tinkered and drawn, finish tinkering and start building.

Inventions fall into three basic categories: weak ideas that don't have a chance, ideas that are good but can't generate enough demand for them to make money, and the small number of good ideas with potential for profit. So inventors have to be both lucky and good.

One of the most helpful parts of Levy's guide is his explanation of the role played by brokers in bringing ideas from inventors to large corporations. Their job is to help separate the good ideas from the weak ones. Most large companies prefer to deal with established brokers, rather than speaking directly with inventors.

There's one other alternative available to help you in many medium-size and large cities around the country. They're called nonprofit inventors clubs, and their members share information that can be very helpful. In a real nonprofit inventors club, you won't be asked to sign any licensing agreements. It's a shared self-help organization, with people encouraging and advising you along the way, and you sharing your information and success stories with others.

Inventors as a group are unusually paranoid, with a tremendous fear that everybody is going to steal their idea. There is some justification for that fear, and the question "Whom can I trust?" is a difficult one to answer. My advice is to seek a patent to protect your concept before you present your idea to a corporation.

Employment Scams —

The extraordinary number of corporate layoffs in recent years has provided fertile ground for the growth of ripoff employment recruiters. Particularly vulnerable are those people who worked in a job for a long time and thought they were going to work for that company for a lifetime. Suddenly, they have found themselves unemployed and suffering a dramatic loss of confidence.

Because of this sense of loss and hopelessness, they are easy prey for organizations that promise to place them in a job. The organizations claim to have special contacts or special influence that enables them to find jobs. That's just someone taking advantage of the unemployed. Nobody can guarantee she'll find you a job and—unless you have a very special skill—no one has special influence with employers.

I urge you not to do business with any employment organization that requires you to pay an up-front fee. If you are really timid about your job search and you want to use a placement service, it should be one whose fee is paid after you are hired. Your preference should be that the employer pays the fee or that the fee is split between you and the employer. It's less desirable for you to pay the full fee.

If you do have an unusual skill that is highly desirable to employers, you may benefit by turning to a recruiter with expertise in your field. People who would be helped by a specialized recruiter might have skills in engineering, medicine, or the sciences. But such areas are by far the exception, and for these job candidates the employer would pay the fee and would never have any up-front charge.

The most dishonest and evil employment cons are those promising work in foreign lands. They entice victims to pay phony application fees, or dial expensive 900-number information services, with talk about exotic locales and high salaries. In some cases the ads will scream about supposedly tax-free income.

- Tips on - Employment Scams

- Placement offices can't guarantee that they'll find you a job, and—unless you have a very special skill—none have special influence with employers.

- Don't do business with any employment organization that requires you to pay an up-front fee.

- The worst employment cons are those promising work in foreign lands. The odds of an American finding work in a foreign country, especially a Third World country, are near zero.

- Work-at-home offers almost always are scams. If you have had so much trouble finding a job, it's unlikely you suddenly would be able to earn several hundred or several thousand dollars a week doing a job in your home.

- If you think you need help looking for a job, try an informal networking group. Formal networking groups, which use computerized job listings and charge a fee, don't work for everyone, but they can be helpful.

The odds of an American finding work in a foreign country, especially a Third World country, are near zero. Unless you have very specialized skills, the country can hire locals for far less pay than would be required to lure an American to that job.

After the Persian Gulf War, all the con artists came out and advertised for people to help with the reconstruction of Kuwait. Typically the jobs required no special skills and paid at least $50,000 a year. Of course, it was all a bunch of baloney. The only thing that changes with the foreign scams is the angle. We went through a wave of Australia scams, for example, back when the Crocodile Dundee films heightened Americans' interest in that country. The number of Americans getting jobs in Australia is limited strictly to those who are appointed to work in the U.S. embassy and consulates. Australia has very restrictive labor laws that keep out foreigners. This is just another way to con people and steal their money.

Work-at-home offers are another popular employment ripoff. They almost always are scams. You can steer clear of these with a little common sense. After all, if you have had so much trouble finding a job, why would you suddenly be able to earn several hundred or several thousand dollars a week doing a job in your home? In most of these cases, someone is supposedly willing to set you up in business without having interviewed or screened you in any way.

I had a call from a woman who heard about a work-at-home scheme in which she would pay $7,000 for lesson books and software that would allow her to process medical claims for doctors' offices. The software supposedly would let her hook up to a mainframe computer in another state and this business was supposed to make her filthy rich. A medical consultant told me this was complete baloney. According to the expert, most doctors use their own employees to process their claims, or they use independent processing companies. The tipoff in this case was that the woman would hook up to a mainframe in another state, which would never allow her to be a truly independent business.

When you hear about a scheme like this, one of the best ways to check it out is to call someone in the profession it involves. In this case, I suggested the woman call doctors' offices and ask the office managers if they were interested in this service and, if they were, what fees they would be willing to pay to have claims processed. She compared her research against the claims being made by the work-at-home company and found out that this was not a legitimate way for her to make money.

Another employment ripoff I've spoken with callers about concerns the sale of vending machines. One company promised this fellow he could work four hours a week, on his own routes, and earn $400 a week in supplemental income. That's simply not true.

It's extremely difficult to place vending machines because the high-traffic locations are already taken up by large national vending machine companies or by small businesses who own their own machines. To get business, you have to contact the owner of the business, either to supply machines or to service the business's own machines. Going up against the big guys isn't easy; you don't have the leverage to get your machines into the places you need in order to make money. The sad thing is you'll end up with $5,000 to $7,000 worth of vending equipment sitting in your garage, because these ripoff artists require you to buy a number of machines. You also have no way of knowing if their equipment will be of decent quality.

Ironically, the warehouse clubs sell vending machines, so you can walk right in and buy your own soft drink or candy-dispensing machine. They're really good quality and sell for a lot less money than the machines from these vending machine companies. If you're really interested in developing vending routes, you could buy a single soft drink machine for about $1,500, try placing it in a store, and see if you're any good at this business. If your machine does well, you could buy a second. Why buy $5,000 worth of machines in advance?

People can sometimes work at home successfully. You might start making something as a hobby and, because you're good at it, create a natural demand for what you produce and expand it into a business. The most famous example of that is Apple Computer. Another possibility is if you already have a skill. Due to the technology that exists today, people can communicate with an office almost as if they were on site.

I know a paralegal who's been running a business out of her home for several years. She loves it. She gets up in the morning and goes over to her computer, and there are instructions waiting for her on the machine. It's as if she's in the office. That's how I communicate with the *Atlanta Journal and Constitution* for my travel columns. I write my columns on my computer and transmit them to the newspaper's mainframe computer. I also have a link, through a travel agency, with an airline reservation system. I do research for my travel columns, my TV travel stories, and my radio show right in my home. You can work out of your home, but generally it will be by using a technical skill.

If you believe you need help looking for a job, I have several recommendations. A number of informal networking organizations have sprung up that don't charge a fee and meet in local churches. I heard about one group that meets at a cafeteria once a week. These groups gather people who are looking for jobs to share ideas, leads, and contacts.

Almost all jobs found in America are found through direct contact with employers or through friends and relatives. The number of jobs found through classified ads or any form of advertising is less than 15 percent of the total openings. Because most people are passive in their job search, the overwhelming majority of people end up competing for the very limited number of advertised jobs. Very few people are out there looking for the vast majority of jobs through informal and formal networking.

In a formal network, you pay a fee to join and you have access to their database. When you become employed, or if you hear about jobs that don't suit you, you return the favor to the network by making leads available. This is a legitimate thing to do and it is a fruitful approach for some people. However, informal networking is probably superior.

If you've lost a job, you may become passive and even have trouble getting started in the morning. One of the ways people can pick themselves up, build confidence, and move toward getting a job is by treating the job search as a job. Give yourself specific assignments every day: people you're going to see and things you're going to do. One of the first things you should do is sit down with three-by-five index cards or a computer and list every single person you know. It may sound like busywork but actually it's not, because there are many people you know or knew in the past who may be able to help you in your job search. By going through the mental exercise of making this list, you give yourself a very helpful tool with which to start your job search.

One major word of caution: when you start contacting people who are potential job leads, don't call and ask if they know about work, because people hate that. Ask for advice or information, not for a job. People love to be asked for their advice. People hate to be asked for a job.

Modeling Schools —

This ripoff appeals not only to a person's vanity and dreams but to parents' dreams for their children. Modeling scams give individuals and families false hope of a brilliant new career and then shatter those dreams by just taking their money.

They tend to target parents with young children, but they're willing to take anybody's money. Other common victims are young men and women in their late teens and early twenties.

I call them modeling road shows because these groups take the con on the road. They'll come into a city and advertise their modeling tryouts or seminars. If you think you or your child has what it takes to be a model, they want you to come to their show—usually in a hotel ballroom. By showing up, you're prequalifying yourself to be taken.

When you arrive, there will be a large presentation, kind of like a pep rally. Then they'll meet with each person individually or in small groups. Let's say a parent goes in with three children. To increase the credibility of the modeling road show, they'll take only one child. It'll sound something like, "We think your daughter Letitia has great talent and we'd like to see her some more, but the other two children aren't ready yet." Or, "We like Mark but Sara is too young. Maybe in another year or two." So they pretend they're eliminating people when all they're really doing is setting you up for a squeeze play. The squeeze usually will come in some type of listing fee, modeling fee, lessons charge, or photography charge. They also have something they call a placement fee. Typically they'll take a victim for $200 to $300.

A real modeling agency makes its money off the bookings it gets for you. They're paid a commission for having placed you in an ad. Only fake modeling groups take these road shows all around America. Any time you're hit for money up front from a modeling organization, you should know something is not right.

One of my callers agreed to pay $180 to one modeling company, including a $50 application fee, $25 for an orientation program, and $105 for a photo session. Interestingly, the contract mandated a $200 penalty for rescheduling the photo session, certainly an exorbitant charge.

She had regrets almost immediately and called me for help. A road-show contract would have had a three-day cancellation option, but because it was a local company, a three-day option wasn't required. The company did agree to let her out of the deal and return her money after my staff and I interceded. But she was lucky; they could have kept the money and she would have had no recourse.

One legitimate charge you will have to pay if you want to become a model is for a photo portfolio. To get that, you'll have to go to a professional photographer and pay a fair amount of money. You shouldn't get a portfolio unless a legitimate modeling agency, one that is looking for actual talent, gives you an encouraging evaluation.

I've seen pictures supplied by my listeners who have been taken by these phony modeling agencies and there isn't a chance at all that these kids are going to be models. The problem is the parents absolutely believe their child is the most gorgeous creature who ever walked. Moms and Dads should believe their child is gorgeous, but by that definition, every child is gorgeous. Granted, there are certain "real-people" looks that modeling agencies want, but

for the most part, they want people who have a special look.

Once the modeling road shows have collected their cash, they leave town. It's impossible to go after them because generally they deliver what they promise, usually modeling lessons. They never promise any modeling work, so they haven't done anything illegal. Breaking hearts isn't against the law.

Telemarketing —

How many times have you sat down for dinner with your family and been interrupted by a telephone sales call?

Telemarketing has become a truly intrusive industry. If I get a piece of junk mail, I can choose to throw it away without even opening the envelope. But if a human being has me on the phone, I'll probably listen to the pitch to avoid being rude.

For many marketers, it's actually cheaper and more effective to have a human being call you than it is to send you a piece of junk mail. Since the postal service was cut loose from the federal budget and forced to balance its own budget, the cost of direct mail has skyrocketed. At the same time, because of deregulation, long-distance telephone costs have steadily decreased. That's why the nation's 300,000 telemarketers make 18 million calls each day, according to the American Telemarketing Association.

Telemarketing has divided itself into two different categories—legitimate businesses and charities, whose calls are annoying but not otherwise worrisome, and ripoff telemarketers, who are out to steal your money. You can avoid both by using an answering machine to screen your calls, particularly around the dinner hour, when telemarketers are most bothersome. With an answering machine, you can hear who's calling and pick up the receiver if it's a call you want to take. You can even tailor your message so friends and family will know what you're doing and telemarketers will know you're not interested.

There are some polite things you can say to a telemarketer to get off the hook quickly. If the person asks if it's convenient to talk, say no. Or you could say, "I'm sorry. This just isn't a convenient time for me to talk. Please call me later." Another way to be polite but not listen to the pitch is to say, "I'm sorry. I don't make buying decisions on the telephone. If you would like, you may send me some information."

I heard a very funny way to handle these annoyances on a television show. The actress who answered the telemarketing call said she was busy, but offered, "If you give me your home telephone number, I'll call you later." Predictably, the telemarketer declined to give his home phone number. "So, you don't like to be called at home?" the actress responded. "Well, now you know how I feel."

Dishonest telemarketers are more dangerous than annoying. Because mail and telephone lists are so easily obtained, illegitimate businesses have no trouble getting your name and number. Con artists have found boiler room operations (the name comes from the cheap office space they rent) to be the most efficient way to steal money. They call you from these boiler rooms and try to get you to buy a product or service. If anyone attempts to sell you something on the telephone and says you must make a decision right then, don't have anything to do with it. Ask phone solicitors to mail you information; otherwise, don't do business with them.

In the worst cases, the con artists get you to provide your checking account number or credit card number over the telephone, and use it to steal from your account. The most ironclad rule I can give you is, never give out your credit card number or your checking account number on the telephone, unless you make the phone call, because you will live to regret it.

I got a call from a fellow who was solicited for an $800 vacation trip on the telephone and, somewhat reluctantly, agreed to give out his credit card number. As soon as the call was over, he changed his mind and called back to say he wasn't interested. The telemarketer told him the $800 charge already had been posted to his account.

If you're calling a mail order company like Spiegel or Land's End, and you know it has an outstanding reputation, then it is okay to use your credit card. In fact, in that instance, using a credit card is preferable to sending a check. That way, if something goes wrong, you can get a refund from your credit card company under the chargeback process.

I urge you especially not to give out your checking account number because that's all criminal telemarketers need to withdraw money from your account. The hoodlums simply present your bank with a draft from your account and within 24 hours, they have your money. It's unbelievable what they do in these boiler rooms. They'll have a check encoding machine right there, and as soon as you give them your checking account number, they'll walk over to this machine and create a very professional-looking bank draft.

These schemes work in two ways. Sometimes they get your credit card or checking account number and immediately draw money out of your account. Other times, they'll sell you a product or service and get your account number for the purchase. You may receive the merchandise or you may not. But while you're distracted, they tap your account. By the time you realize what happened, they've left town.

Money can be taken from your account without your knowledge or consent because of the banking system's failure to have any meaningful safeguards. Banks are supposed to pay a draft only when it has been authorized in writing by you. But most banks have no internal security system in place to verify the accuracy of a draft. The bank is fully liable for any money it pays out in unauthorized bank drafts. But why should you have to sue your bank to force it to live up to the law? It's better for you to help prevent a crime by not giving out your checking account number.

Banks are failing miserably in their responsibility to prevent fraud. Often when you call the customer service center to report a fraud, they tell you that your rights to do a chargeback are explained on the back of your statement. Here's what's wrong with that. Let's say the charge posts on your next statement. You then write the bank and protest the charge. From the date of your original complaint, as many as 60 days pass before the bureaucrats at the bank send your protest through to the criminals' bank. By that time, the criminals have stolen a bunch of money. The banks look at this fraud as a cost of doing business. That's wrong and foolish. It gives an open invitation to the hoodlums.

The banks' security departments should consider it their responsibility to limit losses. The security departments should be notified whenever a consumer believes he or she has been hoodwinked by a criminal enterprise. The credit card issuers generally don't care because the criminals' bank ends up being stuck with the chargeback, not the consumer's bank. Instead of realizing that these losses hurt the whole industry, the banks tend to blame the customer for not being more careful and try to find some reason not to honor the chargeback.

I had a caller who had learned that his credit card was sent to someone else and used fraudulently to purchase $1,200 worth of goods. It seemed clear that this was part of a larger scheme to create phony credit cards. The bank agreed to remove the fraudulent charges from the caller's account but didn't want to be bothered to look into the scheme.

One more thing about telemarketing. If

- Tips on -
Telemarketing

● Use an answering machine to screen your calls, particularly around the dinner hour.

● If anyone attempts to sell you something on the telephone and says you must make a decision right then, don't fall for the pressure.

● Never give out your credit card number or your checking account number on the telephone, unless you make the phone call. With these numbers, con artists can steal from your accounts.

you work for a telemarketer, you should be concerned about whether you're going to get paid. I've heard case after case of people who have showed up for work to discover that the telemarketer had packed up and left, without paying them for their final week. So if you work for a telemarketer that doesn't seem legitimate, or you're thinking about such a job, understand that you, too, may lose.

Long-Distance Calling —

Be careful when you make a long-distance call from a pay phone, or any phone away from home. Public phones often are owned by alternative operator services (AOS), who can charge astronomical rates for a long-distance call.

You may think that because you use your AT&T, Sprint, or MCI credit card, you are using one of those systems. But you may not be—an AOS merely bills through those cards and can charge you as much as it wants. I've heard examples of charges that were six or seven times the rates of a legitimate long-distance company.

Keep an eye out for this ripoff when you use any public phone, but particularly those at gas stations, airports, universities, hotels, and hospitals. If you fall prey to an AOS, you could pay $1 a minute for a call, compared to 15 cents a minute on your own long-distance service. For a 15-minute call, that's $2.25 on your system versus $15 for a ripoff AOS.

Take some care when you use any phone away from home. Owners of public phones are now required to disclose who provides the long-distance service, both in writing and through a short audio message. If you don't recognize the name of the company that's posted, you can bypass it and go to the long-distance provider you wish to use. The easiest way to do that is, after you hear the dial tone, punch in an access code before you dial your number. Your long-distance company can provide the code. When you dial that code, you should hear a tone that lets you know you're connected through your long-distance carrier. Some pay phones are rigged to prevent you from reaching your long-distance carrier even if you dial the access code. In that case, you dial an 800 number to access your carrier. The codes and 800 numbers for the three most widely used services (AT&T, MCI, and Sprint) are in the Tips list for this section.

You have to deal with this annoyance because, after long distance was deregulated, phone owners saw this service as a giant profit center. People had no way of knowing when they used an AOS that they were going to pay more, or how much more, until after they got their bill. It is a complete ripoff. The last thing people think about when they're making a call from a hospital bed is which long-distance service they're using. But hospitals are among the worst offenders in this ripoff. There's been such a backlash of consumer complaints over long-distance ripoffs that many of the big hotels are going back to legitimate phone services.

Phone owners have tried hard to block access to the service you want to use, and they are not required by federal law to provide access through a five-digit code until 1997. I was in a fast-food restaurant in Dillon, Colorado, and tried to dial Sprint, but they had it set up to block both the access code and the 800 number. It was the first time I'd encountered that illegal practice. So I drove to another fast-food restaurant and used their pay phone. I didn't have to pay the ripoff rate there.

As far as home use of long-distance goes, there isn't that much difference in cost for people who don't make that many calls. If you're a typical home user with long-distance charges of $10 a month or less, don't even worry about which long-distance vendor you use. If you use long distance frequently, particularly if your bills are $20 a month or more, then you do need to pay attention to the cost. Choose a company that offers a long-distance plan that most suits your calling pattern.

I also recommend that you look to organizations and trade associations for potential discounts. Members of warehouse clubs are eligible for discounts. I get my discount from my insurance company, which has a special group volume rate on long distance. It offers a volume discount for the calls I make each month, plus another rebate for calls made by members of the insurance company group.

If you use a telephone calling card, consider shopping for one that offers a better deal than those from the major long-distance companies. The best deal I've found in a calling card is from American Travel Network in Buffalo, N.Y. With their card, you pay 17 cents a minute for calls from anywhere to any other location in the United States. There's no extra charge for each call, so you save the typical 80-cent-per-call setup charge you pay with calling cards from AT&T, MCI, or Sprint.

American Travel Network offers another fantastic product—an 800 number to your home with no monthly fee and no minimum charge per month. You pay a flat 18 cents a minute for any calls placed to your home. That's a great deal for people with children in college or at summer camp, for divorced parents who live apart from their children, and for traveling salespeople. With an 800 number, your child can call you, but won't have a phone credit card he or she can abuse.

Deals like these come and go, and you may find better bargains. These are the best I've found, and they should be your target to surpass.

Another kind of calling card to consider is the prepaid calling card, or phone debit card. With these, you pay in advance for the amount of calls you want to make, rather than the traditional system of calling first and paying later. Phone debit cards also allow you to bypass any of the ripoff long-distance services that may be in use, because you access your phone debit card by an 800 number. In addition, there's no per-call surcharge with phone debit cards.

The phone companies are marketing debit cards heavily, in part because they reduce the companies' potential for loss through unauthorized use of a card. If you lose a traditional phone calling card, the phone company is responsible for the cost of any unauthorized calls. If you lose a $20 phone debit card, you lose $20. So if you buy a phone debit card, treat it like cash.

Shop before you buy, because different companies charge very different rates. One company's debit card calls may cost 33 cents a minute, while another may be 25 cents a minute. Try to get one that charges 25 cents a minute or less.

Contests —

We've all read stories about people who have won state lotteries and whose lives have been dramatically changed. Who wouldn't want to win a huge sum of money or some valuable prize? Direct-mail contests play upon your desire to win, a ripoff that makes you think you've won when in reality they simply want to take your money.

When you receive a piece of mail saying you have won a prize, run the other way, because you're being set up for a ripoff. Almost always, a letter that talks about prizes or promotions is an attempt to get you to purchase some over-priced product in return for what appears to be a valuable prize but which is actually worthless.

One caller sent me a contest notice he got that proclaimed, "You have won the American Travelers Sweepstakes Giveaway!!" But what he had won was the right to call a 900 telephone number and pay $3.95 per minute to get a "Hawaiian Dream Vacation for Two" that wasn't worth anything.

In the typical prize offer, the postcard or letter will say you are guaranteed to win one of five prizes. A car is always on the list. Usually they'll

also list $10,000 in cash, a stereo system, a piece of jewelry, and a vacation. If it says you have definitely won one of these prizes, it will be the vacation. If it says you've won two prizes, it will be the vacation and the jewelry, both of which are absolutely worthless.

As in timeshare ripoffs, the vacation will be a certificate offer that has no value. What you usually get is a coupon good for "free" plane tickets—provided that you also buy nights at an expensive hotel from the same company. The jewelry tends to be costume jewelry of minimal value.

Ripoffs don't have to come with big price tags. In fact, when the ripoff is below $20, the company knows nobody is ever going to do anything about it. Although we hear more about ripoffs that cost several hundred dollars, the ripoffs of about $20 or less are the ones people get taken by the most.

One of my callers got a notice that said photographic equipment was being held in his name, and that he could pick it up for $13.78. Supposedly, it was a 35mm camera with "50mm optical lens, lens cap, tripod mount, film counter, and hot shoe synchronized for electronic flash." Actually, it was a flimsy, worthless piece of junk.

Sometimes on these prize offers, you'll see the actual odds of winning each prize. For the two least valuable prizes on the list, the chances of winning are 1 in 1 or 1 in 2. For the other prizes, such as the Lincoln-Continental Town Car, the odds will be 1 in 1,000,000 or 1 in 100,000.

Other times, they get around odds with careful wording. One of my favorites was in a letter a caller got from a firm called O'Brian & O'Brian saying they had decided "to consider giving" her a 1992 Cadillac Fleetwood. There was an order form she was supposed to use to select a style, upholstery, and color. All they wanted was an "optional" $38 check or money order. Not bad for a car, but in truth an absolute ripoff.

The purpose of these "contests" can be to take your money directly or get you to buy some sort of product. I had a call from a gentleman who received just such an offer and was asked to buy pens for his business. The pens were priced at 10 times their market value, and if he had done it, he would have thrown away thousands of dollars. Still, he was ready to buy. That's what's so interesting. When we put someone on the air who has received one of these postcards, they are dying for me to tell them that this offer is different from all the others we've heard about. They insist this one is different. People want to believe there's something legitimate about it even when common sense tells them it isn't right.

The rule of thumb here is what I call zero tolerance. If you receive a postcard or telephone call saying you have won a prize, the only answer you can give is that you are not interested. I guarantee that, if you participate, you will be taken 100 percent of the time.

Let's take the example of Publisher's Clearinghouse, which is a legitimate sweepstakes sponsor. If you fill out all the sweepstakes certificates, you might end up being independently wealthy. But one of the things that separates Publisher's Clearinghouse from illegitimate companies is that the latter require you to make a purchase to participate. You can enter the sweepstakes of Publisher's Clearinghouse without subscribing to any magazines, and subscribing does not improve your chances of winning. I think people probably assume buying a magazine will help or that their name won't be put in the drawing if they don't subscribe. But that doesn't happen. In fact, one winner of the company's $10 million sweepstakes said in a radio interview that she didn't order any magazines. They have to play this one straight and they do.

All you need to know is, do you have to pay to enter the contest? If you do, you know it's a con. If you can enter for free, then it's okay.

Charities —

How do you know when you're donating money to a legitimate charity? A lot of folks collect money for fake charities, and because criminals have become more clever and technology has improved, it's become harder to tell a true charity from a fake one. The frustrating thing for consumers and small businesses is that many of these groups have names that are very similar to those of real charities.

- Tips on - Charities

● If possible, pick a cause that you know personally so you can be sure your money will be spent efficiently.

● To help verify that a charity is legitimate, always request literature from the organization.

● Plan your charitable giving, making all decisions at one time each year.

● If you own a small business, decide how much to give and have a committee of employees hand out the money.

● Never give any money to door-to-door solicitors.

● Watch out for phony charities that telephone and ask you to buy a product at inflated prices.

● Never allow anyone to pressure you into giving to a charity.

Contact:
National Charities Information Bureau
19 Union Square West
New York, NY 10003
212-929-6300

A good approach is to pick a cause that you're involved in, such as helping the homeless or fighting cancer. That way you'll know it's something you believe in and whether your money is being efficiently spent. If you're not actually involved in a cause, but you still want to give money to charity, request literature from the organization. That's a good idea, whether you're solicited in person or on the phone.

Even better, don't make decisions about giving to charity in a haphazard manner. Instead, take one particular time per year and make all your charitable-giving decisions. Some people do that at the end of the year when they have a snapshot of their income tax picture. Then they can make charitable donations with an eye toward their personal finances. When you know how much you can give and make all your donations at one time, you're able to figure out exactly where you want your money to go. If you avoid just pulling out the checkbook or wallet, and instead plan your donations, you'll be much wiser in giving to worthwhile causes. You'll be giving your money in a way that comes from the heart by using your head first.

This works very well for small businesses. If you have your own small business, you no doubt get solicitation calls frequently from charities and quasi-charities such as civic organizations. If you require that they make a written request and explain that you review requests at a set time each year, many of those companies go away and you never hear from them again. The others that actually do write need to be patient and realize you'll consider them during the time of year that you make donations. I recommend that small companies have three employees sit on a committee to decide how the money is handed out. You as the owner of the business decide how much money is going to go to charity each year. Then empower the employees to hand it out.

A friend of mine did this in his business, and he said it was the greatest suggestion I ever had. He used to get bogged down with calls from people trying to convince him their cause was worthwhile. Now that requests have to be submitted in writing and they're only considered one week of the year, most of the hassle he went through has been eliminated.

My advice on door-to-door solicitors is never give them one cent. If you want to give money to that cause later on, that's fine. Ask for literature from the solicitor, but do not give one penny at the door. You need an opportunity for perspective, to think about whether this is a cause you really want to support. You're just never going to know whether that person coming to your door is legitimate.

When you're asked for contributions that amount to pocket change, 25 or 50 cents for the Shriners or Salvation Army, for example, just make your own best decision. Do what you feel like doing at the moment—you're not going to miss the quarter. I'm not as worried about people being taken in that way as much as I am the contributions of $5, $10, or more that con artists try to get you to give on impulse.

Ripoff charities that use the telephone definitely are something to avoid. What often happens with these pseudo-charities is you're supposed to make a purchase rather than a contribution. Such groups will call and say they're with the "Handicapped Veterans of America." They'll tell you they don't want charity but would like you to consider buying their "long-life light bulbs," which supposedly last eight times longer than normal light bulbs. If you buy, they'll tell you, you'll be helping the veterans stay off welfare. These types of pitches are thinly disguised con games. This is not the way to give to a cause. If you're interested in helping the disabled find employment, then give to a vocational or educational training program. Don't buy overpriced light bulbs.

There are organizations that report on the

performance of charities and can tell you exactly what portion of your money actually goes to those in need. The National Charities Information Bureau publishes a list that rates charities.

If you follow my system of determining how much to give each year to charity and use this list to help decide which charities will get that money, you'll feel really good about your system for giving money. You'll be confident that you've served society well with your dollars.

Interestingly, I don't get a lot of calls from people complaining that they've been ripped off by a charity. Perhaps people just write it off to experience. But what these ripoffs do is prevent people from giving to worthwhile charities. If somebody has been burned by a phony charity, she's reluctant to open the checkbook the next time for a legitimate cause.

In any case, never allow anyone—the solicitor, your employer—to pressure you to give to a charity. The money you give should come from your heart.

Advance-fee Loans —

It's sad whenever people lose money to con artists, but it's worse when desperate people are ripped off. That's why I think advance-fee loans are one of the worst scams of all time.

The ripoff artists are small companies that promise to find loans for individuals or businesses. They demand an up-front fee for the loan, then take the money and run. These phony loan companies destroy people who already are near the abyss, struggling either with a small business or on their own. The main targets of the advance-fee loan scams have been businesses, not individual consumers. Unable to get bank loans, many entrepreneurs can't buy inventory or handle the normal cost of operating the business.

A phony loan broker will approach these

> ## - Tips on -
> ## Advance-Fee
> ## Loans
>
> ● Never pay an up-front fee to get a loan. Con artists sucker desperate people into paying the fees, then run with the money and never deliver a loan.
>
> ● A fee that is paid at the time a loan check is cut, such as a bank's loan-origination fee, is not desirable but is acceptable.

scared business owners either by phone or mail or in person and say they may be able to help with the business's cash-flow problem. The broker promises to look for loan money in exchange for an up-front fee. The fee can run from $200 for an individual to $10,000 for a business, which is why businesses are targeted. That's where the savvy business owner or consumer should stop. Any advance fee for a loan is a giant red flag that should warn you to stay far, far away.

One of my callers got taken for $800 from an advance-fee loan company called the Association for Small Businesses and Entrepreneurs. The company had promised to find him a loan for $80,000 to expand his business and provide working capital, but once they had his $800, he never heard from them again.

Many banks charge loan-origination fees, but those are paid as the loan is made. When I took out a loan for my travel agency, for example, I paid a $50 origination fee at the time the check was cut. That's not desirable but it is acceptable. If you're paying a fee before you get any money, you're asking for trouble.

Usually with these scams, a company will target people from out of state. For example, Los Angeles scam artists will contact a small business in Chicago, or someone from Cincinnati will contact a business owner in Dallas.

I got a call from one woman whose tale is typical of this scam. The woman had paid the ripoff up-front fee and never got a loan. She went back and forth with them and they gave her excuse after excuse. Then she realized what had happened. One day she called and the phone had been disconnected.

Normally with these cons, they get your money up front, then give you fish stories about the loan. The whole concept is to delay you and other victims from complaining to the authorities until they can rip off enough people to collect a whole bunch of money. Then they go away. Usually they open up somewhere else with a new name but the same modus operandi.

I'm pleased that this ripoff is not victimizing as many people as it did a few years ago, largely because many states have outlawed this practice, making it more difficult for the con artists to run from state to state.

Those who can elude the authorities know that this con works because people are desperate. If you have a business that you've been building for most of your adult life, and you see that business going down the drain because of cash-flow problems, you're going to believe just about anything. That's why people are willing to pay such high up-front fees, because they're drowning and somebody's throwing them a rope. Unfortunately, it turns out nobody is holding the rope on the other end.

Credit Life Insurance —

Credit life and disability—also known as croak-and-choke insurance—is a terrible buy for you but a big moneymaker for those who sell it. Not surprisingly then, people who want you to buy credit life are almost everywhere you turn.

Your bank or mortgage company will try to rip you off with credit life and disability, as will the lender that finances your automobile. When you buy a major appliance, the store will also make an attempt to sell you croak and choke.

This is the most worthless product that has ever been dreamed up by the insurance industry. Croak and choke pays off your loan balance if you die or if you become disabled. But it protects the lender, not you. By buying it, you are paying to protect the lender.

People agree to buy credit life in the mistaken notion that they're protecting their loved ones from their debts. Let's say you have an outstanding mortgage balance of $50,000 and you're concerned that your family will lose the house if you die. The better thing to do is buy a term life insurance policy that pays your loved ones directly. Then they can decide how to use the money. It may be better for them to keep the mortgage in existence and use the insurance proceeds to pay for living expenses. But if you have this ripoff credit life and disability, all it does is pay off the loan on the home or car and your family has no choice in the matter. That money may have been better used for something else.

The cost of buying credit life insurance is far higher than the cost of legitimate life insurance, if you were to compare the cost per $1,000 of coverage. So by buying term life instead of credit life, you pay a lot less for the same amount of coverage. Or, if you spent the same amount on insurance, term life would provide a much larger death benefit.

For example, a 40-year-old could buy $100,000 worth of term life insurance for as little as $109 per year, or $1.09 per $1,000 of coverage. By contrast, I received a quote on credit life insurance of $660 a year (or $55 a month) to cover a mortgage of just $66,000. That's $10 per $1,000 of

— Tips on —
Credit Life
Insurance

- Credit life and disability insurance, also known as "croak and choke," is worthless.

- It protects the lender if you die or are disabled. It doesn't protect you.

- If you're concerned that your family will lose the house if you die, buy a term life insurance policy that pays your loved ones directly. They can decide how to use the money.

- The cost of buying credit life insurance is far higher than the cost of term life insurance.

coverage, or more than nine times the cost of term life.

To make matters worse, the balance of any installment loan will decline as the consumer makes payments, but the cost of credit life doesn't decline, making credit life even more expensive. If you pay $9 a month for credit life on a $15,000 car loan, you'll pay the same $9 a month a few years later, when you owe just $5,000 on the loan. You pay the same amount for less coverage.

Even after rate cuts in many states, Americans who purchase credit life insurance are being overcharged by more than $500 million each year, according to the National Insurance Consumer Organization and the Consumer Federation of America. Insurers have paid an average of just 44 cents for every dollar collected in premiums, according to a study conducted by those groups. In only three states—New York, Maine, and Vermont—are con-

sumers getting a respectable 60 cents in benefits for each premium dollar. To insure a $10,000, 12 percent loan in either of those three states, it costs $155 over 48 months, including finance charges. But in Louisiana, the worst offender in the study, the cost of credit life for the same loan would be an astronomical $673.

You may not even need to protect your family from a car note or any similar debt. If you die, and have a car note under your signature alone, then the responsibility for that car goes to your estate, not to your family. It will be up to the executor or the executrix of the estate to decide what to do. He or she can either give the vehicle back to the lender or make arrangements to continue payments on the loan and decide how to distribute the vehicle. If the vehicle was worth less than the amount still owed, the lender would have a right to make a claim on the estate for the difference. Turning the vehicle in could not hurt the credit rating of any member of your family.

Some people believe that they will not be approved for a loan unless they agree to buy credit life and disability, and lenders will lie to loan applicants to make them believe it. But legally that cannot be a determining factor in whether you get the loan.

Insurance is one of life's obligations. None of us wants to have insurance for anything, but we buy it because it's necessary. Because of our reluctance to deal with insurance, we tend to buy it hurriedly. We buy too little of some insurance and too much of other kinds. This chapter is designed to guide you painlessly through the things you need to know about insurance.

One piece of advice applies to all your insurance problems. Most states have a consumer help line in the insurance department to provide assistance. These folks are overwhelmed with calls, so get the name of the person you speak with and follow up with her so you're not forgotten. They're busy, but with a little effort they can get results. When dealing with an insurance claim of any kind, keep every letter and document every phone call and promise that the insurer makes.

Life Insurance —

We've probably all heard at least one awful joke about life insurance salespeople, usually about not wanting to get near one. I think people make fun of life insurance agents because we don't like to think about anything connected with death, be it wills, funerals, or insurance.

But many of us need to have life insurance to protect our loved ones from financial chaos in the event we die unexpectedly. Consider your own situation to see if life insurance makes sense for you, how much you need, and which type of life insurance would be best.

If your family would be unable to make the mortgage payments without your income, you need life insurance. But if you're single or married with no children, you might not. Some married people without children don't buy

life insurance, believing their spouse could make do without their income. That's really a personal family decision.

I've seen formula after formula to determine how much life insurance to buy, but none supplies a definitive answer. My rule of thumb is to buy insurance equal to six times your annual salary, before taxes. So if you make $30,000 a year, get $180,000 of life insurance, to replace your income for six years. If both spouses work, both should have life insurance to replace their own income. If either works at home, consider insurance to cover the cost of child care if the homemaker dies. Don't buy insurance on your children. A three-year-old doesn't earn a salary, so there's no need to replace his income.

There are two main types of life insurance: term life and whole life. Term life provides a payment only if you die. Whole life builds a cash value and serves as a savings vehicle.

Term life is like automobile insurance in the sense that you buy it year to year and if you stop paying, the coverage stops. Although term life premiums rise as you get older, the annual cost is far less than for whole life. For example, a 35-year-old nonsmoking woman could get $200,000 worth of term life for $180 a year. The same $200,000 death benefit on a whole life policy would cost $2,224 a year.

Whole life not only provides a death benefit but also serves as a kind of savings account. Part of each premium payment you make is set aside and accumulates value; eventually it can amount to a sizable sum. In addition, you can set up a whole life plan so that you pay premiums for 10 years, then stop, but you maintain coverage for the rest of your life. Because life insurance gets more expensive as you get older, having lifetime coverage has some appeal.

But whole life premiums are high and the policies contain high commissions, making it a favorite of insurance salespeople.

A 25-year-old man who doesn't smoke could buy $200,000 worth of term life insurance for as little as $200 a year, versus $1,886 a year for a whole life policy. But after 10 to 15 years or so, it's likely the whole life policy would be worth more than he'd have if he paid $200 a year for term life and invested the difference in the premiums, $1,686 a year, in mutual funds.

If you can afford the premiums and can dedicate yourself to making the payments for at least 15 years—no small feat—whole life is a better deal. Most of us don't fit either of those circumstances and are far better off with term insurance.

There are other types of life insurance, such as universal life and variable life. These 1980s concoctions are designed to mimic the characteristics of investments available through mutual funds or brokerage houses. I recommend that you explore these options only if you've already fully invested in tax-advantaged retirement plans such as a 401(k) plan or Individual Retirement Account.

If you decide to get term life insurance, the best way to buy is by calling an independent shopping service, such as the Massachusetts-based Insurance Information Inc., to get some quotes. For a fee, these companies will quote you the five lowest-cost policies for your age and sex in your state. You will be amazed how much you will save in premiums by using one of these services. But insist that the services include in their quotes only companies that are rated at least A+ by the A. M. Best Co. If you want to be extremely cautious, ask for quotes from companies that are rated A++, which means they are top-rated for financial stability and strength. A rating of AAA from Moody's Investor Service, Standard and Poor's, or Duff & Phelps is also advisable. The death benefit is of little use if the insurance company goes out of business first.

If you buy a whole life policy, don't cancel it and convert to term insurance or you'll lose a lot of money. Typically 30 to 50 percent of the premiums you pay in the first year of a whole life policy go to pay commissions and other expenses, including underwriting and set-up fees. A 50-year-old woman who pays $4,648 in premiums ($387 a month) in the first year of a whole life policy would lose most of that money to fees. Her policy would have a cash value of just $189 after one year. So canceling the policy after a year or a few years, before the policy started working for her, would be a terrible mistake. It takes 10 or more years, depending on the circumstances, before a whole life policy starts to produce returns equal to what you could earn if you bought term insurance and invested the rest of your money.

Older readers have to weigh a few different factors. Many times they buy insurance through age 65, then drop coverage. If that's your situation, it's okay to buy term insurance. But if your survivors would need replacement income in addition to what they would inherit, shop for insurance based on a need that goes into your 70s or beyond. In many cases, that would mean buying whole life, rather than term, while in your 50s. The cost of $200,000 worth of term life coverage for a 50-year-old nonsmoker would be quite high, at least $538 a year for a man, $420 a year for a woman. At age 70, the annual cost would be nearly $3,000 annually for a man, $1,600 annually for a woman. In those cases, it might make sense, at age 50, to buy a whole life policy that would cost $5,894 a year for a man, $4,648 a year for a woman. The whole life policies would build cash value and the premiums would never increase.

Whichever insurance you prefer, avoid buying more than one policy for any person. Every insurance policy you buy has fees hidden in it. So two $50,000 policies would cost more than one $100,000 policy. Some of the worst

- Tips on -
Life Insurance

● Consider your own situation to see if life insurance makes sense for you, how much you need, and which type of life insurance would be best. If your family would be unable to make the mortgage payments without your income, you need life insurance.

● Life insurance is meant to replace your income. My rule of thumb is to buy an amount equal to six times your annual salary.

● If both spouses work, both should have life insurance to replace their own income. Don't buy insurance on your children.

● There are two primary types of life insurance. Term coverage provides a payment only if you die. Whole life builds a cash value and serves as a savings vehicle.

● Buy whole life only if you can afford it and can dedicate yourself to making the premium payments for at least 15 years.

● If you decide to get term life insurance, the best way to buy is by calling an independent shopping service to get some quotes. You will be amazed how much you will save.

● Don't cancel a whole life policy. Once you've purchased it, it's best to keep it.

● Avoid buying more than one policy for any person. Every insurance policy you buy has fees hidden in it. So two $50,000 policies would cost more than one $100,000 policy.

Contact:

U.S. Office of Consumer Affairs
(For consumer and insurance questions, and to ask for a free copy of the *Consumer's Resource Handbook*)
202-634-4310

Insurance Information, Inc.
23 Route 134
South Dennis, MA 02660
1-800-472-5800

abuses I've seen concern poor people who've ended up with a dozen or more small life insurance policies when they could have bought one large policy for the same amount of money.

Disability Insurance —

Your odds of being disabled are far greater than your odds of dying during your working years,

yet few people buy disability insurance. People have an aversion to the idea they might be partially or completely disabled, so they don't protect themselves financially.

Imagine the powerlessness you would feel as the breadwinner for your family if you were disabled, could not work, and had no source of income. Your family wouldn't have any money to live. With disability insurance, you're buying a financial safety net for your family.

The cost of disability insurance is affected dramatically by some of the purchase decisions you make. Disability insurance that kicks in after 30 days or 60 days costs a lot more than coverage that takes effect six months after you are disabled. I recommend six months. That holds down the premium and still gives you good coverage. It's wise to have enough savings so that you can survive for six months if you lose your job or in case of any other emergency. If you don't have enough savings to cover a six-month loss of income, consider a disability policy that pays benefits after 90 days.

At the other end, people sometimes buy disability coverage that stays in effect for too short a period. Don't get a policy that will pay for only three or five years. Get a policy that covers you through age 65.

The next question is how much coverage to buy. I recommend you get an amount equal to 60 percent of your gross pay. That will give you about what you take home after taxes.

Look very closely in these policies at the definition of a disability. Because the Social Security Administration has such a strict definition of a disability, it pays benefits on just a third of its claims. If your policy has the same definition, you could lose twice. Social Security might determine that you're not disabled under their guidelines, and your insurer will make the same determination. The top insurers use this definition: "The insured is totally disabled when he (or she) is unable to perform the principal duties of his (or her) occupation."

The Social Security Administration pays Americans up to $1,300 a month if it accepts their claim of total disability. Private insurers offer disability policies that pay $2,000 a month in benefits, tax-free, for a cost of about $670 a year (with benefits taking effect after 90 days). It costs more if you're older or have a high-risk job, or if cost-of-living adjustments are built into the benefits.

- Tips on - Disability Insurance

● Your odds of being disabled are far greater than your odds of dying during your working years, so disability insurance is more important than life insurance.

● It's best to get a disability policy that begins making payments three or six months after you are disabled and continues until retirement.

● Buy coverage equal to 60 percent of your current pay before taxes.

● Get a policy that uses a more liberal definition of disability than the one used by the Social Security Administration.

I don't recommend buying either life or disability insurance through your employer. The coverage may cost more, and it won't go with you if you change jobs. Worse, if you develop a health condition that makes you unable to buy these types of insurance, you will have squandered the opportunity you had to buy them while you were healthy.

Health Insurance —

In spite of the country's inability to come up with a consensus on what changes to the health-care system are needed, health care remains a potential time bomb for you. Health-care costs continue to rise, with annual increases about double the general rate of inflation.

Everyone is feeling the cost pressure—insurance companies, employers, employees, and the government. If you ever wondered what ate the federal budget and caused the enormous budget deficits, medical costs have had more of an impact than any other single factor. Health care now makes up 14 percent of America's economy.

If you've dealt with a health insurer in the last few years, you know they have become experts at aggravating the health-care problem. Health insurers have violated every term of the social contract with their policyholders. They've adopted a policy called cost shifting, which is a euphemism for "We're not paying." Health insurers have a vast array of gimmicks they use to put the burden on you. As you go to make claims for health insurance, you'll learn to hate the term "usual and customary." That's a figure an insurer pulls out of thin air and says is the maximum it will pay for a certain procedure or visit. The quote is usually far below the actual cost of the procedure from any physician. It's a dishonest practice health insurers use to make you pay.

Let's say a doctor visit and test for high blood pressure cost $300. Under a traditional health plan, the insurer would pay 80 percent, or $240, and you would pay the remaining 20 percent, or $60. But let's say the insurer says the usual and customary cost of the visit and test in your area is $200. That makes their 80 percent $160 and leaves you responsible for the remaining $140 of the $300 charge. Insurers will not—in fact they're not allowed to—disclose to you what usual and customary costs are before you have the procedure done. So it's impossible for you to price shop or to know with any assurance that they're not going to break you financially.

Maybe overpaying by $80 seems like just an irritation. But what happens on a major surgery? I had one caller whose insurance company claimed the charges for an operation were $5,000 above usual and customary costs. The patient called seven different doctors and got the cost from each. None were anywhere near the insurance company's usual and customary figure. Some were even higher than what the patient's doctor had charged. As things stand today, the consumer has no protection from the cynical abuse and mean-spirited behavior of insurance companies.

The idea behind insurance should be taking care of the sick with the premiums paid by the healthy. When the sick get healthy, they contribute and provide for the newly sick. But the health insurers have turned that philosophy on its head and decided they will only insure people who are never sick. People with "pre-existing conditions" are being dumped by these cynical insurers onto the federal/state Medicaid system or local charity hospitals.

It doesn't appear that Congress is going to enact a major restructuring of the American health-care system, so corporate America has taken the redesign work upon its shoulders. As that trend grows, your employer is likely to have greater control over which doctors you see.

In the current environment, the best alternative is HMOs, or Health Maintenance Organizations. An HMO is a membership group you join through your employer, or join directly, in the case of some HMOs. In exchange for a monthly premium and a co-payment that's normally less than $15, all doctor service is provided, regardless of the cost to the HMO of providing that service. If you have to go into the hospital, your expenses are limited, often to less than $200, regardless of the cost. Prescriptions typically are $3 but can range from nothing to market price. You have peace of mind because there's no financial exposure beyond the cost of your premiums.

Although there's no financial exposure for you, there's a tradeoff that makes many people not like HMOs. You must go to their facilities, their doctors, and their designated hospitals. In exchange for financial security, you waive your freedom of choice. HMOs, being large

- Tips on - Health Insurance

● As things stand today, the consumer has no protection from the cynical abuse and mean-spirited behavior of insurance companies that are determined not to pay claims.

● In the current environment, the best alternative is HMOs, Health Maintenance Organizations. They can't kick you out, and, as a member, you'll have no serious financial exposure. However, service can be annoying and you can't choose your own doctors.

● Make your decisions for health coverage based on what exists where you live and work now, when you read this, not on what the future may hold.

bureaucratic organizations, vary tremendously in quality of customer service. With some HMOs, you have to fight to be seen by a doctor. You have to wait endlessly on the telephone to talk to him or her. And if you feel the need to see a specialist, you have to go through a gatekeeper personal physician first, before you can receive a referral. But an HMO truly shines when you come down with a major illness. Not only will you get care without having to worry about the cost; you won't have to worry that your rates will soar or that your coverage will be dropped. Even if I get terminal cancer, my HMO can't bounce me.

Another solution that many people like is a Preferred Provider Organization, or PPO. PPOs use a carrot-and-stick approach. Your out-of-pocket cost is minimal if you choose to see doctors and go to facilities on your approved list. But fees can be quite large if you go to someone not on the plan.

However, although a PPO has HMO-type features, it is much more like regular insurance than an HMO. Many of the same games people experience with regular health insurance occur with PPOs.

The types of health-care coverage available will continue to vary a lot by company and by region of the country. Make your decisions for health coverage based on what exists where you live and work now, when you read this, not on what the future may hold.

Car Insurance —

The most important thing to know about auto insurance is that you should carry it. It's been estimated that between 10 percent and 50 percent of all motorists in America don't have any auto insurance.

People don't carry insurance because of the cost. Premiums are high and many can't, or won't, pay. But not carrying insurance is a false savings. If you have no insurance and are involved in an accident, you could end up with no car and no money. Worse yet, if you have a car loan and you don't get insurance, the lender has the right to force-place insurance and may not tell you what they've done until the end of your loan. That means the lender buys insurance for your car, at a cost five or six times what you would normally pay. It's a giant profit center for the lenders and a rude surprise for many borrowers. I heard of one case in which the borrower thought he'd made his last car payment when a bank officer told him he still owed $2,600, plus interest, for not carrying insurance.

There are several types of auto insurance, and you should think about how much you need of each. Collision coverage takes care of damage to your car from an accident that is at least partially your fault. Normally you'll be responsi-

- Tips on -
Car Insurance

- It's very foolish not to carry auto insurance, yet perhaps 10 percent to 50 percent of all motorists don't have any.

- If you have a car loan and don't carry insurance, the lender may buy insurance for you at five or six times what you would normally pay.

- Collision coverage takes care of damage to your car from an accident that is all or partially your fault. Normally you'll be responsible for a deductible of $250 or $500, and your insurer pays the rest.

- Comprehensive coverage takes care of noncollision calamities, such as damage from a break-in, theft, or windshield cracking.

- Liability is the most important component of auto insurance and the one to which people pay the least amount of attention. It pays for damage to property and physical injury from an accident that is your fault.

- Medical coverage riders, available in some states, often duplicate your own health insurance. If you don't have health insurance, consider getting it rather than adding medical coverage to your automobile insurance.

ble for a deductible of $250 or $500, and your insurer pays the rest. You should maintain collision coverage in almost all circumstances.

If you have an older car that's worth very little, it may not make sense to carry collision coverage. The other exception is for people with substantial assets, who may prefer to self-insure an older car worth $6,000 or less. I had a car that was six years old and a borderline case of maintaining collision coverage. I was paying $262 a year for collision. If the car had been totaled in an accident, I would have received about $2,700 from my insurance company. It really wasn't worthwhile to keep the coverage.

One way to limit the cost of collision coverage is to carry a higher deductible. If you can afford to pay the first $500 in damage, you can save $50 to $100 a year by carrying a $500 deductible instead of a $250 deductible. Over 5 to 10 years, that's a substantial savings. Plus, you don't want to make a lot of small claims because insurers tend to count against you the number of claims, not the dollar cost to them. But don't carry a high deductible if you can't afford to pay that amount if you have an accident.

Comprehensive coverage takes care of noncollision calamities, such as damage from a break-in, theft of the car, windshield cracking, or damage from natural disasters such as flood or hurricane. Use the same rules of thumb for deductibles as you would for collision coverage.

Liability is the most important component of auto insurance and the one to which people pay the least amount of attention. This is the type of insurance many states require you to carry, because it pays for damage to property and physical injury from an accident that is your fault. Most people try to save money by buying the absolute minimum liability coverage, often $15,000 per person up to a maximum of $30,000 per accident. That's okay if you don't own anything. But if you have personal assets, you need to protect them against the threat of personal-injury lawsuits. If you injure somebody in an accident, that person's medical bills will exceed the minimum liability coverage very quickly. I recommend you carry coverage of $300,000 per accident, which sometimes has a limit of $100,000 per person. Better to have too much liability coverage than too little. It won't cost you much more.

If you are very wealthy, get an umbrella policy. It shields you from liability in almost every phase of your life. Umbrella coverage, which is sold in amounts of $1 million, $2 million, and above, supplements your auto and homeowners liability coverage. You can buy umbrella coverage around the country for $100 to $350 a year, not a big cost because the potential risk of a catastrophic liability claim against you is very small.

The last decision to make about insurance is a medical coverage rider, available in some states. I'm opposed to such riders, because they often duplicate your own health insurance. If you don't have health insurance, I would consider getting it rather than adding medical coverage to your automobile insurance. Agents will try to sell this by saying it will protect a passenger in your car. But here's my answer to that. If it's a friend, they'll claim against their health insurance. If it isn't a friend, they'll sue you against your liability. You're covered in either case.

There are two important considerations in picking an auto insurer. One is the premium cost. The other is the quality of service. On the issue of premium, first decide what coverages you want in the three major areas—collision, comprehensive, and liability. Then it's a fairly easy matter to call insurers and get quotes. The quotes vary tremendously from company to company, so don't take the first offer.

There's an even larger difference in customer service, from the best insurers to the worst. Ask friends, relatives, and coworkers what companies they use and how they've handled claims. Another good source is *Consumer Reports* magazine, which occasionally surveys

customers to determine service quality. In the Cars chapter of this book, the section on auto accidents lists the top 10 insurers as rated by *Consumer Reports*. They're ranked by service quality.

Homeowners Insurance —

Shop for homeowners insurance the same way you buy other kinds of insurance. Figure out what limits you want and what value you need to insure, then call several insurers for quotes. Sometimes you'll get a better deal if you buy your homeowners and auto insurance from the same company. If you're happy with your auto insurer, get a quote from your agent and ask about a multi-line discount.

Make sure you get a quote for insurance that would pay to replace your belongings, rather than pay you based on their depreciated value. There's a big difference. If your television is stolen, replacement coverage would allow you to buy another, instead of giving you half of what you paid for it three years ago.

Ask your agent what documentation you need to substantiate a claim, in case of theft or fire. The insurer makes big money over the years from you in premium payments. You want to make sure that if you have a claim, you will be compensated for your loss. My favorite method of documenting what you own is to use a video camera. If you don't have one, borrow one from a friend. Walk through your house, room by room, and shoot video of your possessions. As you're taping, talk about each item, when you bought it and, if you remember, how much you paid. Make sure to get the electronics, the furniture and anything else you consider valuable. If you have an expensive wardrobe, pan your closet and talk about how many suits or dresses you have. If you have a fire or other loss, you'll be reimbursed for each item. So you'll need to indicate that you have 8 suits and 15 pairs of underwear. There are limits in some basic policies on jewelry. If you have an individual

- Tips on - Homeowners Insurance

● Figure out what limits you want on your homeowners insurance, and what value you need to insure, then call several insurers for quotes.

● Sometimes you'll get a better deal if you buy your homeowners and auto insurance from the same company.

● Make sure you get a quote for insurance that would pay to replace your belongings, rather than pay you based on their depreciated value.

● Ask your agent what documentation you need to substantiate a claim, in case of theft or fire. I think it's easiest to videotape your house and describe your possessions.

● Carry enough liability coverage to protect you against a lawsuit if someone gets hurt on your property.

piece worth more than $2,000, or several pieces collectively worth more than $5,000, you may need to purchase additional coverage.

It's helpful to make a new video once a year, because you may buy new things. When you're done, store the tape somewhere safe— not in your house. If there's a fire, a melted tape won't do you any good.

If you don't like the idea of using video, use a still camera and take pictures of each room and each item of value. Put the pictures in a photo album with a written description of everything, or if you're lazy like me, take a cassette recorder and make an audio description to go with the pictures. Keeping receipts of your purchases is ideal, but the number of us who keep receipts is minuscule.

As with auto insurance, liability coverage is an important consideration in your homeowners policy. You need to have enough liability coverage to protect your assets in case someone gets hurt on your property, or if your dog bites someone. Many policies offer minimum liability coverage of $100,000, but it costs only about $20 more for $300,000 in coverage.

If an incident like this happens, it's a good idea to express your concern about the injured person and to say you're sorry that it happened. Just be careful not to admit fault. Sometimes people are sued just because they've hurt the injured person's feelings. A lot of lawsuits could be prevented just through that simple act of human decency.

I have a nephew in Washington, D.C., who lived next door to a police officer and the officer's police dog. The dog got loose one day and badly bit my nephew. He needed some stitches and some minor plastic surgery and ran up a few thousand dollars in medical bills. His mother never would have sued if someone with the police department had shown some common courtesy. When nobody did, she sued and won $17,000.

I was in the travel business for six years and was fortunate to do very well in it. I ended up with a chain of travel agencies, which I sold in 1987. Since I got into the business, I've traveled constantly. I've visited every continent in the world, except for Antarctica. (My visit to the Arctic Circle, the flip side, will easily suffice.)

Traveling around the world is incredible fun, I've found, but it has also taught me something—the importance of saving money. Many people around the globe, I've observed in my travels, make things last; they don't have to have the latest of everything, unlike many in our consumption-oriented society. I've also seen a lot of people in poor countries who were very happy despite their lack of material things.

Because of economic factors, many people in recent years have chosen to travel less. But in many cases, unless we're on an austere family budget, we choose to spend money on things that are important to us. Sometimes that includes travel and sometimes it doesn't. Travel does not have to be hugely expensive. Many people learned during the deregulation of the airline industry that you can find bargains in travel if you go at the right time.

I want readers to know that travel is within their reach. Travel does not mean you have to eat in expensive restaurants or stay in expensive hotels. It can be very reasonable and affordable if you combine a good price on an airline ticket with affordably priced lodging and spend the rest of your time without drastically changing your lifestyle from what it would be at home. If you don't eat in $50-a-person restaurants at home, don't eat in them on the road, unless that's a lot of the joy you get from traveling. You don't even have to eat out a lot. In Europe, I'll eat breakfast at the bed and breakfast, which is included in the price of the room. I'll go to a supermarket and get pic-

nic items and, at lunch time, go out and have a picnic in a park. It doesn't have to be expensive.

Because of the advent of discount airlines, which are spreading like wildfire across the United States, there's no longer a direct relationship between the distance you fly and the price of a ticket. As a result, price-oriented travelers are looking closely at the cities offered by the discount airlines before choosing their destinations.

In this chapter I'll tell you more about how to travel for less, what hazards to avoid, how to save on hotels and car rentals, and where to visit some great places.

Saving Money on Travel —

If price is your key motivator in buying travel, certain strategies work no matter what's going on with the economy and no matter what is your special interest.

The best strategy is to do the reverse of what everyone else does. Obviously if you go to the beach Christmas week, you will pay the highest possible prices of the year. But believe it or not, if you go from December 1 to December 15, you'll pay a fraction of the cost, even though you're still aiming for a warm-weather getaway. One of the key secrets to unlocking savings in travel is to know the calendar. Ideally, you go to a place at a time when the weather is right and the rates, because of a quirk of the calendar, are especially low. If you're willing to live with less-than-ideal conditions, you'll go during the opposite season, such as a visit to south Florida in the summer.

Europe is a perfect example. From November 1 through March 31, the very lowest rates are offered on airfare to Europe. On the other hand, summertime is very expensive. It would not be unusual for a summertime ticket to Europe to cost 2 1/2 times the winter equivalent of the same seat. Prices to the Caribbean work similarly, although the swings in price are not as extreme. Rates from April 15 through December 15 usually are about 30 percent below the prices from December 15 through April 15. I love going to the Caribbean or Florida during the off-season or summer. Some people worry about hurricanes, but the chances are very small, even during hurricane season, of you being in the wrong place at the wrong time. With modern forecasting technology, seldom could you be in any danger. The greater threat is of having your vacation cut short or canceled by bad weather.

You can also use the calendar to save on your hotel bill. I've taken combined vacations to San Francisco and Lake Tahoe, Nevada, and paid bargain rates at hotels in both cities. In an urban area such as San Francisco, hotel rates are lowest on weekends, when volume from business travelers is minimal. In a resort area, it's just the opposite, with the best deals available during the week. So I visit both cities during the same trip and spend the weekend in San Francisco and the rest of the week skiing in the mountains. In Florida, it's not unusual for the hotels to give you a bonus night free if you arrive Sunday through Thursday and spend several nights. The highest rates are Friday and Saturday nights.

The key to saving money on travel is flexibility. The ultimate bargain hunters, people like me, will go anywhere as long as it's a deal. I went from Atlanta to Rochester, New York, once because it was $69 round trip. I went to Kansas City for the same price. I went to Washington, D.C., on an introductory special, for $20 round trip. I had no reason to go, but went for two days just because of the price.

Most people aren't as flexible or bargain oriented as I am. But you can save a lot of money if you're willing to be flexible about the dates you travel and the airports you fly out of or into. Be willing to travel on a Saturday, rather than a Friday, for example. Fly into Newark airport in New Jersey instead of LaGuardia airport in New York. Flying to cities in Texas and the Southwest often is far cheaper if you leave from Little Rock, Arkansas, rather than Memphis, Tennessee. So people drive from Memphis to Little Rock to catch those flights. But it works the opposite way for flights to many cities in Florida, the South and the East, which are much cheaper out of Memphis than Little Rock. So travelers drive from Little Rock to Memphis for those deals.

All fare competition is local, and you increase your chances of getting a bargain if you look at alternate cities and airports. But be careful, because things change quickly. At one time, flights to Southern California were much cheaper from Oakland than from San Francisco, which is just across the Bay. But now the fares are about equal.

Another thing that has always amused me is how desperately people want nonstop flights. So often you'll find a moderate to huge discount by taking a connecting flight. I think it's worthwhile spending two hours of your time to get a much better deal on a connecting flight.

Be flexible, too, about the airline you use, and don't be fixated on frequent flier miles. A thousand frequent flier miles is worth about $10 in free travel. If you're going on a 2,000-mile round trip, that's $20 in frequent flier value. If you can get a fare $30 cheaper by flying on a different airline, do it.

While I don't think you should overvalue frequent flier miles, I do recommend that you join every airline's frequent flier program, even if you fly infrequently. There's no cost to do so and it takes no more than three minutes. All you do is call the airline reservations office in your city and they will immediately enroll you. By joining the frequent flier programs, you can take advantage of off-the-books discounts, a great way to save money on air travel. Each airline mails special offers to members of its frequent flier program, so by joining, you can take advantage of these private sales. Continental traditionally has been the most aggressive in this, offering special fares to all points of the globe. Northwest has been most aggressive with certificate offers, giving you special rates on domestic tickets or special rates for companions who fly with you.

Airlines and private organizations have established travel clubs that provide you with special rates in return for a one-time membership fee or an annual fee. I'm unhappy to report that most such clubs are not a real value. However, there are several that do seem to offer a good deal. TWA has a club that operates in 60 cities around the country. You pay a membership fee of $50 and receive access to a hotline that gives you an ever-changing menu of discount flights. Prices are about 30 percent less than the lowest fare normally available between the two cities. If I'm considering a club and I'm not sure of the total benefit, I look to see what immediate benefit there is to joining. It's a plus if there's a certificate or voucher that gives me a discount for a service I already use, such as an airline discount or a free day of car rental. If I can make back the membership fee and more just by joining, that's an automatic yes, even if I never use any other service of the travel club.

A good way to save on hotel rates is to buy a half-price hotel program. There's been a proliferation of these programs in the last two years. You get a listing of hotels around the United States or, in some cases, the world, that offer rooms at half the retail price, known as rack rate. There are even hotel discount books for Europe that provide half-price for moderate to high-end hotels.

I'm a member of four such programs and have had great success using them. When I travel to, say, San Diego, I look to see what each program has there and whether the rate is being honored at the time I want to travel. Only a travel nut like me would own four of them. Most people would buy one. Each varies tremendous-

- Tips on - Saving Money on Travel

● The best way to save money on travel is to do the reverse of what others do. Buy airfare and hotel rooms during off-peak seasons, when rates are lower. Plan vacations so you can take advantage of weekend specials in urban areas and mid-week specials in resort areas.

● Be flexible about the dates you travel and the airports you fly out of or into.

● Consider taking trips that involve connecting flights. They're cheaper and often don't take much longer.

● Be flexible, too, about the airline you use, and don't be fixated on frequent flier miles. A thousand frequent flier miles is worth only about $10 in free travel.

● Join every airline's frequent flier program, even if you fly infrequently. It's easy, costs nothing, and allows you to receive mailings that advertise private sale fares.

● Most travel clubs are of mediocre value, but some can provide good savings. Look at them carefully.

● You can save on hotel rates by buying a half-price hotel program. You can buy them from $15 to $50.

ly in price. Sometimes they're offered for sale in combination with something else. You might get a hotel membership for $15, instead of $50, when you buy a $10 coupon book for dining and entertainment. So you would get both for $25.

Sometimes you get the added bonus in hotel coupon books for air travel or car rentals. If you find a book that has an air travel coupon you'll definitely use, and the coupon's value exceeds the cost of the hotel program, buy it. Any value you get out of the hotel program is a bonus.

No list of hotel discount programs is complete, because new ones enter the market all the time. A few I recommend are: ITC 50 (404-813-9895), America at 50 Percent Discount (410-882-9726), Entertainment National Hotel Directory, and Entertainment Europe (both at 1-800-285-5525).

Here's a key consumer warning about hotel programs. Half-price off the retail rate may not be the best rate available at a hotel. Always ask what weekend specials or other discount rates may be available. If the rate is lower than half the retail rate, most travel programs will give you an extra 10 percent off. Let's say the retail rate is $100. The discount program would give you the room for $50, but there might be a weekend special rate of $39. You would get 10 percent off the $39, driving your rate down to $35.

Opportunities and Hazards —

Airlines routinely overbook flights, because of the frequency of no-shows. That creates a big opportunity for people who are flexible. Every time I show up at a gate and I see a big crowd, I go straight to the podium and volunteer to give up my seat if they're overbooked. It works like a charm, because volunteers are placed on the list in the order they give their names. If you're picked, ask to fly out on your airline's next flight or the next flight on any other air-

line, whichever is sooner. Always remember to ask when the next flight is, so you'll know if you can live with the delay. For your trouble, you usually will get a voucher for a free airline ticket, good for one year to anywhere in the continental United States. With some airlines, the voucher is good for a free flight anywhere in North America. I earn about three free tickets a year and use them during holiday periods, when airfares may be extra high or seats may be hard to find.

Sometimes an airline will be oversold and will not have enough volunteers. That triggers a game of musical chairs that leaves someone without a seat. There are very specific rules governing what you get for being involuntarily denied a seat. For details, go to the airline ticket counter and ask to see the contract of carriage.

If you're changing planes and miss your connection, and find yourself stranded somewhere, don't panic and don't allow it to ruin your day or your trip. If I get stranded, I'll take the free shuttle to an airport hotel and eat there, or check my bag in a locker and go jogging.

In addition to putting you on the next flight, the airline usually will compensate you if you're stranded—but don't take just any offer. If you get stranded overnight, don't accept anything less than an airline-provided hotel room, plus meal vouchers and long-distance calls to alert others where you are. For a minor delay, up to four hours, ask for a free meal and free long distance at the airport terminal. Be nice to the gate agent, even if you don't feel like it, because agents have a lot of power.

If your bags are lost, file a claim immediately with the airline baggage service desk. Don't leave the airport without filing a claim. Many airlines have extremely hostile policies about lost baggage claims. While it's still fresh in your mind, try to detail every item that was in your bag and keep a copy of the claim.

On a domestic flight, the airlines have a

maximum liability of $1,250 per passenger for lost bags. Do not put any jewelry, electronics, rare manuscripts, breakable items, cash, or prescription medicines in checked baggage. The airlines don't have to reimburse you fully for their loss, plus they invite theft. Put these items in your carry-on baggage. International rules are even more restrictive. Payments made for lost or stolen items are minimal, based on a rate of $9.07 per pound of checked baggage.

My staff and I had a terrible lost-baggage case with the commuter carrier Atlantic Southeast Airlines, in which the caller left the airport without filing his claim and didn't do so for two or three days. The airline refused the claim, saying the passenger's delay in filing had made it impossible for them to locate the luggage. He lost $8,000 worth of Swiss-made precision tools. The airline's maximum liability would have been only $1,250 anyway, but he got nothing.

You can purchase excess valuation insurance, which costs about $1 per $100 of declared value. But I follow the simplest rule of all. I don't trust the airlines with my luggage. I have a carry-on bag on wheels and if I can't carry it on, I don't take it. That goes even for a long trip. If they have laundries here, they have laundries where I'm headed.

Hotel overbookings are another big travel hazard. Even if you have a reservation, it's possible the hotel won't have any rooms. In industry lingo, that makes you a "walk." If a hotel walks you, they should pay for a free night for you at an equivalent property, and move you back the next night. If you arrive by cab, they should transport you to the alternate hotel or pay for your cab there. The hotel also should allow you to call business associates or family, at no charge, and give them your new location.

You have a right to be happy with the hotel, even if your reservation is guaranteed pre-

- Tips on - Opportunities and Hazards

● By volunteering to give up your seat on an overbooked flight, you usually get a free ticket for travel anywhere in the continental United States.

● If you miss a connecting flight and are stranded, ask the airline to provide a free meal and long-distance calling. If you're stranded overnight, ask for a free hotel room, meals and long-distance calls.

● If your bags are lost, file a claim at the airline's baggage service desk before you leave the airport.

● Be careful what you put in checked baggage. On a domestic flight, the airlines have a maximum liability of $1,250 per passenger for lost bags. On international flights, you get just $9.07 per pound of checked baggage.

● If a hotel sends you away despite a reservation, the hotel should pay for a free night at an equivalent property, and move you back the next night.

● If you check into a hotel and it's dirty or dumpy—or if you feel unsafe there—go back to the desk immediately and ask for your money back.

● To check on the quality of a hotel, ask a travel agent or get the "Mobil Travel Guide." Certain brands of hotel are consistently outstanding, including Courtyard by Marriott, La Quinta, Fairfield Inn, Sleep Inn, and Hampton Inn.

paid. If you check into a hotel and it's dirty or dumpy—or if you feel unsafe there—go back to the desk immediately and tell the clerk the hotel is unacceptable to you and you're going to leave. It's traditional in the hotel industry to release you from your obligation if you are unhappy or afraid.

People are more likely to be unhappy with hotels when they rely on the brand name alone to choose. There are certain brand names that don't maintain consistent quality. One hotel might be nice, but another old and in disrepair. To learn if a particular hotel is good, have your travel agent check in the "Travel Planner," a publication that rates hotels from one to five stars. Consumers can also buy the "Mobil Travel Guide," which does the same thing. Members of the Automobile Association of America (AAA) should rely on the recommendations of the company's tour books. I prefer to stay at hotels that rate two stars or above in the Mobil Travel Guide or three diamonds or better in the AAA books. Hotels are rated in all price ranges, so it's useful for car trips as well as resort vacations.

There are certain brand names of hotels that deserve mention for the consistent quality of their product from city to city. Among them are Courtyard by Marriott, La Quinta, Fairfield Inn, Sleep Inn, and Hampton Inn.

Some hotels have affinity programs that are useful. You pay a nominal fee to join and in return get discounts and sometimes amenities packages, such as free local phone calls or free faxes. These programs are worthwhile only if you travel several times a year.

Consolidator Fares —

Most airfares for international travel continue to be influenced or controlled by agreements between governments. So your ticket to France or Greece will carry an artificially high price.

As a result of such controls, a group of entrepreneurs called consolidators developed a free-market outlet for international fares. When tickets on an international flight aren't selling well at the official price, the airlines sell them at a discount to consolidators, who then resell them, through travel agents, to bargain hunters. Consolidators are high-volume ticket brokers who act as intermediaries between the airlines and the travel agents, although some consolidators also sell directly to the public.

Consolidators promise in advance to sell a percentage of the airlines' tickets, in exchange for a lower price. The more tickets they sell, the better price they can negotiate from the airline. So they want to move as many tickets as possible.

If ticket sales are soft, airlines also may lower prices to consolidators as the departure date approaches. So if you're flying to England in November, the consolidator likely will quote you a higher price in July than if you wait until October to buy your ticket. A few weeks before takeoff, the airline has a better feel for how many tickets it is going to have to dump. While airlines normally will advertise a sale to perk up slow-selling domestic tickets, they discount international fares privately through consolidators.

Consolidators started out serving the ethnic market, offering deals to immigrants who came to this country from nations such as India. Airfares between the United States and India were very high, so Indian entrepreneurs saw an opportunity to make money by selling off-price tickets to Indians. Korean consolidators emerged to serve growing Korean communities in areas such as Los Angeles. And other consolidators have followed the growth of large ethnic communities throughout America.

Consolidator fares have been more available to the public in the 1990s, as the concept of competitively priced airfares has spread around the world. Even though governments have been slow to recognize the value of increasing demand for tickets by cutting prices, the airlines have accepted the realities of price competition.

Consolidators vary widely in quality and professional ethics, so it's important to follow some key steps when you buy consolidator tickets. First, have your travel agent check the published fare for your destination. Sometimes the consolidator fare isn't that great a deal. Next, ask the travel agent to check with her preferred consolidators to see what's available. If you don't like the quote the travel agent gives you on a consolidator ticket, buy a Sunday newspaper and look for advertisements from consolidators in the travel section. Point the ads out to your travel agent, and see if she can find you a better deal than she first quoted. Ads can be misleading, however.

It's very important to buy consolidator tickets from a travel agent or a consolidator in your city. Always pay by credit card, so you are protected in case the consolidator doesn't deliver the ticket. If you pay by check or cash to an out-of-town consolidator, you're in the worst possible position if the company takes your money and doesn't send you a ticket. We got a call recently from a consumer who sent $5,300 to a consolidator a thousand miles away and never got his tickets. If you use a credit card and that happens, you can get a refund easily from your credit card company. If not, you could lose your money.

Make sure to tell your travel agent if you would prefer not to fly on certain airlines. Sometimes the very best consolidator rates will be on an airline you've never heard of, from a country you don't know much about. I'm not kidding. You'll find the best deals to London from New York to London on third-world airlines. Quite often to Asia, the cheapest tickets will be on the airline of a third-world Asian country, rather than one of the first-tier Asian airlines. The irony is that Asia has the world's two best airlines, Singapore Airlines and Cathay Pacific, as well as some of the most unreliable air-

- Tips on - Consolidator Fares

● Consolidators are high-volume ticket brokers who sell international airfares for an average of 20 percent less than the regular price.

● The best consolidator fares often are available a few weeks before your departure date and on less well-known airlines.

● Always buy consolidator tickets from a travel agent or consolidator in your city, and always use a credit card to pay for your tickets.

● Ask your travel agent to check the published fare for your destination, and the consolidator fares that she can find. You can also check the travel section of your Sunday newspaper for consolidator advertisements.

● Tell your travel agent if you would prefer not to fly on certain airlines. Sometimes the best consolidator rates will be on obscure airlines

lines in the world. You need to know the airline as well as the price.

Despite some potential hazards, everybody who flies internationally should at least compare the cost of consolidator tickets to a published airfare. When my family took a vacation in Asia in 1994, six of us used free tickets from frequent flyer miles. But my brother Neal used a consolidator ticket. He flew with us on the same plane; the only difference was he saved 30 percent on the cost of his fare.

Normally you'll save about 20 percent on the cost of an international ticket by buying a consolidator fare, depending on how flexible you are about airline and schedule. Sometimes it can be as much as 55 percent, but other times the savings are meaningless. Check the price and recheck the price. Tickets, like almost all airline tickets, are nonrefundable.

Car Rentals —

I get more complaints about car rentals than about any other phase of travel. It's because people don't rent cars very often and are sometimes confused by the transaction at the car rental counter.

Most upsetting is the array of choices car renters are hit with for insurance-type products. When you rent a car, you'll often get a very heavy-handed pitch for collision damage waiver, or CDW, also known by the codes LDW or PDW. This is a ripoff fee whose sole purpose is to build profits for the car rental company. By paying it, you supposedly waive your responsibility in the event the car is damaged or destroyed in an accident. Nationwide, the fee averages $12 a day. On an annual basis, that's more than $4,000, a lot more than you pay for total coverage on your personal automobile. Some states have banned collision damage waiver, while other states have put caps on it to end the abuses.

My advice is to reject collision damage waiver, which is your option, under almost all circumstances. Check with your auto insurer before you go on a trip, because many times your own policy will cover you for temporary use of a rental car. Another way to avoid CDW is to use a credit card, such as Gold Visa or Gold MasterCard, Diners Club, certain American Express cards, or the premium Discover Card. They will provide collision coverage if you use their card to rent the car. If you've dropped collision coverage on your personal automobile, you should use one of these pre-

mium credit cards or see if you can purchase a short-term rider from your insurer. The regular Discover Card has an option that allows you to buy coverage for $6.95 per rental. Just contact Discover before you rent and they will automatically add the charge to your bill. For a one-week rental, paying $6.95 is a much better deal than paying $84 for CDW.

Whether you take the collision damage waiver or not, check the rental car carefully before you leave the rental lot. Quite often I'll see a dented fender or a broken tail light after looking closely at a rental car. At night, I pull the car up underneath a light to check it. If you see any damage on your rental car, have an official of the company note it on the rental contract before you leave. If you don't, you'll probably have to pay for the repair.

I had a caller whose rental company claimed his wife had broken an outside mirror and wanted him to pay $371 for it, an outrageous price even if she had broken it. My staff called the company and got him out of that.

The second type of insurance you'll normally be offered is excess liability coverage. Again, check with your own automobile or homeowners insurance provider, because either or both may provide you with such coverage, making it unnecessary to purchase it from the car rental company. The cost is about $7 a day.

There are two other optional insurance coverages you'll see quite often on a car rental contract. Personal effects coverage, or PEC, is to cover you against theft of your possessions from the rental car. Normally your homeowners or renters insurance will cover that. Personal injury protection covers some of your medical bills if you're injured in an accident. This coverage is completely unnecessary if you already have health insurance.

I have some specific strategies for saving money on a car rental. First, the best place to shop, hands down, is through your travel agent. Travel agents have shopper screens on their computers that allow them to see the rates offered by all car rental companies at one time. From there it's very simple to tell who has the best deal.

My second trick is to rent the smallest car available at the cheapest rate. I always rent the smallest car, but I get a larger car for the same price 80 percent of the time. Car rental companies load their fleets with larger cars, so they rarely have the smaller car you ordered when you show up. When you book a small car, the rental company may try to sell you up to a larger car, at a higher cost, when you get to the counter. Just remember that four out of five times you'll get the larger car without paying for it. You have me to blame if you end up with five people stuffed into a subcompact because all they had left is the small car. But I've never heard of that happening.

Some rental companies will offer you fuel options. You can pick the car up with a full tank and drop it off with a full tank. Or pick it up full and bring it back empty. The only option to choose is taking it out full and bringing it back full. Just stop at a service station on your way back to the rental lot and fill the tank. If you forget, they'll charge you two to four times the normal retail price for gas.

Don't fool with any of the other options that require a calculator and a mathematics degree. Any of the plans that require you to bring the car back with an empty tank are dangerous. With crime so prevalent, it's not smart for you to play it cute and run out of gas trying to coast in on fumes.

If I rent on a weekend, I usually find the best rates with one of the major on-airport rental companies, such as Hertz, Avis, National, and Budget, which rely almost exclusively on business travelers. There's little business travel on weekends, and those companies have huge fleets they need to push into the marketplace, so they discount heavily.

- Tips on - Car Rentals

● When you rent a car, don't accept the insurance options the company wants you to buy. Check with your own auto insurance agent to see if you're covered under your policy, or use a premium credit card that offers travel insurance.

● Check the rental car carefully before you leave the rental lot. If you see any damage, have an official of the company note it on the rental contract before you leave.

● For the best deals, shop for a rental car through your travel agent.

● Rent the smallest car available at the cheapest rate. Four out of five times, the rental company won't have the small car you ordered and will have to give you a larger car at the small-car price.

● Always take the car out with a full tank of gasoline and return it with a full tank.

● If you're renting for five days or more, a weekly rental will provide a large discount.

If your rental is for weekdays, you'll usually pay a high price per day with on-airport rental companies, and find much better prices with "second-tier" companies. The largest second-tier renters are Thrifty and Alamo. There is a substantial number of third-tier renters in major markets, but the quality of service varies tremendously.

If you're renting for five days or more, a weekly rental will provide a large discount. A seven-day rental usually costs less than a three-day rental. That's because car rental companies have high costs for processing a rental. With a short-term rental, you're paying mostly for the cost of the people needed to prepare the car for rental and accept it for return. If you begin Thursday at noon and return the car usually by the same time Monday, you're eligible for weekend rates that are up to 70 percent below weekday rates.

Where to Buy Travel —

If you don't take vacations often, you're more likely to be conned by scam operators who pretend to be in the travel industry. These organizations use many different techniques in their attempts to steal your money, the most common being a prize drawing offering a free vacation to the winner. No one ever wins the trip, but almost anyone who enters will be called and told he's won. The catch is that winners are expected to pay a registration fee, an administrative fee, a deposit, or taxes. The fees for this supposedly free trip will be more than it would cost you to buy a vacation on your own.

One of my callers got taken for $398 on a "free" trip that was actually just a promotional offer to sell him a trip. He got a call saying he had won a trip with a hotel stay in Fort Lauderdale, Florida, a cruise to the Bahamas, and then a hotel stay in the Bahamas. He was told his cost was $398. He paid the money, and all he got for it was the opportunity to spend a couple of nights in Fort Lauderdale, a five-hour ferry crossing to the Bahamas and the possibility of a couple of nights in the Bahamas. He certainly didn't get $398 worth of travel. Many times these companies don't give anything in return for the money they take. They just vanish with everybody's money.

The legitimate way to buy travel is from a local travel agent, who can find you the best deals available and at no further cost to you, since the customer doesn't pay the agent. A real travel agent has met financial and managerial standards that qualify him for what's known as "appointment." It's like licensing, but more

- Tips on - Where to Buy Travel

● Don't accept "free" trips for which you have to pay any fee.

● Buy travel from a local travel agent that is a member of the ARC, Airline Reporting Corp., or IATAN, the International Air Transport Association Network.

● There's no cost to the consumer to use a travel agent. The airline pays for the travel agent's services.

● Pay for travel only on a credit card. You'll be able to get a refund if the company goes out of business.

● There's a big difference among travel agents in their outlooks and specialties. Choose one who's good at the trips you take most often.

● If price is your main consideration with a travel agent, it's especially important to choose an agent who will take a few minutes to help you and offer you different options.

● Never call an airline directly to buy tickets. Many try to sell the traveler the most expensive ticket he will buy.

● When you buy a cruise, use a travel agent who specializes in cruises.

difficult to obtain than licensing. You have to show that you have financial worthiness and a staff in the agency with the experience necessary to operate a travel business.

Before you do business with a travel agent, ask if she's a member of the ARC, Airline Reporting Corp., or IATAN, the International Air Transport Association Network. If the organization doesn't know what you're talking about, you're not dealing with a real travel agency.

When you buy travel, pay for it only on a credit card. Normally I advise you to use a credit card to protect against getting scammed; but with travel, you need to use a credit card because the entire industry is so tumultuous. You could buy a ticket from a perfectly legitimate company that might go out of business before your trip. Airlines, tour operators, and cruise lines go bust regularly. In a single week a few years ago, for example, two large international tour operators went bust. If you pay by check or by cash and an operator folds, you lose your money. If you pay by credit card, you're protected by your chargeback rights.

It's not easy to choose a travel agent out of the vast numbers of them. For one, you'll want a very personal relationship with your agent. I put the emphasis on the agent because choosing the individual you work with at an agency is even more important than the agency itself. Ask friends, coworkers, and relatives for travel agents they've used and liked. Then call these agents with a trip you're thinking of taking and see who seems on the ball and interested in you. If you're new to an area, call a half-dozen agents at random for suggestions on a particular trip. You'll find out quickly who's interested in you and wants your business.

Travel agents have widely varying outlooks and specialties. I was an extremely price-oriented travel agent—no surprise there—and I was not the right person for someone who wanted to stay in the very best hotels and resorts. But I was as good as you could get on finding deals. Some agents are really good at business travel; others specialize in cruises. Some are great at planning Caribbean trips, while others are really good at European vacations. You can't find one agent who does everything well, so choose one who's good at the trips you take most often. Many agents will be up front about their specialties. If you call an agent who does all your business travel about a trip to the Galapagos Islands, he may refer you to another agent in his office.

If price is your main consideration with a travel agent, it's especially important to choose an agent who is willing to take a few minutes to help you. If you want to find the cheapest way to fly from Dallas to Los Angeles, a thorough agent will ask you questions and give you options. Are you flexible about the day and time you leave, the airport you fly out of or into, and the airline? You want someone who thinks in a third dimension.

Unfortunately, most agents are judged on their productivity—how many dollars' worth of tickets they book per hour and per day—and as a result are under intense pressure. The more time an agent spends with you to find you a better deal, the less revenue she generates. If an agent gets a 10 percent commission, she'll make $50 for selling a $500 ticket. If she spends five minutes helping you find a $200 deal, her income drops from $50 to $20, and she's spent time that could have been used to sell tickets to other customers. The most customer-oriented agents look to build a relationship with you over time, rather than worrying about the transaction time involved in one purchase.

Never call an airline directly to buy tickets. If you do, you almost certainly will pay more for your flight. Seven or eight airlines may offer fares between two cities, but an airline will give you only the fares it offers. Worse, many airlines embargo fares. That means the airline instructs its employees not to quote certain fares unless the traveler knows to ask specifically for that fare. They try to sell you the most expensive ticket they can. A travel agent, on the other hand, can check the fares of each airline in a more thorough effort to find the best fare.

More than 80 percent of airline tickets sold in this country are issued by travel agents, because it's a more efficient way for the industry to distribute tickets. Airline employees are paid much more in salary than travel agents, so in most cases it's cheaper for the airline to pay a commission to the travel agent than to use its own employees to sell tickets. In any case, the consumer pays nothing. The airline pays for the travel agent's services.

Generally, you should call a travel agent when you're buying an airline trip or other services, such as a rental car or hotel, or when you buy a tour package. When a travel agent helps you with a smaller vacation, such as a weekend driving trip, he's doing it out of good will because the commissions aren't worth his time. He might do it as an investment in future business or a thank-you for past business.

When you buy a cruise, use a travel agent who specializes in cruises. That could be a cruise specialist within a travel agency or an agency that does cruises exclusively. Don't buy a cruise through an out-of-state 800 number unless you are an extremely experienced cruise passenger and you purchase it by credit card. Otherwise, buy it locally and from someone who does a big volume in cruising. A large-volume agency can offer you special low rates that are not available through other travel agents. If a cruise line has a sailing date that's selling terribly, it won't put out a special to all agents, because it doesn't want to hurt the retail price of all its cruises. So it offers the equivalent of a private sale through a few high-volume booking agencies.

It's important not to buy a cruise just because it's cheap. Cruise ships have their own per-sonalities, and if you get a cruise on a ship that doesn't fit your lifestyle or interests, that's not a bargain at any price. Someone may go on a cruise seeking some peace and quiet to recharge her batteries. If the cruise is host to the senior class of a local high school and the students drink and party all night long, that would ruin a dream vacation. I won a cruise once as a travel agent, when I was in my twenties, and the average age on the ship was 71. A good cruise specialist might tell you, for example, that a particular ship is older, has large cabins, and doesn't have much entertainment, but the service is very personal. Ask her if the ship you're considering has what you want.

Cruise lines have done a mediocre job in food standards and cleanliness. The U.S. Public Health Service publishes ratings on ships, and your travel agent can show you the figures. The ABC Star Guide also has a section on cruise ships that you can see at your travel agency.

Places to Go —

Infrequent travelers often lose out on a great vacation by choosing the security of a travel package over the spontaneity of a less-structured vacation. In a package, everything is arranged in advance—air, hotel, and ground travel.

I hear a lot of complaints about travel packages designed for the budget traveler, particularly trip packages to Nassau, Jamaica, or Cancún. In fact, I hear more complaints about those three places than everywhere else in the world combined. Sometimes travelers are victims of overbooking; they arrive at the destination and the accommodations they paid for are not available. Other times it's just a general problem of poor service.

But what leaves a bitter taste in people's mouths is the attitude they encounter when a problem arises. Nobody seems to care or does anything to resolve it. Many people who go to these places have a wonderful time and go back

- Tips on - Places to Go

- Travel packages offer security at the expense of spontaneity. Budget travel packages, such as those to Nassau, Jamaica, or Cancún, generate a lot of complaints.

- If you're interested in the Caribbean, buy one of the comprehensive guides to the Caribbean, such as *The Caribbean Islands Handbook*.

- The big advantage of going on your own to Europe is that you can concentrate on visiting the smaller towns and villages, where prices are lower and people are friendlier.

- If you have frequent flier miles, try to use them for international travel, rather than domestic. For international travel, Asia is a better deal than Europe.

- Airlines offer lower frequent flier mileage requirements to Asia, Europe, and Latin America during off-peak periods. So if possible, try to schedule your international trip during the winter.

year after year without problems. But it's too risky to plan your vacation around the hope that everything will go perfectly.

If you haven't traveled a lot and want to get real value for your dollar, start off with trips to familiar places. If you're looking for a beach, go to a nice one in Florida. As you get more comfortable as a traveler, then maybe look to the Caribbean. There are lots of wonderful islands in the Caribbean. But be careful what you ask for; a lot of times I hear people say they want to go someplace where there's absolutely nothing to do, a place of absolute peace and tran-

quility. When they get there, they're bored—because there's absolutely nothing to do. Many of us require more activity than we'll find in a completely out-of-the-way spot.

Don't rely on brochures when you're thinking of the Caribbean, because every glossy brochure presents a picture that's not really accurate. Instead, buy one of the comprehensive guides to the Caribbean. My favorite is *The Caribbean Islands Handbook*. These books give you enough information to select the island that fits your lifestyle. Another thing you need to know when you fly to the Caribbean: you'll have to change planes at least once, and many times twice. By the time you've been through all of that, you'll give up one day in each direction in travel time.

Of the Caribbean destinations, Aruba has become increasingly popular because it's reasonably affordable and has good air transportation and decent accommodations. Grand Cayman is a great spot to go to, with beautiful beaches and great snorkeling and scuba diving. It has decent air services, although prices tend to be sky high once you get there.

Florida has a handful of places I really like. On the Gulf Coast, I love Marco Island, Naples, Sanibel Island, Sarasota, Destin, and Pass-A-Grille. On the Atlantic side, I recommend Ponte Vedra Beach, Melbourne Beach, and Indian River Shores. All have nice stretches of sand and are relatively uncrowded. The main difference between the Gulf Coast and Atlantic beaches is the water tends to be very calm on the Gulf side, while the waves are moderate to rough on the Atlantic side.

First-time travelers to Europe seem to have an unnatural fear of moving around once they land, so they remain sealed in a tour bus. The tour offers the safety and security of traveling with a group and removes worries about handling money, picking a hotel, and communicating with someone who doesn't speak English. But if you lock yourself in a tour bus, you'll miss the essence of Europe. When I go to Europe, I do it with reckless abandon. I book my airline ticket and my car rental in advance, and that's it. I make no hotel reservations and I usually don't have an itinerary. When I get there, I am completely on my own. I land, get in the car, and drive. One time I was in France and the highway was about to split in two directions. One direction was to Amsterdam and the other was to Paris. I had two kilometers to decide which way to go. At the last second, I decided to go to Amsterdam.

The big advantage of going on your own is you can concentrate on visiting the smaller towns and villages of Europe, where prices are lower and people are friendlier. You can stay in small hotels and bed and breakfasts, meet local people, and enjoy local flavor. The bigger cities in Europe are so international in size and outlook that there isn't much difference between them. It makes little sense to spend three days in London, three in Paris, and three in Rome. Better to fly into Paris and spend the rest of the trip visiting the French countryside.

I realize there are some cities people desperately want to see, and Paris is one. But Frankfurt has no charm or redeeming value, and you should get out of it as quickly as you can. There are some great cities in Belgium, including Bruges and Ghent, but Brussels is a complete waste of time. While northern Europe is generally cleaner and things run like clockwork there, people seem to have a better time in southern Europe.

For those of you who think my unstructured form of travel is nuts but are willing to take a little more of a chance than with a fully escorted tour, there is a third choice in Europe. It's called a hosted itinerary and it allows you to take local tours when you get to a city. You have a tour representative in each town you can call for help and your hotels are preplanned and prepaid. To me that's a good compromise for people who are willing to step out a little bit but who don't want to wing it.

If you have more money and want more planning, there's a fourth option called an FIT. Under this format, the travel agent customizes the trip for you, planning details even down to dinner reservations at a particular restaurant.

If the whole idea of going to Europe scares you because of the language gap, make your first trip to Great Britain.

My favorite continent in the world is South America. In spite of the similarity in language, the difference from country to country in South America is greater than that between countries in Europe.

I've been to Latin America five times. I loved Chile, Argentina, and Bolivia, an odd choice because Bolivia is one of the world's poorest countries. Latin America is dramatically different from either Europe or the United States. People are unusually friendly. Lots of people resist going to South America over fear of political instability or crime, but I've never been afraid anywhere in South America, except in Brazil, and even Brazil knows it has a major crime problem. I particularly enjoyed the rural scenery of South America and the people. But the beaches were a disappointment. Even the most famous beaches of South America don't touch the quality of a Florida beach. The best travel guide to South America is the *South American Handbook*. Nothing else comes close.

My favorite city in the world is Hong Kong. If you would like to see this jewel before the Chinese take over, you have only until 1997. Hong Kong has a spontaneous vitality that no other city I've been to even simulates. It's a living, breathing, exciting place, full of opportunity, not to mention the best service in the world.

If you have frequent flier miles, try to use them for international travel, rather than domestic. You often can travel abroad for about the same number of frequent flier miles as you would spend flying to another American city, even though the cost of the tickets in cash would be far higher for the international trip.

For international travel, Asia usually is a better deal than Europe. The airfares to Asia are much higher than those to Europe, so if you're thinking of taking two trips, buy your trip to Europe and use your frequent flier miles to go for free to Asia. Most airlines offer lower mileage requirements to Asia, Europe, and Latin America during off-peak periods. So if possible, try to schedule your international trip during the winter.

Using your frequent flier miles for domestic travel can, however, make sense in the event of an emergency. I know someone who had to travel quickly because of a family crisis, and he used 60,000 frequent flier miles for a pair of tickets instead of paying $800 per ticket. That's smart.

Handling Money —

You can save money before you leave town if you follow a few tips on getting cash. Travelers planning a foreign trip traditionally buy foreign currency before they go, but that's a bad decision because banks in the United States tend to offer terrible rates of exchange. The difference from these poor rates to your best deal may be as much as 20 percent of the money you're changing. That can make a huge difference in the final cost of your trip.

If you do want to get money before you leave, one organization that offers better rates than the banks is Ruesch International.

There are several other options. AAA members can buy American Express Traveler's checks, at no commission, in U.S. dollars, British pounds, and certain other major European currencies. The exchange rate on those is okay. You can exchange the U.S. dollar checks at American Express offices in Europe at no commission, or you can exchange foreign currency checks in specific countries.

- Tips on - Handling Money

● When planning a foreign trip, don't get foreign currency before you leave town.

● For a great exchange rate on your money overseas, use credit cards as often as possible and get cash from automated teller machines using your bank ATM card.

● If you're exchanging currency, don't just go for the posted rate of exchange at a change booth or bank. Make sure you know if there's any service fee.

Contact:
Ruesch International
(Currency exchange)
1350 I Street NW
Suite 1010
Washington, D.C. 20005
1-800-424-2923

But technology has provided a better solution. I go to Europe with no foreign currency and use credit cards as often as I can. When you use a credit card, you get the banker's buying rate of exchange, the wholesale rate, plus a small service fee. That's much better than any rate of exchange you could get changing money.

The other technique that works very well in some countries, but just fairly well in others, is to use the automated teller machine card from your bank. If your bank is a member of the Cirrus or Plus network, you can get cash at an increasing number of ATM machines around Europe. I have used my ATM card with a fair amount of success in Europe. Once again, you get the wholesale rate of exchange, plus a small transaction fee.

Here's a key warning. If you're exchanging currency, don't just go for the posted rate of exchange at a change booth or bank. Make sure you know if there's any service fee or any minimum transaction charge. London is infamous for change places that advertise great rates of exchange on the dollar. But when you look at the fine print, the service charges are even bigger. It's a huge ripoff.

When I visit a foreign country, I walk into the arrival hall without a bit of their currency. I always find a teller machine or a money-change facility somewhere. Even at a foreign airport, where the rate of exchange offered is poor, you'll usually get a better deal than at an American bank.

In 1992, I arrived in Spain with no money, got a rental car, and drove several hours out of Madrid. My traveling companion and I had no Spanish pesetas and no food and were hungry. When we got to a town, the teller machine network was down. So we changed U.S. dollar traveler's checks at a local bank. Even in a situation where nothing was working, it was no crisis. For the rest of the trip, we used credit cards and teller machines.

Bed and Breakfast Inns —

Bed and breakfasts have served a very useful purpose in Europe by providing travelers with affordable lodging, because in Europe there isn't yet a widespread industry of affordable hotels. In fact, no country on earth has the kind of high-quality, affordable lodging that we have in the United States.

Because of that, bed and breakfasts have taken a completely different tack in the United States than they have in Europe. Since they can't compete at the low end, bed and breakfasts have tried to be a fantasy-type getaway. That's worked well in resort areas but not well in other locations.

The bed and breakfast industry has fallen on hard times in part because the novelty has worn

---

- Tips on -
Bed and
Breakfast Inns

● Bed and breakfast inns are designed as budget accommodations in Europe, while they're chosen more in the United States as a homey, charming alternative to standard hotels.

● If you want to stay at a bed and breakfast in Europe, you can book in advance through some advance reservation services or some travel agents. But usually you're better off just getting a room when you get there.

---

off for travelers, who at first loved the individuality and the homey spirit of a bed and breakfast, but have since decided that they miss the privacy and the no-surprises consistency of a standard hotel.

When the bed and breakfast craze was at its height in the mid-1980s, many well-educated, upper-middle-class people decided they would love to run a bed and breakfast inn. Many lost their enthusiasm and left the industry as they realized it wasn't all so charming. Owners still had to change bed linens, clean toilets, deal with sometimes difficult guests, and wake up early to fix breakfasts for visitors. A fatigue factor took over and lots of people got out of the business. What was a huge fad may yet find its proper level in the United States.

I stayed at a bed and breakfast in a nonresort area in the United States and paid $49 off-season for a room with no bathroom and heat that barely worked. It was a neat, charming house, but not worth the price for this location.

On the other hand, my co-author and his wife stayed at a wonderful bed and breakfast in a

Maryland resort area, on the Chesapeake Bay, and absolutely loved it. Because it was a resort area, there was a reason to go in addition to staying at the inn.

If you want to stay at a bed and breakfast in Europe, you can book in advance through some advance reservation services. In some cases, your travel agent can help you with them. But usually you're better off just getting a room when you get there. It's your choice. If that makes you nervous, call and book a room. It may give you a chance to practice your high school French.

The Workbook section is what makes this book a true "Survival Kit." In it, you'll find tools to help you in your consumer battles.

Keep the worksheets in the book, or make photocopies and keep them with your important records. Some of the letters, like the "drop-dead" letter, can be copied and mailed. Just fill in the collector's name and your account number and sign it. Others, like the sample complaint letter, can be quickly modified and retyped to fit your situation.

Documentation Sheet

The problem: _____

_____

_____

Action Log

Date of action	What you did (Called? Wrote?)	Name of person you contacted
_____	_____	_____

What action was promised or taken: _____

_____

_____

Date of action	What you did (Called? Wrote?)	Name of person you contacted
_____	_____	_____

What action was promised or taken: _____

_____

_____

Action Log

Date of action	What you did (Called? Wrote?)	Name of person you contacted
_____	_____	_____

What action was promised or taken:

_____

_____

_____

Date of action	What you did (Called? Wrote?)	Name of person you contacted
_____	_____	_____

What action was promised or taken:

_____

_____

_____

Date of action	What you did (Called? Wrote?)	Name of person you contacted
_____	_____	_____

What action was promised or taken:

_____

_____

_____

Date of action	What you did (Called? Wrote?)	Name of person you contacted
_____	_____	_____

What action was promised or taken:

_____

_____

_____

"Drop-dead" Letter to Collection Agencies

Date: _____

To whom it may concern:

I have been contacted by your company about a debt you allege I owe.

I am instructing you not to contact me any further in connection with this debt.

Under the Fair Debt Collection Practices Act, a federal law, you may not contact me further once I have notified you not to do so.

Sincerely,

_____

Account Number _____

Date: _____

To whom it may concern:

I have been contacted by your company about a debt you allege I owe.

I am instructing you not to contact me any further in connection with this debt.

Under the Fair Debt Collection Practices Act, a federal law, you may not contact me further once I have notified you not to do so.

Sincerely,

_____

Account Number _____

Model Letter of Complaint

Date: _____

John Jones
Regional Vice President
ABCD Company
500 Main Street, Suite 1000
Anywhere, USA

Dear Mr. Jones:

I regret having to write to you about an unpleasant experience I've had with your company. I prefer to contact a company only in praise of an employee or the company's actions.

Unfortunately, my situation is such that it is necessary for me to forward a complaint to you.

Give the specifics of the complaint. Say whom you've spoken with about the problem, what attempts you've made to solve it, and what specific action you would like the company to take.

_____

_____

_____

_____

I look forward to hearing from you. I hope you can respond within 30 days so that we are able to resolve this problem in a speedy fashion.

Sincerely,

Getting Your Name Off Mailing Lists

Date: _____

Mail Preference Service
Direct Marketing Association
P.O. Box 9008
Farmingdale, N.Y. 11735

To whom it may concern:

I am writing to register with your Mail Preference Service.

Please inform your members that I do not want my name sold to any company for the purpose of placing me on a mailing list and sending me advertising mail.

In addition, I would like my name removed from existing lists.

Thank you very much for your help.

Sincerely,

Name: _____

Street: _____

City: _____ State: _____

Zip Code: _____

Account Numbers

Credit Cards
Your maximum liability if a credit card is stolen is $50 per card. You have no liability for charges made after you report the card as lost or stolen.

Creditor/phone	Account number	Credit limit	If lost, call this number	Interest rate
_____	_____	_____	_____	_____
_____	_____	_____	_____	_____
_____	_____	_____	_____	_____
_____	_____	_____	_____	_____
_____	_____	_____	_____	_____
_____	_____	_____	_____	_____
_____	_____	_____	_____	_____
_____	_____	_____	_____	_____
_____	_____	_____	_____	_____

Banks
If you lose your ATM card, you could lose all the money in your account plus your credit line. Call your bank within 48 hours and your maximum liability is $50.

Institution/ phone	Type of Account	Account No.	Branch	Contact
_____	_____	_____	_____	_____
_____	_____	_____	_____	_____
_____	_____	_____	_____	_____
_____	_____	_____	_____	_____
_____	_____	_____	_____	_____
_____	_____	_____	_____	_____
_____	_____	_____	_____	_____
_____	_____	_____	_____	_____

Insurance

Life
Company:_____
Agent: _____
Phone #: _____
Account No.: _____
Policy Type: _____
Benefit Amount: _____
Beneficiary: _____

Disability
Company:_____
Agent: _____
Phone #: _____
Policy No.: _____
How long after disability does coverage take effect? _____
How long does the policy remain in effect? _____
What is the benefit amount? _____

Homeowners
Company:_____
Agent: _____
Phone #: _____
Policy No.: _____
Features: _____
Does the policy include protections against inflation? _____

Insurance

Health
Company: _____

Account No.: _____

Deductibles: _____

Other features: _____

What is the co-payment? _____

Is there a maximum out-of-pocket cost? _____

Is there an annual or lifetime cap on benefits? _____

Auto
Company: _____

Agent: _____

Phone #: _____

Policy No.: _____

Features: _____

Liability coverage: _____

Collision coverage: _____

Comprehensive coverage: _____

Other features: _____

Is there reimbursement for towing or car rental expenses? _____

Letter to Request Copy of Credit Report

Date: _____

Equifax Information Service
P.O. Box 740123
Atlanta, GA 30374

To whom it may concern:

Please send a copy of my current credit report. I am enclosing a check to cover the $8 fee.

I am:

Name: _____
Address:_____
_____

My Social Security Number: _____

Thank you.

Sincerely,

Letter to Request Copy of Credit Report

Date: _____

TRW Complimentary Report Request
P.O. Box 2350
Chatsworth, CA 91313

To whom it may concern:

Please send my "annual complimentary copy" of my current credit report.

I am:

Name:_____

Address: _____

_____

My Social Security Number: _____

My previous address: _____

My birthdate: _____

My spouse's first name: _____

A copy of my driver's license (or a household bill) is enclosed.

Thank you.

Sincerely,

Letter to Request Copy of Credit Report

Date: _____

Trans Union
P.O. Box 7000
North Olmstead, OH 44070

To whom it may concern:

Please send a copy of my current credit report. I am enclosing a check to cover the $15 fee.

I am:
Name:_____
Address: _____

_____

My Social Security Number: _____
My previous address: _____
My birthdate: _____
My daytime telephone number: _____
My employer: _____

Thank you.

Sincerely,

Sample Credit Report

Please address all future
correspondence to this address ▶

```
EQUIFAX CREDIT INFORMATION SERVICES
P O BOX 740256
ATLANTA, GA 30374

(000)000-0000
```

CHRISTOPHER N BRANDON
1500 ASHWOOD WAY
LAWRENCEVILLE GA 30243

DATE **07/08/92**
DATE OF BIRTH 07/02/55
NUMBER OF DEPENDENTS 18

CREDIT HISTORY

Company Name	Account Number	Whose Acct.	Date Opened	Months Re-viewed	Date of Last Actvity	High Credit	Terms	Balance	Past Due	Status	Date Reported
SYS PL&SUP		I	08/90		400	1450				01	06/92
SYS PL&SUP		I	06/90		400	1450				R1	06/92
SYS PL&SUP		I	05/91		400	1450				I1	06/92
GAFED BKHD		I	05/91	01/92	400	1450				I1	06/92
GOLDOMESVG		I	05/91	05	01/92	400	1450			I1	07/92
GMAC	123613286	I	05/91	05	01/92	25K 450		22K	O	I1	06/92
UNTDCREDIT	613286	I	05/91	05	01/92	400		450	O	I1	05/92
SEARS	123456			05/92						R5	05/92

GOLDOMESVG
 NO ACTIVITY SINCE DATE REPORTED

GMAC
>>> PRIOR PAYING HISTORY - 30(01)60(00)90+(00) <<<
 NO ACTIVITY SINCE DATE REPORTED

UNTDCREDIT
 NO ACTIVITY SINCE DATE REPORTED

SEARS
>>> PRIOR PAYING HISTORY - 30(00)60(00)90+(02) 04/91-R5.03/91-R5 <<<

>>> COLLECTION REPORTED 05/92. ASSIGNED TO BUS & PROF 02/92. CLIENT-NOT AVAILABLE
 AMOUNT-$123, PAID 02/92, BALANCE-$0 02/92
 DATE OF LAST ACTIVITY 02/92, INDIVIDUAL, ACCOUNT NUMBER 12345

 ******** ADDITIONAL INFORMATION **********

 FORMER ADDRESS 1500 ASHWOOD, WAY, SUWANEE, GA

 FORMER ADDRESS 423 STONEWOOD, DR, STONE MOUNTAIN, GA

 CURRENT EMPLOYMENT - TEACHER, GWIMMWTT CO, SUWANEE, GA

 ******** THE FOLLOWING ITEMS WERE REPORTED BY ANOTHER CREDIT BUREAU: **********
   RALE, NC DATE REPORTED - 01/01/92

 ********** COMPANIES THAT REQUESTED YOUR CREDIT HISTORY **********

07/08/92 ACRO SUPT	07/08/92 SYS PL&SUP
07/08/92 EQUIFAX	07/06/92 EQUIFAX
07/01/92 EQUIFAX	05/12/92 ACIS 205000008.999AA00074
05/05/92 SYS PL&SUP	03/03/92 DAT EMPLACRO SUPT
09/12/91 SEARS	05/13/91 SYS PL&SUP
04/18/91 CBI RALE	

Request for Repairs to Rental Property

Date: _____

To whom it may concern:

We are distressed that you have not responded to several requests to make repairs on our apartment.

Briefly describe the nature of the problem and what action you would like the landlord to take.

Please take care of this in the next 48 hours, or it will be necessary for us to hire a repairperson ourselves and deduct the cost of their services from our next rent check.

Thank you.

Sincerely,

Apartment No. _____

What to Do When You're in an Auto Accident

1) Wait for a police officer to write a report.
2) Exchange information with the other driver about yourselves and your insurance companies.
3) Get the names and telephone numbers of as many witnesses as you can.
4) While the accident is fresh in your mind and you're waiting for the police, draw a sketch of the accident scene.
5) As soon as possible, report it to your insurance company, even if you don't plan to make a claim.
6) Contact the other driver's insurance company.

Long-Distance Calling Codes

Keep an eye out for an expensive ripoff when you use any public phone, but particularly those at gas stations, airports, universities, hotels and hospitals. Phones operated by ripoff companies can cost you six or seven times the rates of a legitimate long-distance company. If you don't recognize the name of the company that's posted on the phone, you can bypass it with the following access codes, and go to the long-distance provider you wish to use. Try the five-digit code first. If that doesn't work, dial the 800 number.

AT&T	10288 or 1-800-CALL-ATT
MCI	10222 or 1-800-950-1022
Sprint	10333 or 1-800-877-8000

Car-Buying Worksheet

	Model #1	Model #2	Model #3
Base cost:	_____	_____	_____
Options:			
Automatic transmission	_____	_____	_____
Air conditioning	_____	_____	_____
_____	_____	_____	_____
_____	_____	_____	_____
Transportation:	_____	_____	_____
Total dealer cost:	_____	_____	_____
Cost to insure:	_____	_____	_____

Bids from Dealers

What is the lowest price at which they will sell the vehicle I want, with the options I want? Take bids by phone, and ask the top three to fax their bid to you. If anyone refuses to bid, don't buy from that dealership.

Name of Dealer (and phone #)	Salesperson	Their Best Price
1) _____	_____	_____
2) _____	_____	_____
3) _____	_____	_____
4) _____	_____	_____
5) _____	_____	_____
6) _____	_____	_____
7) _____	_____	_____
8) _____	_____	_____

Sample Living Will

Living will made this _____ day of _____ month _____ year.

I, _____, being of sound mind, willfully and voluntarily make known my desire that my life shall not be prolonged under the circumstances set forth below and do declare:

1.　　If at any time I should (check each option desired):

    ( )　　have a terminal condition,

    ( )　　become in a coma with no reasonable expectation of regaining consciousness,

    ( )　　become in a persistent vegetative state with no reasonable expectation of regaining significant cognitive function,

as defined in and established in accordance with the procedure set forth in paragraphs (2), (9), and (10) of Code Section 31-32-2 of the Official Code of Georgia Annotated, I direct that the application of life-sustaining procedures to my body (check the option desired):

    ( )　　including nourishment and hydration,

    ( )　　including hydration but not nourishment, or

    ( )　　excluding nourishment and hydration,

be withheld or withdrawn and that I be permitted to die.

2.　　In the absence of my ability to give directions regarding the use of such life-sustaining procedures, it is my intention that this Living Will shall be honored by my family and physician(s) as the final expression of my legal right to refuse medical or surgical treatment and accept the consequences for such refusal;

3.　　I understand that I may revoke this Living Will at any time:

4.　　I understand the full import of this Living Will, and am at least 18 years of age and am emotionally and mentally competent to make this Living Will; and

5.　　If I am a female and have been diagnosed as pregnant, this Living Will shall have no force and effect unless the fetus is not viable and I indicate by initialing after this sentence that I want this Living Will to be carried out _____ (initials) _____ (date).

Signed: _____

_____ (City), _____ (County), and

_____ (State of Residence).

I hereby witness this Living Will and attest that:

(1)   The declarant is personally known to me and I believe the declarant to be at least 18 years of age and of sound mind;

(2)   I am at least 18 years of age;

(3)   To the best of my knowledge, at the time of the execution of this Living Will, I

    (a)   am not related to the declarant by blood or marriage;

    (b)   would not be entitled to any portion of the declarant's estate by any will or by operation of law under the rules of descent and distribution of this state;

    (c)   am not the attending physician of declarant or an employee of the attending physician or an employee of the hospital or skilled nursing facility in which declarant is a patient;

    (d)   am not directly financially responsible for the declarant's medical care; and

    (e)   have no present claim against any portion of the estate of the declarant;

(4)   Declarant has signed this document in my presence as above-instructed, on the date above first shown.

Witness: _____

Address: _____

Witness: _____

Address: _____

An additional witness is required when the Living Will is signed in a hospital or skilled nursing facility.

I hereby witness this Living Will and attest that I believe the declarant to be of sound mind and to have made this Living Will willingly and voluntarily.

Witness: _____

    Medical director of skilled nursing facility or staff physician not participating in the care of the patient or chief of the hospital medical staff or staff physician or hospital designee not participating in the care of the patient.

Courtesy of Piedmont Hospital, Atlanta

The Phone Book

Academy of Family Mediators
(Divorce mediation)
355 Tyrol West
1500 S. Highway 100
Golden Valley, MN 55416
612-525-8670

American Bar Association
Attorney Complaints & Fee Arbitration
750 North Lake Shore
Chicago, IL 60611
1-800-621-6159

American Homeowner's Foundation
(Remodeling contracts)
1724 South Quincy Street
Arlington, VA 22204
703-536-7776

American Institute of Architects
(For a remodeling contract, ask for the standard form of agreement between owner and contractor: A101, A111 or A201)
AIA Orders
2 Winter Sport Lane
P.O. Box 60
Williston, VT 05495
1-800-365-2724

American Institute of CPAs
1211 6th Avenue
New York, NY 10036
1-800-862-4272

American Movers Conference
Dispute Settlement Program
1611 Duke Street
Alexandria, VA 22314
703-683-7410

American Society of Home Inspectors
85 West Algonquin Road
Suite 360
Arlington Heights, IL 60005
1-800-743-2744

American Travel Network
1160 Main Street
Buffalo, NY 14209
1-800-477-9692

AutoSolve Manufacturers Arbitration
Program
(Auto arbitration for Toyota or Lexus vehicles)
1000 AAA Drive
Heathrow, FL 32746
1-800-477-6583

Bankcard Holders of America
(For a guide to low-interest, low-fee credit cards)
524 Branch Drive
Salem, VA 24153
703-389-5445

Bureau of the Public Debt
Division of Customer Services
Washington, DC 20239
202-874-4000

Center for Auto Safety
(Auto recalls)
2001 S Street N.W., Suite 410
Washington, DC 20009
202-328-7700

Child Support Enforcement
370 L'enfant Promenade, S.W.,4th floor
Washington, DC 20447
202-401-9373

Children's Support Services
(To find a collection agency specializing in
child support)
P.O. Box 691067
San Antonio, TX 78269
1-800-729-2445

Council of Better Business Bureaus
Autoline
4200 Wilson Boulevard
Suite 800
Arlington, VA 22203
1-800-955-5100

Equifax Information Service
(Credit reports)
P.O. Box 740123
Atlanta, GA 30374
1-800-685-1111

Federal Trade Commission
(For a copy of the brochure "Fair Debt Col-
lection Practices Act")
Publications Division
Washington, DC 20580
202-326-2222

Fidelity Investments
82 Devonshire Street
Boston, MA 02109
617-523-1919
1-800-544-6666

Ford Consumer Assistance Center
(Auto arbitration, Ford vehicles)
300 Renaissance Center
P.O. Box 43360
Detroit, MI 48243
1-800-392-3673

Funeral and Memorial Societies of America
(For a directory of memorial societies in
your area)
6900 Lost Lake Road
Egg Harbor, WI 54209
414-868-2729

GEICO
(Extended warranties)
One Geico Boulevard
Fredericksburg, VA 22412-3004
1-800-841-1003
In Texas: 1-800-841-5432

Housing & Urban Development
(Questions regarding landlord/tenant disputes)
Washington, DC
202-708-0547
(Ask to speak with the desk officer representing your state)

Insurance Information, Inc.
(Insurance price quotes)
23 Route 134
South Dennis, MA 02660
1-800-472-5800

International Fabricare Institute
Garment Analysis Laboratory
12251 Tech Road
Silver Spring, MD 20904
1-800-638-2627

INVESCO
7800 E. Union Avenue
Suite 800
Denver, CO 80237
303-930-6300
1-800-525-8085

IRS Problem Resolution National Office
Taxpayer Ombudsman's Office
Washington, DC
202-622-6100

Janus Capital
100 Fillmore Street
Suite 300
Denver, CO 80206
303-333-3863
1-800-525-3713

MasterCard International
Public Affairs Department
888 7th Avenue
New York, NY 10106
212-649-5476

Morningstar Inc.
225 West Wacker Drive
Chicago, IL 60606
1-800-876-5005

Mortgage Bankers Association of America
(Mortgages and refinancing)
1125 15th Street
Washington, DC 20005
202-861-6500

National Association of Professional
Remodeling Contractors
4301 North Fairfax Drive
Suite 310
Arlington, VA 22203-1627
1-800-966-7601

National Association of Securities Dealers
(Investments)
Disciplinary History: 1-800-289-9999
Licensing Information: 301-590-6500

National Charities In
(Performance rating
19 Union Square We
New York, NY 1000:
212-929-6300

National Foundation
Counseling
8611 2nd Avenue
Suite 100
Silver Spring, MD 2
303-589-5600

National Highway T
Safety Administratic
Auto Safety Hotline
1-800-424-9393 (Tou

National Pest Contro
Washington, DC
1-800-858-PEST

Postal Inspector
(Mail fraud)
North and Northeast
Central and Western
South and Southeast

Ram Research
Card Trak
(For a comprehensiv
credit cards, no-fee
credit cards)
460 West Patrick Str
P.O. Box 1700
Frederick, MD 2170
1-800-344-7714

The Remodelors Co
Association of Home
1201 15th Street, N.
Washington, DC 20(
1-800-368-5242, ext.

Resor
(Infor
Clinto
P.O. B
North
708-29

Ruesc
(Curre
1350 I
Suite 1
Washi
1-800-

Charle
101 Mc
San Fr
415-62
1-800-6

Scudde
P.O. Bo
Boston
617-439
1-800-2

T. Rowe
100 E.
Baltimc
410-547
1-800-6

TRW Cc
(Credit
P.O. Bo
Chatsw
1-800-6

perty Owners Association
on on vacation timeshares)
rr, President
95
k, IL 60062
10

ernational
exchange)
et, N.W.

n, DC 20005
2923

hwab Corp.
omery Street
isco, CA 94104
00
5300

291
A 02107
40
2470

rice Associates Inc.
tt Street
, MD 21202
308
5660

plimentary Report Request
port)
350
th, CA 91313
-7654

Trans Union
(Credit report)
P.O. Box 7000
North Olmstead, OH 44070

Twentieth Century
4500 Main Street
P.O. Box 419200
Kansas City, MO 64141
816-531-5575
1-800-345-2021

USAA Life Insurance Co.
USAA Building
San Antonio, TX 78288
210-498-6505
1-800-531-8000

U.S. Office of Consumer Affairs
(For consumer and insurance questions,
and to ask for a free copy of the *Consumer's
Resource Handbook*)
202-395-7904

Vanguard Group
P.O. Box 2600
Valley Forge, PA 19482
610-669-1000
1-800-662-2739

VISA International
P.O. Box 8999
San Francisco, CA 94128
1-800-227-6811

Reference

Many of these books may have gone out of print and may be located at your local library.

The Banker's Secret
Random House (book);
Good Advice (software)
1-800-255-0899

Buying Stocks Without a Broker
McGraw
1-800-962-4369 ext. 2222

Caribbean Islands Handbook
Edited by Ben Box and Sarah Cameron
Prentice-Hall Travel

The Complete Guide to Buying Your First Home
by R. Dodge Woodson
Betterway Publishing

The Complete Guide to Managing Your Money
by Jane Bryant Quinn
Consumer Reports Books

Consumer Reports Car Buying Guide
(Or *Consumer Reports'* April Auto Issue)

Edmund's car guides
Edmund Publications Corp.

Everybody's Guide to Small Claims Court
by Ralph Warner
Nolo Press
1-800-992-6656

Guide to Mutual Funds
The American Association of Individual
Investors
625 North Michigan Avenue
Suite 1900
Chicago, IL 60611
312-280-0170

*The Handbook for No-Load
Mutual Fund Investors*
by Sheldon Jacobs
Irwin Professional Publishing
1-800-252-2042

The Homeseller's Kit
Dearborn Financial Publishing Co.

How to Buy a House, Condo or Co-op
Consumer Reports Books

How to Protect Your Driver's License
by Ralph Robinson

*The Inventing and Patenting Sourcebook:
Desktop Companion*
by Richard Levy

*Kiplinger's Personal Finance:
Buying and Selling a Home in Today's Real
Estate Market*
by Joe Meyers
Kiplinger Books

Lemon Law: A Manual for Consumers

*Mom's House, Dad's House: Making Shared
Custody Work*
by Isolina Ricci
Macmillan

The Money Guide
Consumer Reports Books
1-800-500-9760

The Mortgage Kit
Dearborn Financial Publishing Co.

The Parents Book about Divorce
by Richard Gardner
Bantam

Patent It Yourself
by David Pressman
Nolo Press

South American Handbook
Prentice-Hall Travel